Currency Crisis

Currency Crisis

Special Issue Editor
Faridul Islam

MDPI • Basel • Beijing • Wuhan • Barcelona • Belgrade

Special Issue Editor
Faridul Islam
Department of Economics,
Morgan State University
USA

Editorial Office
MDPI
St. Alban-Anlage 66
4052 Basel, Switzerland

This is a reprint of articles from the Special Issue published online in the open access journal *Journal of Risk and Financial Management* (ISSN 1911-8074) from 2018 to 2019 (available at: https://www.mdpi.com/journal/jrfm/special_issues/currency_crisis).

For citation purposes, cite each article independently as indicated on the article page online and as indicated below:

LastName, A.A.; LastName, B.B.; LastName, C.C. Article Title. *Journal Name* **Year**, *Article Number*, Page Range.

ISBN 978-3-03921-578-2 (Pbk)
ISBN 978-3-03921-579-9 (PDF)

© 2019 by the authors. Articles in this book are Open Access and distributed under the Creative Commons Attribution (CC BY) license, which allows users to download, copy and build upon published articles, as long as the author and publisher are properly credited, which ensures maximum dissemination and a wider impact of our publications.

The book as a whole is distributed by MDPI under the terms and conditions of the Creative Commons license CC BY-NC-ND.

Contents

About the Special Issue Editor vii

Preface to "Currency Crisis" ix

Faridul Islam
Currency Crisis: Are There Signals to Read?
Reprinted from: *jrfm* **2019**, *12*, 128, doi:10.3390/jrfm12030128 1

Colin Ellis and Emilia Gyoerk
Investigating the Economic and Financial Damage around Currency Peg Failures
Reprinted from: *jrfm* **2019**, *12*, 92, doi:10.3390/jrfm12020092 5

Agus Salim and Kai Shi
A Cointegration of the Exchange Rate and Macroeconomic Fundamentals: The Case of the
Indonesian Rupiah vis-á-vis Currencies of Primary Trade Partners
Reprinted from: *jrfm* **2019**, *12*, 87, doi:10.3390/jrfm12020087 21

Georgina M. Gómez
Money as an Institution: Rule versus Evolved Practice? Analysis of Multiple Currencies
in Argentina
Reprinted from: *jrfm* **2019**, *12*, 80, doi:10.3390/jrfm12020080 38

Patrick Collins, Jameel Ahmed and Ahamed Kameel Meera
Simulation of the Grondona System of Conditional Currency Convertibility Based on Primary
Commodities, Considered as a Means to Resist Currency Crises
Reprinted from: *jrfm* **2019**, *12*, 75, doi:10.3390/jrfm12020075 52

**Linh My Tran, Chi Hong Mai, Phuoc Huu Le, Chi Linh Vu Bui, Linh Viet Phuong Nguyen
and Toan Luu Duc Huynh**
Monetary Policy, Cash Flow and Corporate Investment: Empirical Evidence from Vietnam
Reprinted from: *jrfm* **2019**, *12*, 46, doi:10.3390/jrfm12010046 72

Mohsen Bahmani-Oskooee and Majid Maki-Nayeri
Asymmetric Effects of Policy Uncertainty on the Demand for Money in the United States [†]
Reprinted from: *jrfm* **2019**, *12*, 1, doi:10.3390/jrfm12010001 86

Matthew Harrison and Geng Xiao
China and Special Drawing Rights—Towards a Better International Monetary System
Reprinted from: *jrfm* **2019**, *12*, 60, doi:10.3390/jrfm12020060 99

About the Special Issue Editor

Faridul Islam is a Professor of Economics at Morgan State University, Baltimore, MD. Farid earned his MS from the London School of Economics and his PhD from University of Illinois-Urbana under the supervision of Paul Newbold. His dissertation used quarterly seasonal US data to forecast the performance of the major macroeconomic series. After graduation, he worked at the erstwhile Wharton Econometric Forecast Associates, PA, before joining the ranks of faculty. His current research broadly covers different areas of economics/finance, with implications for public policy. He is currently interested in our opioid crisis, which he considers a real challenge and perhaps the nation's most serious test, requiring immediate public policy intervention by the US government. Aside from academic activities, he is engaged in service to the profession, the University, and the community. He has served on over two dozen Ph.D. dissertation committees in the US and abroad.

His papers have appeared in quality outlets, including *Economics Letters*, *Industrial Relations*, *Economic Modelling*, *International Trade Journal*, *Journal of Asian Economics*, *Journal of Economic Education*, *Structural Change & Econ Dynamics*, *Australian Economic Papers*, *Empirical Econ*, *Economic Change & Restrg.*, *Journal of Econ Dev*, *Journal of Developing Areas*, *Indian Econ Review*, *Indian Econ Journal*, *Econ Bulletin*, *Journal of Bus Econ & Mgmt.*, *South Asian Econ Journal*, and *Bangladesh Dev Studies*. He has several manuscripts with review/resubmit status. He presents papers regularly at national and international conferences, which helps to establish and expand his professional network and to stay engaged effectively in research and publishing.

Preface to "Currency Crisis"

The 2008 financial crisis was the worst economic calamity since the Great Depression. By some estimates, the toll it took runs into the trillions of dollars. The collapse of Lehman Brothers, which required huge sums of money for a bail out, nearly brought down the global financial system. This was contained by a monetary and fiscal stimulus, which prevented another great depression. The pace of recovery has remained feeble relative to prior post-war upturns. Europe's crisis evolved into the euro crisis, as GDP failed to pick up. The Fed has mostly remained monetary policy-centric.

Faridul Islam
Special Issue Editor

Editorial

Currency Crisis: Are There Signals to Read?

Faridul Islam

Department of Economics, Morgan State University, Baltimore, MD 21251, USA; Faridul.Islam@morgan.edu

Received: 18 July 2019; Accepted: 23 July 2019; Published: 2 August 2019

Abstract: Financial crisis is nothing new in the annals of history of the capitalistic path of economic development; it is a part of the business cycle. The theoretical basis is well entrenched in the concept of 'Keynesian Cross'. The tale of crisis, dating back centuries, has taken a new turn with the call for more globalization—liberalize trade and open up the financial sector. This has made many nations vulnerable to crises that are likely to be repeated, perhaps frequently. Based on recent experience, warning signs can be read from the dollar-centric exchange rate, the mainstay for the stability of the current global financial system. To a careful observer, fatigue in the system cannot be overlooked.

Keywords: China; Special Drawing Right; international monetary system; reserve currency; RMB internationalization; mortgage crisis; default swap; derivative; Asian crisis; LIBOR

The 2008 financial crisis was the worst economic calamity since the Great Depression. By some estimates, the toll it took runs into the trillions. The collapse of the Lehman Brothers, which required huge sums of money for bail out, nearly brought down the global financial system, was contained by monetary and fiscal stimulus and prevented another great depression. The pace of recovery remains feeble relative to prior post-war upturns. Europe's crisis evolved into the euro crisis, as GDP failed to pick up. The Fed has mostly remained monetary policy-centric.

The first sign of trouble surfaced in 2006 when housing prices started to fall. Realtors failed to realize that many homeowners had dubious credit sources, blamed on the subprime loans when the real culprit was the banks' ability to engage in trading with profitable derivatives, and then sell them to investors. The derivatives created an insatiable demand for even more mortgages. While hard to believe, the Fed had thought the subprime mortgage crisis would stay within the housing sector alone or that they didn't understand the actual causes of the crisis until much later (well, so they claim).

Hedge funds and other financial institutions owned the mortgage-backed securities, spread to mutual- and pension funds; and corporate assets. The banks had chopped up the original mortgages and resold them in tranches. This made it impossible to price the derivatives, which are contracts that allow businesses, investors, and municipalities to transfer risks and rewards associated with commercial or financial outcomes to other parties. Holding a derivative contract can reduce the risk of bad harvests, adverse market fluctuations, or negative events like a bond default.

Each derivatives transaction is like a stock or bond trade—one party wants to increase its exposure to a specific risk as the other moves in the other way. Derivatives derive their values from its price, volatility, and risk of an underlying stock, bond, commodity, interest rate, or exchange rates. The price is a function of the price of the above listed items. Some derivatives, like stock equity options and credit default swaps remain contingent on future events. Others, such as commodities, futures contracts, and interest-rate swaps, are more explicit contract exchanges, such as a specified number of items on a specified date in the future for a certain price.

The pension funds bought risky assets thinking that the insurance product—credit default swaps—would protect them. The American International Group (AIG) sold these swaps. As the derivatives lost value, AIG lacked the cash flow to honor every swap. Banks panicked and stopped lending to each other, fearing that they would have to absorb the loss and that other banks would dump the useless mortgages as collateral. This raised interbank borrowing costs—the LIBOR. The growing mistrust was part of the financial crisis. The Fed's action to pump money via Term Auction Facility, a temporary program managed by the Fed to address elevated pressures in the short-term to support markets, was inadequate.

Clearly, multiple players, in different roles, were acting behind the crisis. Central bankers and other regulators were no less to blame for tolerating this mess. The "Great Moderation"—years of low inflation and stable growth—fostered risky enterprise (See Batabyal et al. 2018). In Asia, a "savings glut" pushed global interest rates down. In Europe, banks borrowed from the US money markets before the crisis to purchase suspicious assets. These factors created a corrosive chemistry leading to a debt surge that had the appearance of a less risky world.

The most obvious feature of the onset of a currency crisis, or the result a manifested in a sharp and large decline in exchange-rate for the affected countries/region before it transmits to others. The severity varies by the strength of the trade and financial linkage. A shock in the exchange-rate can be initiated by the actions of a powerful organization, government or large corporations, triggering a loss of confidence in a government or its monetary policy. The case in point is illustrated by the Asian flu (1997), which raises much controversy about the outside players. In Malaysia, the Prime Minister Mahathir stood his ground and took decisive steps that many see as the gold standard for dealing with crisis for his nation to date. (Collins et al. 2019)

Although widely acclaimed, it remains a mystery why his actions were ignored by the "mainstream economists" and the US media. How can one believe that the American economists were unaware of the fragility of the US financial system, or that they knew but kept silent? Some even ask who they are: "Do these so-called experts really understand the problem? Or would their advice aggravate the problem? Or do they have an agenda of their own?". (See Collins et al. 2019). Much the same criticisms apply to the 2008 crisis. Solving a problem of this magnitude is the central goal of the Public Banking Institute (PBI) and the American Monetary Institute. As we know, at the heart of the collapse of the Lehman Brothers (2008) was the loss of money from holding too many toxic securities and loans, linked to the then chaotic US property market. World Trade Org. (WTO) reports that trade fell in every country. Credit supply to the real economy fell to the tune of $2 trillion in America alone.

Curiously, even when a government/business is following sensible policies, the currency may still be targeted for destabilization for political reasons. This includes the threat of "regime change" in places such as Russia, North Korea, Iran, Venezuela, and Syria. The US continues to use its dollar power to arm-twist others and pressure them to follow America's position, regardless. Because of such abuses, many nations are trying to bypass the US dollar through bilateral trade by paying in their own currencies, which assumes that the currencies preserve an acceptable level of stability in their relative values (Collins et al. 2019).

The historical context may help us to learn and take lessons from the experience for the future. Two papers seem to have identified several weak spots that could prove to be Achilles heel: (i) the current state of the international monetary system (IMS); and (ii) China's monetary relations with the rest of the world. A solution might be to find ways to expand the use of the International Monetary fund's (IMF) Special Drawing Rights (SDRs), where China can unilaterally kick-start an SDR market to transact with other nations. Emerging markets suffer more from rising US interest rates. Their indebtedness (mostly domestic) has reached 225% of GDP—higher than the post 2008 financial crisis. Central banks were forces to pour some $10 trillion to ease the post 2008 crisis.

Some authors see the present monetary setup as 'a deficient, non-system' (White 2015; Ocampo 2017); and inherently crisis-prone because of the following drawbacks such as the IMS's reliance on the US dollar, which is the global currency, but which appears unstable, in need of some reform. The most recent uptick in tension includes the Sino–US trade war, along with rising domestic indebtedness of China. The brighter spots however are, a political will on all sides to resolve the war, China's sizeable US dollar chest, and her policy to internationalize the RMB[1]. This final point will help to stay outside the dollar arena. For this to work, China will need to open its capital account and establish financial links with the world. A fully-fledged currency of SDRs might shrink global imbalances. It will happen if the cooperating members for multilateral initiatives show interest. If the SDR takes effect, as a different currency, it would help China to open up its capital account and pave the way to easier dollar–RMB fungibility. The Hong Kong–China axis can be helpful in this regard. Is the time rife for taking a closer look with an open mind for a workable solution before it is too late?

The dollar-centric single currency system is an enormous economic gift for the US. Sadly, it is being used more as a political tool against the actors deemed unfriendly to US interests by denying banking access. Such a policy is likely to backfire and harm American leadership. Poorer developing countries thus must hold precautionary surplus dollar as insurance against the potential future balance of payments (BOP) problem for related adjustments when they are least able to do it. The G20 comes close to an economic policy coordinator, but is mostly ineffective. The US, the largest beneficiary, favors the status quo to gain seigniorage and prestige. The problem is in the attempts to leverage on excessive foreign policy—clearly, a mistake. To maintain the status, the US must run unsustainable current account deficits to provide the world with enough dollars. Nations buy US debt, which explains why the US can afford to run such reckless fiscal policy. The tax cuts by Trump are considered by many as irresponsible. The above narrative suggests that the dollar likely will come under considerable pressure in the times ahead. Should that happen, it is plausible that we will see significant rise in disorders in the global economy—perhaps just the tip of the iceberg. Whether or not it will take place, or where it would lead us to, is anybody's guess, and remains to be seen.

The world is cognizant of potential vulnerability in the global financial order and the risk each economy might end up bearing. In this regard, the risk associated with the economies that maintain pegged exchange rate has been highlighted by Ellis and Gyoerk (2019). The choice for a country's exchange rate regime has wide implications for the effectiveness and the flexibility of policy tools, and for economic and financial stability[2]. The author examines the interaction of currency peg abandonment with the occurrence of a banking crisis. He finds that countries that simultaneously suffered a systemic banking crisis during the period of exchange rate regime shift saw a greater economic and financial damage following the change. Regardless of a banking crisis, countries begin to recover after the same gap in time since the float.

To shield from shock, several reform proposals have been tabled including granting the SDR a larger role. The IMF appears to favor the idea. It is hard to assess if an SDR-based true global currency will achieve better macro-economic coordination. Some suggest that an IMS with a multicurrency arrangement is a viable option, with a broader role for the SDR. This may not materialize for lack a geopolitical alignment and the veto power of the US in the IMF (Harrison and Xiao 2019). However, given a changing global order, rooted in rising nationalism and populism, things likely will have to change for better or worse. While access to global markets and currencies is seen as a matter of right, the openness to private capital flows has made more diversification possible, and created opportunity for improved returns in the post Bretton–Woods world. One wonders if the genie is already out of the bottle. A top-down reform of the current IMS might have to be replaced by a bottom-up one.

China and the IMS need each other. If China were to unilaterally make the SDR central to its next phase of capital account opening, the Chinese institutions, corporates and individuals would embrace it. China, with the support from the rest of the world and Hong Kong, could

---

[1] The official currency introduced by the Communist People's Republic of China in 1949 was named as "Renminbi" (RMB), meaning "the people's currency", while. "Yuan" is the name of a unit of the renminbi currency, like the price is say cost one yuan or 10 yuan etc.

[2] He examines 21 instances where exchange rate pegs were abandoned to assess the potential economic damage associated with pegs failing. The sample includes major exchange rate shifts over the past thirty years, covering 1990's Latin American crises and the peg abandonment in Egypt (2016). Given the close link of banks to the sovereign and the real economy, risks tend to flow through, and possibly be magnified by the banking system.

promulgate SDR, ushering in an era of reduced tensions where China will have a more prominent role. (See Harrison and Xiao 2018, 2019).

Fast forward to 2017. Growth rose in every big advanced and most emerging economies (except a few European ones). Global trade surged, America boomed, and the slide of China into deflation had been out of consideration; even the Euro zone was thriving. In 2018, the story is very different. The stock markets tumbled a few times due to worry about a slow-down in global growth and its broader ramifications.

Despite some unusual surges here and there, the overall economic scenario across the world in 2018 saw some notable unevenness. In the US, President Trump's tax cuts have helped lift annualized quarterly growth above 4%, although it is likely to be short-lived. Unemployment is at its lowest since 1969, a historic episode! Yet the IMF thinks US economic growth will see slow-down, and maybe every advanced economy too. The situation in the emerging markets appears soft, which is a sign of broader trouble.

Against the above backdrops of the global economic condition, many predict rough days ahead. It would help to gain a better understanding of the scenario occurring across the globe, through the prism of political economy and finance. This special issue, a collection of well thought out papers from well-known academics working in the field of international money and finance, is a modest and timely effort, offering a logical perspective of professionals. The collection will hopefully add to the list of resources and be considered of much import for students, and perhaps, for the policymakers engaged in global finance and economics, despite whatever limitations it might have.

Funding: This research received no external funding.

Acknowledgments: The help from the *JRFM* editorial staff in this special issue on currency crisis is gratefully acknowledged, without which it would have been a real challenge, to complete the job. Standard caveats apply.

Conflicts of Interest: The authors declare no conflict of interest.

References

Batabyal, Sourav, Islam Faridul, and Khaznaji Maher. 2018. On the sources of the Great Moderation: Role of monetary policy and intermediate inputs. *Economic Modelling* 74: 1–9. [CrossRef]

Collins, Patrick, Jameel Ahmed, and Ahamed Kameel Meera. 2019. Simulation of the Grondona System of Conditional Currency Convertibility Based on Primary Commodities, Considered as a Means to Resist Currency Crises. *Journal of Risk Financial Management* 12: 75. [CrossRef]

Ellis, Colin, and Emilia Gyoerk. 2019. Investigating the Economic and Financial Damage around Currency Peg Failures. *Journal of Risk Financial Management* 12: 92. [CrossRef]

Harrison, Matthew, and Geng Xiao. 2019. China and Special Drawing Rights—Towards a Better International Monetary System. *Journal of Risk Financial Management* 12: 60. [CrossRef]

Harrison, Matthew, and Geng Xiao. 2018. Enhanced Special Drawing Rights—How China Could Contribute to a Reformed International Monetary Architecture. *China & World Economy* 26: 41–61.

Ocampo, José. 2017. *Resetting the International Monetary (Non)System. A Study Prepared by the United Nations University World Institute for Development Economics Research.* Oxford: Oxford University Press.

White, William. 2015. Point of View: System Malfunction. In *Finance & Development*. Washington, DC: IMF, vol. 52, pp. 44–47.

© 2019 by the author. Licensee MDPI, Basel, Switzerland. This article is an open access article distributed under the terms and conditions of the Creative Commons Attribution (CC BY) license (http://creativecommons.org/licenses/by/4.0/).

Article

Investigating the Economic and Financial Damage around Currency Peg Failures

Colin Ellis [1],* and Emilia Gyoerk [2]

1 Department of Economics, University of Birmingham, Birmingham B15 2TT, UK
2 Formerly Moody's Investors Service, London E14 5FA, UK; emilia.gyork@gmail.com
* Correspondence: c.ellis@bham.ac.uk

Received: 1 May 2019; Accepted: 22 May 2019; Published: 30 May 2019

Abstract: The choice and structure of a country's exchange rate regime has wide implications for the effectiveness and flexibility of monetary policy tools, as well as for economic and financial stability. We examine 21 instances where exchange rate pegs have been abandoned in the past, to gauge the potential economic damage associated with pegs failing. The sample includes major exchange rate shifts over the past thirty years, spanning from the Latin America currency crises of the 1990s to the peg abandonment in Egypt in 2016. Given the close interconnection of banks to the sovereign and the real economy, risks often flow through to, and can also be magnified by, the banking system. We therefore examine the interaction of currency peg abandonment with the occurrence of a banking crisis to investigate the different circumstances and impacts of exchange rate pegs failing. We have found that countries that simultaneously suffered a systemic banking crisis during the period of exchange rate regime shift also experienced significantly greater economic and financial damage following the adoption of a freely floating exchange rate. Nevertheless, regardless of whether there was a banking crisis, countries start showing signs of recovery after the same amount of time once the currency floated.

Keywords: exchange rates; currency pegs; banking crises

1. Introduction

The choice and structure of a country's exchange rate regime has wide implications for the effectiveness and flexibility of policy tools, as well as for economic and financial stability. One option is to peg the domestic currency to a foreign one; but if that peg proves to be unsustainable, the macroeconomic and financial damage when the peg breaks can be substantial. Recently, the dollar pegs of certain Gulf Cooperation Council (GCC) countries came under pressure after the fall in oil prices in 2014–15 exacerbated fiscal and current account deficits, leading to substantial declines in foreign exchange reserves. In particular, the Bahraini and Omani pegs became vulnerable and were exposed to market speculation as a result of weak balance of payments positions, strong reductions in foreign exchange reserves, and rising public debt. Before this, a number of pegged currencies among Commonwealth of Independent States countries also experienced significant pressure in the aftermath of the fall in oil prices and sanctions on Russia.

In some instances, past pressures of maintaining an exchange rate peg have ultimately led countries to abandon them in favour of a floating exchange rate. Such institutional shifts have often been preceded by factors including (1) instabilities in the banking sector stemming from its ties to the real economy and the sovereign; (2) depletion of foreign reserves and a lack of policy tools for the central bank to support the economy; (3) broader economic deterioration leading to defaults; and (4) political turmoil, has led many countries to abandon their exchange rate pegs in favour of a floating exchange rate and regained policy control. Importantly, policy stances and broader macrofinancial conditions can often be highly detrimental for the domestic credit environment before the peg is abandoned, such that continued defense of the peg would have caused significantly greater economic and financial damage than the abandonment did.

Whenever exchange rate pegs fail, the macroeconomic and financial fallout associated with the failure can be substantial, with widespread associated negative effects across a range of domestic issuers. In this paper, we examine 21 instances where exchange rate pegs have been abandoned in the past, to gauge the potential economic and financial turmoil associated with pegs failing. The data sample covers a select number of major exchange rate shifts over the past thirty years, spanning from the Latin America currency crises of the 1990s to the recent peg abandonment in Egypt at the end of 2016. Whether the shift from a managed exchange rate regime to floating occurs in conjunction with wider systemic economic and financial stress, or whether it takes place in a more contained fashion, has implications for the magnitude and persistence of the economic and financial turmoil at the time the peg is abandoned. Given the close interconnection of banks to the sovereign and real economies, the build-up of risks often flows through to, and can also be magnified by, the banking system. We therefore examine the interaction of currency peg abandonment with the simultaneous occurrence of a banking crisis to investigate the different circumstances and impacts of exchange rate pegs failing. We find that countries that simultaneously suffered a systemic banking crisis during the period of exchange rate regime shift also experienced significantly greater economic and financial damage following the adoption of a freely floating exchange rate. Nevertheless, in general, the timing of the peak impact of peg failures on growth and other economic variables were broadly similar across countries that saw banking crises, and across those that did not. This suggests that all countries generally began to see some degree of recovery at a similar point in time following peg abandonment.

This paper is organized as follows. The subsequent section provides a motivation for our study and an introduction to the theories surrounding monetary policy design with regards to fixed exchange rate regimes as well as the transmission channels from the exchange rate to the broader economy. The third section outlines the data used, while the fourth section illustrates the results found. The fifth section is our conclusion.

2. Background

The choice, structure, and alteration of a country's exchange rate regime has important credit implications, as can any shift in policy regime. One well-known description of the choices facing monetary policymakers is the so-called "impossible trinity", or monetary policy trilemma, coined by Mundell (1960, 1963) and Fleming (1962). This states that it is impossible to simultaneously pursue all of the following: a fixed exchange rate, an independent monetary policy (most often to target domestic inflation), and allowing the free flow of capital.

The trilemma can be understood from various viewpoints. As an illustration, suppose a central bank is pursuing a fixed exchange rate policy and there is free movement of capital, but then the central bank independently sets a policy interest rate that is lower than that of the foreign anchor currency issuer (the supplier of the peg currency). There will be an economic incentive to sell the domestic currency, which yields a lower interest rate in favour of the foreign currency that yields more. The domestic currency would thus depreciate in value and fuel domestic inflationary pressures. To keep the value of the domestic currency, the central bank has the following options: (1) buy the surplus domestic currency in exchange for the foreign currency. But this is only viable as long as there are sufficient foreign exchange reserves available, and therefore may not be a long-term solution; (2) the central bank has to mirror the interest rate of the foreign country to reduce depreciation pressures. This will cause the central bank to lose monetary policy independence, as it cannot freely set its policy interest rate while maintaining the exchange rate peg; or (3) the central bank needs to limit the flow of capital to maintain the domestic currency value and its chosen interest rate. The country and its citizens, therefore, might not gain from the benefits of free transfer of funds.

In practice, two out of these three features are achievable. Importantly, however, the trilemma still implies that the domestic central bank needs to pay close attention to external developments: whatever the choice of policy goals and instruments, the implementation of policy will not be immune to global developments.

Recent academic literature (e.g., Rey 2015) has argued that, given the emergence of a global financial cycle, the trilemma effectively transforms into a dilemma in which the central bank is faced with an irreconcilable arrangement where independent monetary policy is possible if and only if the capital account is managed, regardless of the exchange rate regime. In one sense, this is akin to global factors having a greater (or even dominant) role in the determination of the optimal domestic monetary stance. However, this dilemma perspective does not obviate the fact that domestic monetary policy can only focus on a single nominal anchor—either an inflation target, or a fixed exchange rate (essentially, an exchange rate target)—despite the fact that the suitable policy choices for either will depend at least in part on external developments.

Other authors have also investigated the fallout from currency regime changes, and the interaction with the banking sector. One notable contribution is from Hutchinson and Noy (2005), who examine the output costs of currency and banking crises, using an emerging market data sample ending in 1997. They find that both currency and banking crises have separate negative effects on output, yet also find that there is little sign of a multiplicative effect—extra output losses from banking and currency crises occurring simultaneously. This contrasts somewhat with Aghion et al. (2001), who consider how a banking crisis may be exacerbated if a currency crisis occurs at the same time, where a sharp devaluation can push near-insolvent banks into bankruptcy. It is noteworthy that the modelling approach used by Hutchinson and Noy (2005) fails to capture most of the variation evident in emerging market output growth, and we have seen a number of currency crises in recent years that have exhibited different characteristics.

Another notable contribution is from Chang and Velasco (2000), who posit that the nature of the exchange rate regime may influence the likelihood of each type of crisis (banking and currency), brought by self-fulfilling runs. They find that international illiquidity is fundamental in the joint occurrence of banking and currency crises, reflecting either common factors or spillover effects. In a similar vein, Kaminsky and Reinhart (1999) find common causes in the incidence of so-called twin crises (banking and currency), but notably do not conclude that a twin crisis will always be larger than the combined effect of the two crises measured independently.

Other research has focused on various aspects related to these studies. For instance, Cavallo et al. (2005) and Gupta et al. (2003) focus on the output cost of currency crises, while Arteta and Eichengreen (2002), among others, focus on output costs of banking crises. Other work has focused on the transmission channels of financial crises to output losses, such as Corsetti et al. (1998) and Dekle and Kletzer (2001).

However, it is notable that much of this work pre-dates the global financial crisis in 2007/8, and hence does not account for the significant financial and economic changes seen since the mid-2000s, or, as noted above, the currency and banking crises seen since that time. As globalisation has spread and capital controls have been seen as relatively less effective or desirable, countries that have opted to peg their exchange rates[1] have effectively sacrificed autonomy over domestic monetary policy. In other words, allowing for free movement of capital while pursuing a fixed exchange rate means the domestic central bank must apply an interest rate policy that is aligned with that of the country issuing the currency it is pegged to.

As long as economic fluctuations are aligned and both economies can support synchronous movements in the exchange rate, a fixed exchange rate helps add stability and anchors inflation

---

[1] The value of the domestic currency may be pegged against a single foreign anchor currency or against a basket of different foreign currencies.

expectations. This has been highly beneficial for many emerging market economies and encouraged capital inflows. However, passive adoption of the monetary policy stance of the anchor country is also a key reason why exchange rate pegs can fail.[2] If economic cycles start to deviate across countries, applying the same monetary policy can be procyclical and exacerbate these fluctuations, exposing the pegging country to an interest rate that is too high or too low given domestic macroeconomic conditions.

As an example, if the US—which has served as the anchor currency issuer for several other countries[3]—experiences stronger growth and appreciation pressures, it may apply a higher policy interest rate to prevent economic overheating. If at the same time, the pegging country experiences headwinds to growth but maintains its currency peg to the US dollar (USD), it not only adopts a too-high interest rate relative to domestic activity, but also adopts an appreciating exchange rate (relative to other currencies) that reduces the relative competitiveness of that country's products. This combined effect weighs on domestic growth, with the associated negative effects for a range of market participants. The mechanism naturally works in reverse as well, with accommodative US monetary policy fueling economic overheating in pegged countries.

Once a currency peg starts to come under pressure and it is deemed unsustainable to defend the peg, countries choose a range of options in the transition to a floating regime: from abruptly breaking the peg to progressively allowing increasingly large deviations from the stated peg.[4] These different regime shifts, in turn, further shape not just the exchange rate adjustment itself, but also the macroeconomic consequences. All instances that we consider have originated from periods of increasing instability leading ultimately to pegs being abandoned. Speculation, policy uncertainty and political turmoil often prompt exchange rate liberalisation as a way to restore stability.

The economic impact of a fall in the exchange rate, as is typical following peg abandonment, will depend on its trigger and the wider circumstances of exchange rate regime shift.[5] A decline in the exchange rate is essentially a re-pricing of the economy, relative to other economies. As such, domestic firms that use foreign inputs will suffer higher costs; this will hit profitability and/or result in higher domestic selling prices. Higher import prices often feed into higher producer and consumer prices over a long period of time, due to elongated supply chains.

However, domestic firms that compete with foreign firms may see positive impacts. The higher price of imports will likely lead to a fall in import volumes, both if customers switch to buying from domestic producers and because of the general fall in spending due to their weaker purchasing power. And a weaker exchange rate is generally positive for exporting firms, boosting either export volumes or margins, depending on whether firms adjust either the foreign or domestic price of exports. The depreciation of sterling between late 2007 and early 2009 shows that effects can be mixed: UK export prices responded first in sterling terms, rising as the depreciation took hold; and while prices initially fell in foreign-currency terms, UK exporters then offset this. By 2011, the foreign-currency price of UK exports was little changed from 2007, while the sterling price was significantly higher (Figure 1).

---

[2] The ultimate reasons for why certain countries abandon their pegs and others do not vary widely and are often highly idiosyncratic across countries.
[3] The US Dollar has also served as the de facto global reserve currency for the past six decades, and is predicted to continue to serve this purpose for the foreseeable future (Ellis and Smartt 2018).
[4] For further description of the circumstances around the peg failure, see the Tables A1 and A2 in the Appendix A.
[5] The description of transmission channels from the exchange rate to the broader economy draws on work by Ellis et al. (2015).

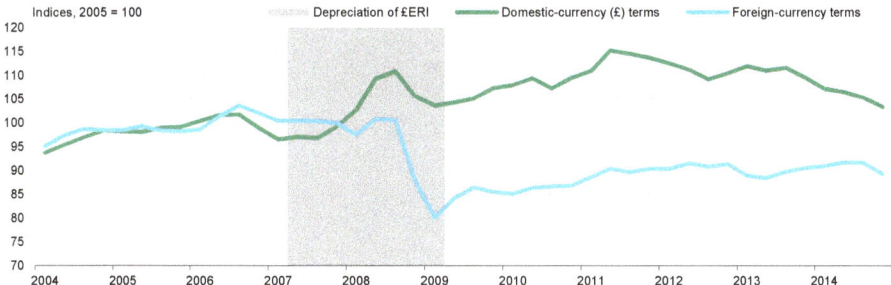

Figure 1. An illustration of diverging foreign- and domestic-currency export prices. The UK goods export prices in sterling terms and in foreign currency terms, around the time of the significant 25% depreciation in the sterling exchange rate index (ERI) from 2007 until 2009.

Over time, a weaker exchange rate will generally boost export values relative to imports, thereby improving trade and current account balances, although in the short term both can deteriorate if prices respond more swiftly than volumes. As such, countries with large current account deficits are likely to be more vulnerable to a depreciation in their exchange rate. Such a depreciation will help to rebalance external and internal demand in the economy, which also typically provides some short-term boost to GDP growth via weaker imports and/or stronger exports. Correspondingly, a currency appreciation can temporarily weigh on GDP growth via weaker exports and stronger imports.

Trade-dependent entities—both sovereigns and corporates—are most exposed to these effects. Companies focused in commoditised goods such as basic raw materials—for instance, some chemicals or metal products—are particularly exposed to these effects of changes in the relative value of currencies. However, commodity producers whose exports are traded in a common currency (typically the US dollar) are generally insulated from these pricing and volume effects. Instead, currency movements will typically have more impact on margins, if some of these costs are in domestic currency terms.

Exchange rates also affect the household sector. Consumers often spend a significant proportion of their income on imports; and the higher prices of these goods and services, following the exchange rate decline, implies a fall in the real consumption wage—households' earnings relative to consumer prices. This often manifests as a short-term rise in consumer price inflation.

A currency depreciation can also affect household and corporate balance sheets. The value of foreign assets will increase, in domestic currency terms, which could mitigate any drag from weaker profitability or real wages; however, this may be offset by increases in foreign liabilities. Domestic assets will also be cheaper to foreigners, which could encourage inward investment flows. However, the trigger for the exchange rate movement is important here; if the currency decline reflects higher risk premia, then capital outflows are likely in the short term and may only stabilise over time, weighing on medium-term growth prospects.

Finally, a fall in the exchange rate may also trigger responses from domestic policymakers. Because exchange rates are relative prices, the impact on (measured) inflation will only be temporary if the central bank credibly targets inflation; if medium-term inflation expectations are anchored, central banks can look through the relative price shock. In contrast, if expectations are not anchored, then there is a risk of second-round effects—higher prices could feed into higher wages, which in turn could feed back into higher prices or unemployment. In these scenarios—or if the fall in the exchange rate is accompanied by a sharp increase in capital outflows—the central bank could be forced to raise policy rates, thereby increasing funding costs for banks, companies and households.

We aim to shed light on the different experiences surrounding the abandonment of a peg, to gauge the potential economic and financial turmoil associated with pegs failing. Given the close interconnection of banks to the sovereign and real economies, we further evaluate how the interaction of an exchange rate regime shift with the occurrence of a systemic banking crisis impacts the observed outcomes. We further add value by assessing the persistence of the economic and financial costs borne by peg abandonment, and how this is impacted by a banking crisis.

3. Materials and Methods

We examine 21 instances where exchange rate pegs have been abandoned in the past, to gauge the potential economic and financial turmoil associated with pegs failing. Importantly, we conduct our analysis using an event study rather than formally adopting quantitative modelling. This partly reflects the wide variation in experience across crises, as reflected in the poor fit of some modeling in past research. Importantly, we do not try to ascribe causality between currency crises and other events such as banking crises; we simply examine deviations in output and other macroeconomic variables following the crisis. In doing so, we hope to establish the broad range of outcomes that other countries may see when future crises occur.

The data sample is described in the appendix, and covers a selected number of major exchange rate shifts over the past thirty years, spanning from the Latin America currency crises during the 1990s to the recent peg abandonment in Egypt at the end of 2016. We are primarily concerned with assessing the impact for the following macroeconomic variables: the exchange rate of the domestic currency to the peg anchor currency (normally the US Dollar), real GDP and its growth rate, inflation, and unemployment. All data are collected from public sources. We apply an event study approach in which we examine the 18 months leading up to, and the 18 months following, the month of peg abandonment to capture and isolate the peak of the impact of currency peg failure. In considering the interaction of currency peg failure with banking crisis, we draw on the definition and database on systemic banking crises developed by Laeven and Valencia (2018). Their definition of a systemic banking crisis fulfils two criteria along the dimensions of severity of crisis and policy responses:

1. There are significant bank runs, losses in the banking system, and/or bank liquidations; and
2. There are significant policy interventions to combat these losses in the banking system.

Figure 2 shows the countries that suffered a systemic banking crisis and when that crisis erupted in relation to the month of the peg breaking. Ten countries, or about half the sample, experienced a banking crisis, and we use this as a means to split our sample in order to investigate the different impacts of exchange rate pegs failing. In most cases where there was a systemic banking crisis, it broke out within a few months after the peg failed, indicating a coincidence of the peak of the pressure on the peg and the systemic banking crisis entering full force.

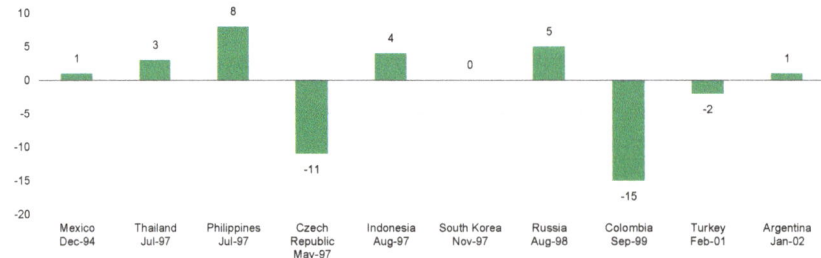

Figure 2. Timing of systemic banking crises in relation to the month of currency peg failure. The figure shows the number of months' difference from the time of the currency peg breaking to the systemic banking crisis erupting, as defined by Laeven and Valencia (2018). A negative number signifies the systemic banking crisis erupted before the peg failed, while a positive number indicates the banking crisis broke out after the adoption of the floating currency. In South Korea, the banking crisis became systemic in the same month as the currency was floated. Although Azerbaijan suffered a crisis in its banking sector when the largest bank, International Bank of Azerbaijan, suspended payments on some of its liabilities in 2017 and restructured $3.3 billion of debt, the crisis was not systemic in nature as defined by Laeven and Valencia, and is therefore not featured in the exhibit.

However, there are also instances where the banking crisis came first. In particular, in both the Czech Republic and Colombia, the banking crises became systemic around a year before the pegs were abandoned. It is likely that the damaging impact of these banking crises provided motivation for the countries' central banks to mitigate pressure on their currencies. Both countries adopted increasingly lax exchange rate arrangements in the year before abandoning their managed regimes altogether. Immediately before the authorities let the pegs fail, the Czech Republic allowed deviations of ±15% around the stated exchange rate peg, while Colombia allowed fluctuations of ±10%. But it also serves to demonstrate that banking crises do not always follow currency crises, and it is possible for causality to run the other way.

4. Results

Although all episodes of exchange rate regime shifts from managed into freely floating have been disruptive in our sample, the macrofinancial damage associated with some cases was more damaging than others. Many factors affect the severity of impact, including risk build-up and contagion across sectors, as well as the adaptability, timeliness and adequacy of policy responses. The currency peg failures in Russia in 1998 and in Argentina in 2002 were both accompanied by sovereign defaults, resulting in particularly severe economic and financial damage. At the other end of the spectrum, Iceland in 2001 and Kazakhstan in 2015 experienced more muted consequences of dropping their exchange rate pegs.

On average, countries that suffered a banking crisis recorded the greatest exchange rate depreciation six months after the peg broke (see Figure 3). The currency had then lost almost half its value compared to its level in the month the peg was abandoned. In contrast, countries that avoided a banking crisis recorded a much milder average impact of 20% depreciation against the time of peg failure, with the nadir of the exchange rate depreciation for these non-banking-crisis countries happening around 15 months following peg failure. This indicates that although the loss in value of the currency was more severe for banking crisis countries, the currency started regaining in value sooner compared to countries that did not see a banking crisis.

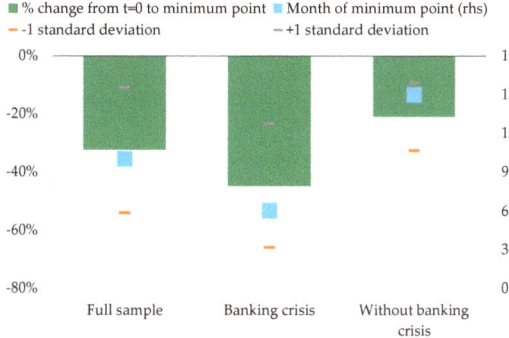

Figure 3. Exchange rate depreciation following currency peg abandonment. This figure demonstrates the largest degree of exchange rate depreciation and month of minimum point after peg failure. Green bars refer to the greatest average percent depreciation in the exchange rate against the anchoring peg currency, and the blue square markers refer to the month in which this depreciation occurred following peg abandonment. Standard deviation markers refer to the sample standard deviation around the minimum point.

On a country by country basis, Figure 4 shows the instances in which the exchange rate depreciation exceeded 50% from the time of peg failure, including Indonesia, Turkey and Argentina, within a few months of abandoning their pegs. Such magnitude of depreciation will have severe consequences for both growth and financial stability.

However, there are other examples where the authorities have moved to floated currencies more gradually, which can result in less violent moves in the exchange rate from the point of flotation. For instance, when Egypt floated its exchange rate in 2016, it saw a 14% depreciation in the second month after flotation, but the exchange rate then stabilised at around 10% below the previously pegged value (see Figure 4). Nonetheless, it is important to note that the authorities had already devalued its pegged currency by 13% some ten months before it moved to a floating currency. Additionally, that flotation only occurred after political and social stability had already improved and coincided with a series of measures aimed at restoring macroeconomic stability, supported by strong financial flows from donors. There have been other instances of shifts in pegs prior to their abandonment: for example, Azerbaijan also moved its peg lower in February 2015—devaluing by 25%—before the currency was ultimately floated in December of that year.

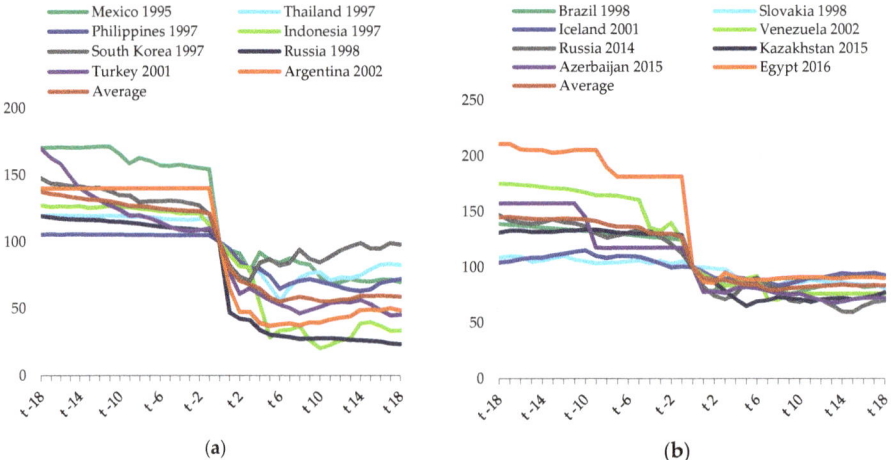

Figure 4. Change in exchange rates around time of peg abandonment. This figure demonstrates the impact on exchange rates around the time of peg failure: (**a**) shows banking crisis countries; (**b**) shows countries without banking crisis. The vertical axis showing the exchange rates against the anchor currency in index terms where the month of peg failure = 100. The horizontal axis reflects the 18 months, on either side, of the point of peg failure.

The impact of a peg failure on economic growth prospects can be very damaging as a result of significantly increased uncertainty, instability and contagion of risk across sectors. As monetary policy is largely unable to respond to domestic developments while the peg remains, support for the economy is typically limited to fiscal policy and is often insufficient.

Average real GDP growth in the year after the peg failed was around −3% for countries that did not see a banking crisis, compared with a figure of around −6.5% for countries that also suffered a banking crisis (see Figure 5). Apart from this initial growth impact, the cumulative damage from exchange rate pegs failing is also substantial. It is hard to gauge this accurately, given that many countries enjoyed strong growth before their pegs broke: our simple assumption is that, if the peg had not failed, growth over the following 18 months would have continued at its average rate over the five years before the peg failure.[6] On this basis, the cumulative GDP shortfall in countries without banking crises was 3.5% on average; but in countries with banking crises it was larger at 6% after 18 months. Both of these figures include some partial recovery over the 18-month period, with a peak

---

[6] This is a critical assumption, notably as some countries may have seen substantial capital inflows and unsustainable growth before the peg failed.

GDP shortfall of 4.5% after nine months where there was no banking crisis, and a shortfall of 7.6% after 12 months for countries with banking crises.

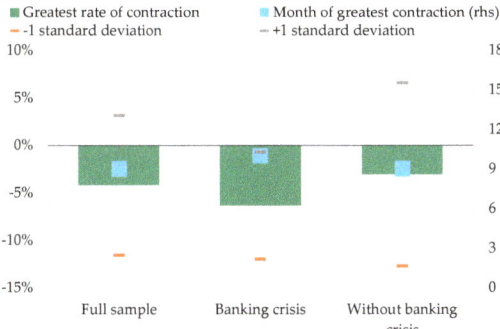

Figure 5. Contraction in annual real GDP growth following currency peg abandonment. This figure demonstrates the largest degree of economic shrinkage in real terms and month in which this shrinkage occurred after peg failure. Green bars refer to the greatest average percent contraction in real GDP, and the blue square markers refer to the month in which this shrinkage occurred following peg abandonment. Standard deviation markers refer to the sample standard deviation around the greatest contraction point.

The fact that the GDP shortfall is higher when both banking and currency crises occur, rather than instances of the exchange rate peg failing (but no banking crisis) is consistent with previous research noted earlier, although the magnitudes are somewhat smaller. While this may suggest that the impact of crises has changed over time, it could also reflect policymakers taking different stances given they have more (global) experience in what happens when risks crystallize. In light of past research, it is also unsurprising that the coincidence of currency and banking crises results in greater output losses. In particular, where economies are already struggling with the higher inflation and negative real wage effects engendered by the currency depreciation, having a banking sector that is experiencing its own crisis—leading to a credit crunch—will also imply a fall in output, and indeed likely result in further negative wealth shocks on corporates and households, as bad debts are ultimately re-structured, and may even spillover to the sovereign balance sheet if public recapitalization is required. Furthermore, if the banking sector is the main source of finance to the real economy (with capital markets being relatively underdeveloped in the countries in our sample), its crisis will also impede the process of (re)allocating funds to new investments and businesses that can facilitate the broader transformation and hence recovery of the economy.

Figure 6 illustrates the impact of peg failure on real GDP growth per country. It is clear that if risks spread to the banking system the reduction in economic activity is substantial, with contraction on an annual basis often exceeding 5% for several months following currency flotation. Although Venezuela circumvented a systemic banking crisis, the recession in 2002 was significant. A fall in oil prices acted as a trigger, but the recession was also fueled by political instability—including a failed coup d'etat and the imprisonment of then-president Hugo Chávez—as well as business strikes and the withdrawal of foreign investment. The peg was abandoned in June 2002. However, following another speculative attack and business strikes in December 2002, Venezuela reinstated a peg in February 2003, alongside extensive capital controls.

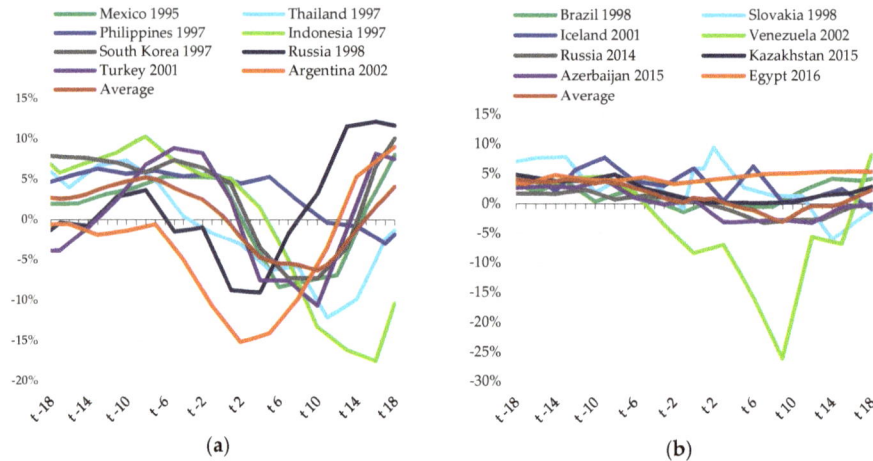

Figure 6. Impact on real GDP growth around time of peg abandonment. This figure demonstrates the impact on real GDP growth around the time of peg failure: (**a**) shows banking crisis countries; (**b**) shows countries without banking crisis. The vertical axis showing the annual growth rates in percentage terms. The horizontal axis reflects the 18 months, on either side, of the point of peg failure.

When the currency starts falling in value, its purchasing power declines, which fuels domestic inflationary pressures. There is a significant difference in the magnitude of impact between banking crisis countries and non-crisis countries in terms of the impact on inflation rates (see Figure 7). The substantial currency depreciation experienced by these countries contributed to inflationary pressures as imports became relatively more expensive. At the peak of impact, annual inflation of crisis countries had on average risen by 35 percentage points from a rate of 11% at the time the peg broke to 46% at its peak a year later. Countries that avoided a banking crisis saw an average increase of 10 percentage points from 9% to 19%.

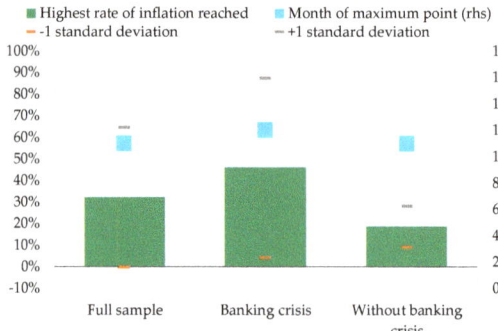

Figure 7. Annual rate of consumer price index (CPI) inflation following peg abandonment. This figure demonstrates the highest CPI inflation rate reached and the month in which this rate occurred after peg failure. Green bars refer to the greatest average rate of annual inflation, and the blue square markers refer to the month in which this inflation peak occurred following peg abandonment. Standard deviation markers refer to the sample standard deviation around the maximum point.

Nevertheless, among the countries that have suffered a systemic banking crisis, the experiences vary widely. Southeast Asian countries saw marginal increases in inflation from the rates prevalent before the currency was floated, while Russia, Indonesia, and Turkey have recorded inflation well over 70% (see Figure 8).

Venezuela and Egypt are the outliers in the set of countries that did not endure a banking crisis. The rise in Egypt's inflation rate was partly driven by the removal of subsidies around the time of the peg dissolution, rather than just the peg abandonment itself. During its crisis, Egypt also received support from its Gulf state neighbours as well as an extended fund facility arrangement of $12 billion from the IMF, which further helped to mitigate the overall economic impact.

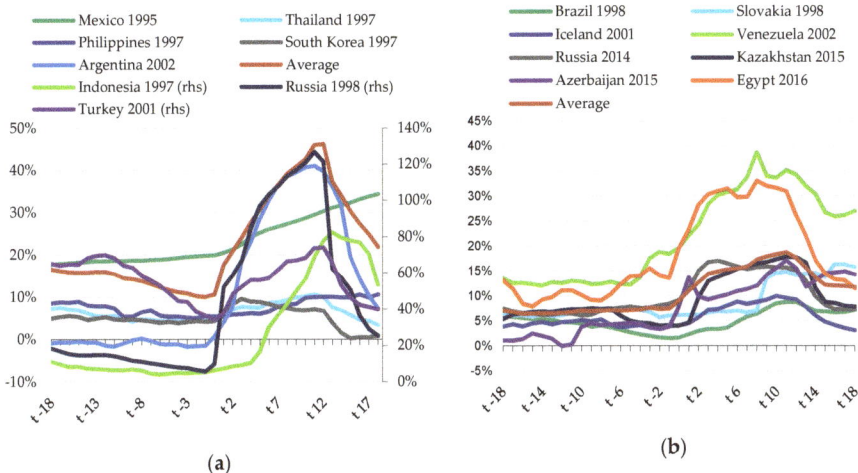

Figure 8. Impact on annual rate of CPI inflation around time of peg abandonment. This figure demonstrates the impact on CPI inflation around the time of peg failure: (**a**) shows banking crisis countries; (**b**) shows countries without banking crisis. The vertical axis shows the annual rates in percentage terms. The horizontal axis reflects the 18 months, on either side, of the point of peg failure.

As uncertainty grows, economic activity slows, inflationary pressures build, and employers pull back on hiring intentions and reduce staff numbers. As a result, unemployment tends to rise following peg failure. Figure 9 shows that countries that avoided a banking crisis reached a higher peak rate of unemployment from the time of peg failure compared with those that went through one, but in part this reflected the higher starting point. The rise in unemployment was greater for banking crisis countries, on average hovering around 7–8% in the months before the peg broke and subsequently rising by 2.2 percentage points to about 10%. On the other hand, countries that avoided such a crisis on average had an unemployment rate of around 12.5% at the time of peg failure, with the rate rising to almost 14% about a year later.

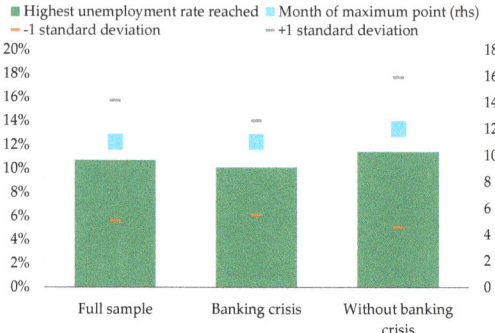

Figure 9. Unemployment rate following currency peg abandonment. This figure demonstrates the highest level of unemployment reached and the month in which this rate occurred after peg failure. Green bars refer to the greatest average level of unemployment, and the blue square markers refer to the month in which this unemployment peak occurred following peg abandonment. Standard deviation markers refer to the sample standard deviation around the maximum point.

Among countries that circumvented a banking crisis, Venezuela and Slovakia recorded the largest increases in unemployment of around 4 percentage points after abandoning their pegs (see Figure 10). In addition to recording the most pronounced rise in unemployment, these countries also started from the highest levels at the time the peg broke, of around a 15% unemployment rate. At the other end of the spectrum, Egypt had declining unemployment rates following the exchange rate regime shift.

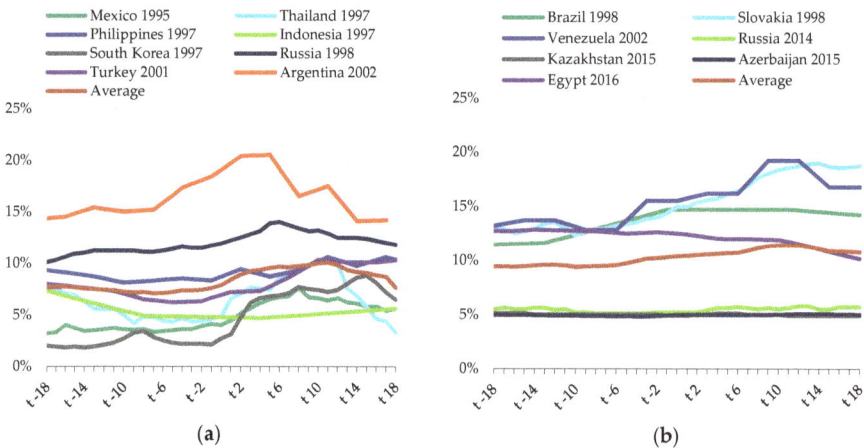

Figure 10. Impact on unemployment around time of peg abandonment. This figure demonstrates the impact on unemployment around the time of peg failure: (**a**) shows banking crisis countries; (**b**) shows countries without banking crisis. The vertical axis shows the annual rates in percentage terms. The horizontal axis reflects the 18 months, on either side, of the point of peg failure.

Overall this analysis demonstrates that, while countries' individual experiences differ, the abandonment of an exchange rate peg in order to move to a floating currency regime is typically associated with a dramatic weakening of macrofinancial conditions. This, in turn, will engender widespread economic and financial damage within the economy. If the peg break also coincides with a banking crisis, the negative credit impact could be much more substantial than would otherwise be the case, as noted in previous research. Nevertheless, regardless of whether there was a banking crisis, countries start to show signs of recovery after the same amount of time once the currency floated.

5. Conclusions

The choice and structure of a country's exchange rate regime has wide implications for the effectiveness and flexibility of policy tools, as well as for economic and financial stability. One choice is to peg the domestic currency to a foreign one, but if that peg proves unsustainable, the macroeconomic and financial damage when the peg breaks can be substantial. In this paper, we examine 21 instances where exchange rate pegs have been abandoned in the past, to gauge the potential economic and financial turmoil associated with pegs failing. The data sample covers a selected number of major exchange rate shifts over the past thirty years, spanning from the Latin America currency crises during the 1990s to the recent peg abandonment in Egypt at the end of 2016. Whether the shift from a managed exchange rate regime to floating occurs in conjunction with wider systemic economic and financial stress, or whether it takes place in a more contained fashion, has implications for the magnitude and persistence of the economic and financial turmoil at the time the peg is abandoned. Given the close interconnection of banks to the sovereign and real economies, the build-up of risks often flows through to, and can also be magnified by, the banking system. We therefore examine the interaction of currency peg abandonment with the simultaneous occurrence of a banking crisis to investigate the different circumstances and impacts of exchange rate pegs failing. We find that countries that simultaneously suffered a systemic banking crisis during the period of exchange rate regime shift also experienced significantly greater economic and financial damage following the adoption of a freely floating exchange rate. Nevertheless, regardless of whether there was a banking crisis, countries start showing signs of recovery after the same amount of time once the currency floated.

Author Contributions: Conceptualization, C.E.; Data curation, E.G.; Formal analysis, E.G.; Investigation, E.G.; Methodology, C.E. and E.G.; Writing—original draft, E.G.; Writing—review & editing, C.E.

Funding: This research received no external funding.

Acknowledgments: The authors are grateful for helpful comments from former and present colleagues at the Bank of England, Moody's Investor Service, and elsewhere. All errors remain our own.

Conflicts of Interest: The authors declare no conflict of interest.

Appendix A

Table A1. Sample of countries that abandoned their currency pegs, first half of sample.

Country	Date of Peg Failure	Starting Currency Regime	New Currency Regime	Start of Systemic Banking Crisis	Date of Sovereign Default
Mexico	Dec 1994	Managed exchange rate versus USD within widening bands	Floating	Jan 1995	-
Thailand	Jul 1997	Fixed peg against a basket of currencies, especially USD	Floating, but with market interventions	Oct 1997	-
Philippines	Jul 1997	Officially floating, but with admitted market interventions	Floating, but with market interventions	Mar 1998	-
Czech Republic	May 1997	Fixed peg versus USD, but towards the end of the regime the currency was managed within widening bands	Managed float, but no stated bands; Currency appreciated after regime shift	Jun 1996	-
Indonesia	Aug 1997	Fixed peg against a basket of currencies, but towards the end of the regime the currency was managed within widening bands	Floating, but with market interventions	Dec 1997	-

Table A1. Cont.

Country	Date of Peg Failure	Starting Currency Regime	New Currency Regime	Start of Systemic Banking Crisis	Date of Sovereign Default
South Korea	Nov 1997	Fixed peg versus USD, but towards the end of the regime the currency was managed within widening bands	Floating, but with market interventions	Nov 1997	-
Russia	Aug 1998	Managed exchange rate versus USD within widening bands	Managed float	Jan 1999	Aug 1998
Slovakia	Oct 1998	Fixed peg against currency basket, but towards the end of the regime the currency was managed within progressively widening bands	Floating, but with market interventions	-	-
Brazil	Jan 1999	Crawling peg versus USD; steady devaluation of centre rate with fluctuations within band	Floating	-	-
Chile	Sep 1999	Crawling peg versus USD with widening bands; steady adjustment of centre rate with fluctuations within widening bands	Floating; Currency appreciated following regime shift	-	-
Colombia	Sep 1999	Crawling peg versus USD with widening bands; steady adjustment of centre rate with fluctuations within progressively widening bands	Floating, but with market interventions. Currency appreciated following regime shift	Jun 1998	-

Table A2. Sample of countries that abandoned their currency pegs, second half of sample.

Country	Date of Peg Failure	Starting Currency Regime	New Currency Regime	Start of Systemic Banking Crisis	Date of Sovereign Default
Poland	Apr 2000	Fixed peg against a currency basket, but towards the end of the regime the currency was managed within widening bands	Floating Currency appreciated following regime shift	-	-
Turkey	Feb 2001	Pre-announced path of exchange rate against currency basket (USD and euro)	Floating	Dec 2000	-
Iceland	Mar 2001	Fixed peg against currency basket, but towards the end of the regime the currency was managed within progressively widening bands	Floating, but with market interventions	-	-
Argentina	Jan 2002	Fixed peg versus USD	Floating	Dec 2001	Nov 2001
Venezuela	Jun 2002	De facto fixed versus USD Officially a crawling peg with bands	Floating (Peg reinstated in Feb 2003)	-	-

Table A2. *Cont.*

Country	Date of Peg Failure	Starting Currency Regime	New Currency Regime	Start of Systemic Banking Crisis	Date of Sovereign Default
Russia	Nov 2014	Progressively widening bands against a dual currency basket (USD and Euro)	Free floating	-	-
Switzerland	Jan 2015	Minimum exchange rate floor against EUR	Floating, but with announced willingness to intervene; Currency appreciated following regime shift	-	-
Kazakhstan	Aug 2015	Fixed peg versus USD	Floating, but with market interventions	-	-
Azerbaijan	Dec 2015	Fixed peg versus USD	Free floating. De facto re-pegged in May 2017	-	-
Egypt	Nov 2016	Fixed peg versus USD, but with frequent discrete devaluations	Floating	-	-

References

Aghion, Philippe, Philippe Bacchetta, and Abhijit Banerjee. 2001. Currency Crises and Monetary Policy in an Economy with Credit Constraints. *European Economic Review* 45: 1121–50. [CrossRef]

Arteta, Carlos, and Barry Eichengreen. 2002. Banking Crises in Emerging Markets: Presumptions and Evidence. In *Exchange Rate and Financial Vulnerability in Emerging Markets*. Edited by Mario Blejer and Marko Skreb. Cambridge: MIT Press.

Cavallo, Michele, Kate Kisselev, Fabrizio Perri, and Nouriel Roubini. 2005. Exchange Rate Overshooting and the Costs of Floating. Working Paper No. 2005-07, Federal Reserve Bank of San Francisco, San Francisco, CA, USA.

Chang, Roberto, and Andres Velasco. 2000. Financial Fragility and the Exchange Rate Regime. *Journal of Economic Theory* 92: 1–34. [CrossRef]

Corsetti, Giancarlo, Paolo Pesenti, and Nouriel Roubini. 1998. What Caused the Asian Currency and Financial Crisis? Part I: A Macroeconomic Overview. NBER Working Paper No. 6833, National Bureau of Economic Research, Cambridge, MA, USA.

Dekle, Robert, and Kenneth Kletzer. 2001. Domestic Bank Regulation and Financial Crises—Theory and Empirical Evidence from East Asia. In *Preventing Currency Crises in Emerging Markets*. Edited by Sebastian Edwards and Jeffrey A. Frankel. Chicago: University of Chicago Press.

Ellis, Colin, and Georgina Smartt. 2018. *Currency Composition of Foreign Reserves Continues to Change only Gradually, with Any Major Shifts Likely Years Away*. London: Moody's Investors Service.

Ellis, Colin, Marie Diron, and Elena Duggar. 2015. *Credit Implications of Exchange-Rate Movements Depend on Source of the Shock and Issuers' Exposures*. London: Moody's Investors Service.

Fleming, Marcus. 1962. Domestic financial policies under fixed and under floating exchange rates. *International Monetary Fund (Staff Papers)* 9: 369–80. [CrossRef]

Gupta, Poonam, Deepak Mishra, and Ratna Sahay. 2003. Output Response during Currency Crises. Working Paper No. 03/230, International Monetary Fund, Washington, DC, USA.

Hutchinson, Michael, and Ilan Noy. 2005. How bad are twins? Output costs of currency and banking crises. *Journal of Money, Credit and Banking* 37: 725–52. [CrossRef]

Kaminsky, Graciela, and Carmen Reinhart. 1999. The Twin Crises: The Causes of Banking and Balance-of-Payments Problems. *American Economic Review* 89: 473–500. [CrossRef]

Laeven, Luc, and Fabian Valencia. 2018. *Systemic Banking Crises Revisited*. IMF Working Paper 18/206, International Monetary Fund, Washington, DC, USA.

Mundell, Robert. 1960. The monetary dynamics of international adjustment under fixed and flexible exchange rates. *The Quarterly Journal of Economics* 74: 227–57. [CrossRef]

Mundell, Robert. 1963. Capital mobility and stabilization policy under fixed and flexible exchange rates. *Canadian Journal of Economics and Political Science* 29: 475–85. [CrossRef]

Rey, Helen. 2015. Dilemma Not Trilemma: The Global Financial Cycle and Monetary Independence. NBER Working Paper No. 21162, National Bureau of Economic Research, Cambridge, MA, USA.

© 2019 by the authors. Licensee MDPI, Basel, Switzerland. This article is an open access article distributed under the terms and conditions of the Creative Commons Attribution (CC BY) license (http://creativecommons.org/licenses/by/4.0/).

Article

A Cointegration of the Exchange Rate and Macroeconomic Fundamentals: The Case of the Indonesian Rupiah vis-á-vis Currencies of Primary Trade Partners

Agus Salim and Kai Shi *

School of Economics, Northeast Normal University, Changchun 130024, China; ags192@nenu.edu.cn
* Correspondence: shik142@nenu.edu.cn

Received: 28 February 2019; Accepted: 25 April 2019; Published: 13 May 2019

Abstract: Since the appearance of persistent research finding a disconnection between the exchange rate and its macroeconomic fundamentals, the empirical debate has not stopped. Studies employ various methods to explain the presence of the exchange rate disconnect puzzle, including applying models to the case of emerging market economies. However, the exchange rate has different determinants in some countries. To revisit this puzzle in an emerging market currency, we analyzed the cointegration of the exchange rate of the Indonesian Rupiah vis-á-vis currencies of primary trade partners and its macroeconomic fundamentals. The empirical results based on Autoregressive Distributed Lag (ARDL) and Nonlinear Autoregressive Distributed Lag (NARDL) models show that the fundamental variables consistently drive the exchange rate. The trade surplus as an extended nonlinear variable revealed high feedback to the exchange rate volatility in the long-run.

Keywords: cointegration; exchange rate disconnect puzzle; macroeconomic fundamentals; emerging market economies; NARDL; trade balance

1. Introduction

Interdependence in international finance affects the correlation of all macroeconomic variables according to several empirical studies, contrary to theoretical concepts. One of the empirical debates is the relationship between exchange rates and macroeconomic fundamentals. Theoretically, exchange rate volatility, in the long run, is determined by several macroeconomic fundamentals such as money supply, real income, real interest rates, inflation, trade balance, etc. (Abhyankar et al. 2005). Another piece of evidence that supports the relationship between exchange rates and fundamentals was provided by Charles and Darné (2009) and Laganà and Sgro (2007), who discussed theoretical developments and explanations. They also revealed econometric techniques, including increasing data and economic value by evaluating the performance of these fundamental models.

Since the introduction of exchange rate disconnect puzzles through empirical studies by Meese and Rogoff (1983), the investigation of the relationship between exchange rates and macroeconomic fundamentals continues. They used a sample of the exchange rates of three developed countries' currencies, namely US dollars against the German Mark, the Japanese Yen, and the British Pound. The macroeconomic variables included in their study are the difference in the money supply, the difference in output, the difference in inflation rates, the difference in interest rates, the US trade balance, and the foreign trade balance. They concluded that the structural model used in the study resulted in low significance. This finding presented a conundrum, which sparked a debate on the so-called "exchange rate disconnect puzzle" in international macroeconomics.

Recently, the study of the relationship between the exchange rate and macroeconomic fundamentals has grown. Engel and West (2005) assessed the determinants of the exchange rate, confirming the existence of the puzzle. They employed the exchange rate of US dollars vis-á-vis the currencies of six industrialized countries: Canada, France, Germany, Italy, Japan, and the UK. The finding illustrates a small influence on some fundamental macroeconomic variables such as the money supply, outputs, inflation, and interest rates in predicting the movements of the floating exchange rates.

Engel and West's (2005) study on exchange rate determination has received considerable academic interest, especially for confirming the exchange rate disconnect puzzle. Bahmani-Oskooee et al. (2015) compared the model using data from the same country with the Autoregressive Distributed Lag (ARDL) model developed by Pesaran et al. (2001). They concluded that the results were the opposite of Engel and West (2005). Besides, they also supported the monetary model of exchange rate determination. Moreover, their results were also supported by Tawadros (2017), who also referred to the model of Engel and West (2005). By using another sample, namely the exchange rate between Australian dollars and five currencies of Australian trading partners, they concluded that there is a relationship between exchange rates and macroeconomic fundamentals. In addition, the fundamental variable "granger" causes the exchange rate.

All studies mentioned above analyze the case of the main currency being form developed countries. However, the study of the relationship between exchange rate and macroeconomic fundamentals in the case of an emerging market economy is also fascinating. AbuDalu and Ahmed (2014) used a sample of several developing countries in Southeast Asia, revealing a significant relationship between exchange rates and macroeconomic variables. Moreover, Ouyang and Rajan (2016) analyzed the real exchange rate determinants in 34 developing economies, although they focused on the effect of inflation targeting, while other macroeconomic variables were also included. The result show that macroeconomic variables affect the volatility of the real exchange rate, especially in developing Asian economies. Thus, a possible extension of study on the presence of the relationship between exchange rates and macroeconomic fundamentals is needed to analyze the case of an emerging market economy.

This study aimed to revisit the Meese–Rogoff exchange rate disconnect puzzle in Indonesia, a Next-11 emerging economy, one of the eleven countries that are expected to become the largest economies in the 21st century after Brazil, Russia, India, and China. As an emerging market economy in Southeast Asia, Indonesia has major trade relationships with several leading economies including China, the USA, Japan, the EU, and Singapore. These relations mean the Indonesian Rupiah is also exchanged with major currencies of those primary trade partner countries. We employed the previous model developed by Tawadros (2017) to examine the cointegration of the Indonesian Rupiah vis-á-vis the currencies of its five biggest trading partner countries, namely Chinese Yuan, United States Dollar, Japanese Yen, Euro, and Singaporean Dollar, and the macroeconomic fundamentals.

Evidence of cointegration between exchange rates and macroeconomic fundamentals in the case of the emerging economy was discovered. Since we employed the linear ARDL approach developed by Pesaran et al. (2001) and nonlinear ARDL by Shin et al. (2011), the results confirm a cointegration of all ten multivariate equations. This manuscript supports and expands the work of Evans and Lyons (2005), AbuDalu and Ahmed (2014), Bahmani-Oskooee et al. (2015), and Tawadros (2017). Moreover, a particular modified variable, i.e. trade balance, showed high statistical significance in both the short-run and the long-run. The remainder of this manuscript is organized as follows. Section 2 presents the previous study of the exchange rate and macroeconomic fundamentals relationship. Section 3 depicts the methodology and econometric modeling process. Section 4 analyzes the result of a causality test and discusses the possible exchange rate disconnect puzzle in the Indonesian Rupiah. Section 5 provides a brief conclusion.

2. Literature Review

After the collapse of the Bretton Woods System, a new system was created to avoid the speculation of the foreign exchange market. Laganà and Sgro (2007) explain that the destruction of the Bretton

Woods System encouraged a test of the exchange rate model using the determination and causality of a theoretical variable. The empirical debates described in the introduction of this manuscript explained that the exchange rate is determined by a set of macroeconomic variables. Empirical results are also diversified in different countries through the level of economy. Most of the studies developed the determinants of an exchange rate model which focused on major currencies from developed countries. However, some previous studies also found the cointegration of exchange rate and macroeconomic fundamentals in the case of emerging market economies.

Gente and Leon-Ledesma (2006) analyzed the consequences of foreign interest rate changes on real exchange rate volatility in East Asian emerging countries. To obtain the equilibrium of the real exchange rate, they estimated the effect of the real interest rate, output, government expenditure, and dummy 1997 Asian crisis using Vector Autoregressive (VAR). The result shows a negative and significant effect of the US interest rate on the real exchange rate volatility for all of the countries, except Thailand. Domestic output confirms the positive and significant effect for three countries, except South Korea. The dummy crisis 1997 variable that was applied for Thailand, Malaysia, and South Korea has a positive and significant effect on the real exchange rate of these three countries' currencies against the US dollar.

Another cross-country study, Lee-Lee and Hui-Boon (2007) tested the volatility of foreign exchange market in Southeast Asian countries using a Vector Autoregressive (VAR) and ARDL approach in order to account the cointegration of exchange rate and macroeconomic fundamentals. The application of the procedure results in a long-run movement among the estimated variables. In the short-run, money supply and trade balance influence the volatility of the Malaysian Ringgit. Money supply and stocks have exerted pressure on the volatility of the Indonesian Rupiah, while the inflation rate influences the volatility of the Thai Baht. Moreover, a similar combination of macroeconomic variables in Indonesia manifest the volatility of the Singaporean Dollar. They concluded that, generally, the interest rate variable shows a small impact on the volatility of exchange rate in Southeast Asian countries.

A more recent analysis of the exchange rate causality by Sarno and Schmeling (2014) who attempted the validity test for macroeconomic fundamentals on exchange rates including the Indonesian Rupiah, the result shows that macroeconomic fundamentals such as the inflation rate, money supply, and nominal GDP, have strong significant predictive power to the exchange rate. They grouped a sample, in which G1 contains 25% of all countries that have depreciated to the US dollar whereas G4 contains 25% of all countries with the highest appreciation against the US dollar. They found that a highly significant number of G1 countries had the strongest experiences in depreciation against the US dollar when their inflation rate increased. Beyond the inflation rate, the variables of money supply and GDP growth differential had indicated a monotonic decline when the sample moved from G1 to G4 countries.

Bouraoui and Phisuthtiwatcharavong (2015) addressed the unresolved issue of the exchange rate model on the Thai Baht against the US dollar. They estimated monthly data used Ordinary Least Square (OLS) to explain the effect of macroeconomic fundamentals on the behavior of THB/USD nominal exchange rate. The result presents an influence of the term of trade and the international reserve to the exchange rate volatility. However, interest rate differential, manufacturing production index, monetary base, and government debt do not exhibit a significant relationship with the exchange rate. Correctly, the lower price of exporting goods in Thailand is responded to by depreciation of the THB/USD rate, while the increase of the international reserve shows an opposite effect.

To explore the issue of the break date effect on the exchange rate, Raza and Afshan (2017) revisited the structural break test to prove the cointegration of exchange rate and macroeconomic variables in Pakistan. They estimated the ARDL bound testing approach, the Johansen and Juselius cointegration approach, and the Gregory and Hansen structural break co-integration. They confirmed a significant relationship of a few considered variables in the long-run. In particular, the long-run estimation provided a positive and significant effect of the money supply and inflation rate. However, an increase in the terms of trade, trade openness, and economic growth has significantly depreciated the value of the Pakistani Rupee against the US dollar.

3. Research Method

3.1. Data Source

The data used for the following analysis includes quarterly data, from 1999: IV to 2017: I for China, USA, Japan, and a total of European Monetary Union, and from 2013: I to 2017: I for Singapore, as the availability of the data. The original dataset mainly obtained from the official site of the International Monetary Fund (IMF), the Organization for Economic Co-operation and Development (OECD), and the Indonesian Statistical Bureau.[1] The dependent variable is the spot exchange rate of the Indonesian Rupiah vis-á-vis foreign currencies. The independent variables are differentiated from broad money using M2 of Indonesia and foreign countries, differential GDP growth between Indonesia and foreign countries, interest rate differential, consumer price index as a proxy of the inflation rate differential, and trade balance between Indonesia and each trade partner country. To ensure that the data are stationary, we applied a logarithmic form for all macroeconomic variables and exchange rate except for the interest rate and inflation rate (the description of measurement and source for each variable is explained in Appendix A).

3.2. Empirical Model

Since the main purpose of this study is to examine the primary relationship of the exchange rate and macroeconomic fundamentals in the form of flexible price monetary model of Frenkel (1976) and Bilson (1978) as well as sticky price monetary model of Dornbusch (1976) and Frankel (1979), we adapted the previous monetary model from the study of Tawadros (2017). We modified the model by including the trade balance variable as Meese and Rogoff (1983) and Obstfeld and Rogoff (2001) have described in order to represent the sticky-price asset model of Hooper and Morton (1982). The original model of this study is transformed into econometrics model as outlined by Equation (1):

$$\text{Logs}_t = \alpha + \beta\left(\log \overline{m}_t - \log \overline{m}_t^f\right) - \varphi\left(\log y_t - \log y_t^f\right) + \gamma\left(i_t - i_t^f\right) + \eta\left(\pi_t - \pi_t^f\right) + \mu \log TB_t + \varepsilon_t, \quad (1)$$

where $\log s_t$ represents the nominal exchange rate; the $\log \overline{m}_t - \log \overline{m}_t^f$ represents the ratio of Indonesia and foreign money supply differential and $\log y_t - \log y_t^f$ represents the ratio of Indonesia to the foreign output differential. The $i_t - i_t^f$ represents Indonesia and foreign interest rate differential and $\pi_t - \pi_t^f$ is the inflation rate differential. Since the result of Frankel (1979) found that $\gamma > 0$, we expect $\eta > |\gamma|$. The $\log TB_t$ represents the trade balance between Indonesia and each trade partner country and ε_t is the disturbance term.

Umit (2016) explained that Indonesian Rupiah is one of weak currency which have encountered to the global shock. It would appear a structural break effect to the exchange rate volatility. Thus, the stationary exchange rate series which contains structural changes should be tested. We addressed this issue by employing Lee-Straizicich unit root test with two breaks developed by Lee and Strazicich (2001, 2003). Two structural time breaks (TB$_1$ and TB$_2$) are allowed to capture the structural change in the two break point which included two dummy variables, DU$_1$ and DU$_2$, respectively. As such the transformation of the original model with two dummy variables becomes:

$$\begin{aligned}\text{Logs}_t = \ & \alpha + \beta\left(\log \overline{m}_t - \log \overline{m}_t^f\right) - \varphi\left(\log y_t - \log y_t^f\right) + \gamma\left(i_t - i_t^f\right) + \eta\left(\pi_t - \pi_t^f\right) + \mu \log TB_t + \\ & \omega DU_{1,t} + \partial DU_{2,t} + \varepsilon_t,\end{aligned} \quad (2)$$

---

[1] All data can be shared under the request for further research.

where DU_1 takes the value of one if $t > TB_1$ and otherwise zero; and finally, DU_2 takes the value of one if $t > TB_2$ and otherwise zero.

3.2.1. Autoregressive Distributed Lag (ARDL) Model

In order to obtain the cointegration of exchange rate and macroeconomic fundamentals, we have to transform Equation (2) into Autoregressive Distributed Lag (ARDL) model. The advantage of this approach is the applicability to either pure stationary variables, integrated process, or their mixture. Mainly, this estimation used the bound testing approach to test the cointegration which developed by Pesaran et al. (2001). The ARDL is also used by some empirical studies to see the effect of the validity of the monetary theories to exchange rate determination. In this manuscript, the ARDL model was used to analyze the existence of a cointegration relationship between the exchange rates and macroeconomic fundamental. Accordingly, we set up the ARDL model as follows:

$$\Delta Logs_t = \alpha + \sum_{k=1}^{n_1} \emptyset_k \Delta logs_{t-k} + \sum_{k=0}^{n_2} \beta_k \Delta \left(\log \overline{m}_t - \log \overline{m}_t^f\right)_{t-k} + \sum_{k=0}^{n_3} \varphi_k \Delta \left(logy_t - logy_t^f\right)_{t-k} \\
+ \sum_{k=0}^{n_4} \gamma_k \Delta \left(i_t - i_t^f\right)_{t-k} + \sum_{k=0}^{n_5} \eta_k \Delta \left(\pi_t - \pi_t^f\right)_{t-k} + \sum_{k=0}^{n_6} \mu_k \Delta logTB_{t-k} \\
+ \sum_{k=0}^{n_7} \omega_k \Delta DU_{1,\,t-k} + \sum_{k=0}^{n_8} \partial_k \Delta DU_{2,t-k} + \delta_1 s_{t-1} + \delta_2 \left(\log \overline{m}_t - \log \overline{m}_t^f\right)_{t-1} \\
+ \delta_3 \left(logy_t - logy_t^f\right)_{t-1} + \delta_4 \left(i_t - i_t^f\right)_{t-1} + \delta_5 \left(\pi_t - \pi_t^f\right)_{t-1} + \delta_6 logTB_{t-1} \\
+ \delta_7 DU_{1,\,t-1} + \delta_8 DU_{2,t-1} + \varepsilon_t, \tag{3}$$

Once the Equation (3) is estimated, the effects of each variable on the exchange rate in the short-run are inferred by the coefficient estimates attached to each of the first-differenced variables. The long-run effects are gained by estimating $\delta_1 - \delta_8$ which are normalized by δ_1. However, we applied an F-test to establish the existence of a long-run relationship which tested the null hypothesis of no cointegration. Pesaran et al. (2001) provide two sets of critical value in the stationary testing which applied inattentive of whether the variables are I(1) or I(0). An upper bound critical value assumes that all variables are I(1) and lower bound critical value assumes that for all variables are I(0). If the calculated F-statistic is above the upper bound, then all variables are jointly significant and indicated a long-run cointegration, respectively to the lower bound of calculated F-statistic.

On the other case, if the calculated F-statistic lies between these two bounds, the result is inconclusive, and we can use an alternative test by forming lagged error correction term of the linear combination of lagged level variables in Equation (3). The model is then re-estimated using the same number of optimum lags that are derived from the ARDL$(n_1, n_2, n_3, n_4, n_5, n_6, n_7, n_8)$ with the following equation:

$$\Delta Logs_t = \alpha + \sum_{k=1}^{n_1} \emptyset_k \Delta logs_{t-k} + \sum_{k=0}^{n_2} \beta_k \Delta \left(\log \overline{m}_t - \log \overline{m}_t^f\right)_{t-k} + \sum_{k=0}^{n_3} \varphi_k \Delta \left(logy_t - logy_t^f\right)_{t-k} \\
+ \sum_{k=0}^{n_4} \gamma_k \Delta \left(i_t - i_t^f\right)_{t-k} + \sum_{k=0}^{n_5} \eta_k \Delta \left(\pi_t - \pi_t^f\right)_{t-k} + \sum_{k=0}^{n_6} \mu_k \Delta logTB_{t-k} \\
+ \sum_{k=0}^{n_7} \omega_k \Delta DU_{1,\,t-k} + \sum_{k=0}^{n_8} \partial_k \Delta DU_{2,t-k} + \rho ECM_{t-1} + \varepsilon_t. \tag{4}$$

In this new specification, we also examined the direction and speed of adjustment in the short-run disequilibrium by estimating the sign and the significance of ECM_{t-1} coefficient. Basically, the ECM_{t-1} links the long-run equilibrium which is implied by the cointegration relationship, with the short-run adjustment process which the variables reacted to any shock in the long-run equilibrium. In the Equation (4) above, a negative and significant $\hat{\rho}_i$ indicates adjustment of the exchange rate toward the long-run equilibrium following any short-run disequilibrium. Finally, the higher absolute value of $\hat{\rho}_i$, the faster adjustment process or convergence rate.

3.2.2. Nonlinear Autoregressive Distributed Lag (NARDL) Model

Equation (3) above has the primary assumption that trade balance has a symmetric effect on the dynamic of spot exchange rate of the Indonesian Rupiah vis-á-vis its five respective currencies. However, it would be possible that there is an asymmetric effect of the trade balance included in the model due to the fluctuation of export and import volume in Indonesia. If there are differences in the expectation of the changing variable over time, it is possible for the variable to have an asymmetric effect towards the dependent variable (Shin et al. 2011; Bahmani-Oskooee and Saha 2017). In order to test the effect of symmetric and asymmetric of trade balance towards spot exchange rate, we generated the trade balance to become two time-series variables. One variable represents a trade surplus, and the other one represents a trade deficit.

Shin et al. (2011) argued that the NARDL model is a flexible analysis model that was adopted from their technique and used in a wide range of economic phenomena. They developed a NARDL model that used an unemployment-output relationship and the Korean gasoline price case. They found a great confirmation that output growth has an asymmetric effect on the sensitivity of unemployment in the long run. Bahmani-Oskooee and Fariditavana (2015) have also run the effect of the exchange rate using the NARDL approach. They found an asymmetric effect of exchange rate on fluctuation of the trade balance. Moreover, Turan and Karakas (2018) employed the current account case and found that changes in the current account deficit have a significant effect on the budget deficit.

To address the symmetric and asymmetric effect of trade balance, we have to rewrite the change of logTB variable as ΔlogTB. The ΔlogTB variable includes positive and negative change based on the study of Turan and Karakas (2018). The positive changes represent a surplus in bilateral trading activities, and the negative changes represent a deficit in bilateral trading activities. We denote the positive changes by $\Delta \log TB_t^+$ and negative changes by $\Delta \log TB_t^-$. The denoted variables are then used to build the partial sum concept to generate the new variables with the following equations:

$$\log TBPos_t = \sum_{k=1}^{n} \Delta \log TB_t^+ = \sum_{k=1}^{n} \max(\log TB_t, 0), \tag{5}$$

$$\log TBNeg_t = \sum_{k=1}^{n} \Delta \log TB_t^- = \sum_{k=1}^{n} \min(\log TB_t, 0). \tag{6}$$

The logTBPos variable is the partial sum of positive change that represents the trade surplus, and the logTBNeg variable is the partial sum of adverse changes that represents the trade deficit. Then we replace logTB variable of Equation (3) by logTBPos and logTBNeg to obtain the new equation as follows:

$$\begin{aligned}
\Delta \log s_t = {}& \alpha + \sum_{k=1}^{n_1} \varnothing_k \Delta s_{t-k} + \sum_{k=0}^{n_2} \beta_k \Delta \left(\log m_t - \log m_t^f\right)_{t-k} + \sum_{k=0}^{n_3} \varphi_k \Delta \left(\log y_t - \log y_t^f\right)_{t-k} \\
& + \sum_{k=0}^{n_4} \eta_k \Delta \left(i_t - i_t^f\right)_{t-k} + \sum_{k=0}^{n_5} \gamma_k \Delta \left(\pi_t - \pi_t^f\right)_{t-k} + \sum_{k=0}^{n_6} \mu_k \Delta \log TBPos_{t-k} \\
& + \sum_{k=0}^{n_7} \sigma_k \Delta \log TBNeg_{t-k} + \sum_{k=0}^{n_8} \omega_k \Delta DU_{1,\,t-k} + \sum_{k=0}^{n_9} \partial_k \Delta DU_{2,t-k} + \delta_1 s_{t-1} \\
& + \delta_2 \left(\log m_t - \log m_t^f\right)_{t-1} + \delta_3 \left(\log y_t - \log y_t^f\right)_{t-1} + \delta_4 \left(\pi_t - \pi_t^f\right)_{t-1} + \delta_5 \left(i_t - i_t^f\right)_{t-1} \\
& + \delta_6 \log TBPos_{t-1} + \delta_7 \log TBNeg_{t-1} + \delta_8 DU_{1,\,t-1} + \delta_9 DU_{2,t-1} + \varepsilon_t
\end{aligned} \tag{7}$$

The adjustment process of generating a partial sum variable above introduces a nonlinear in Equation (7) which so-called as nonlinear autoregressive distributed lag (NARDL), and the Equation (3) is linear ARDL model (Pesaran et al. 2001). The nonlinear ARDL could be estimated with the same procedure as used for estimating the linear ARDL model (Bahmani-Oskooee and Saha 2017). The symmetry and asymmetry effect of the trade balance will be defined by the result of coefficients and signs of ΔTBPos and ΔTBNeg variables. Furthermore, we used a standard Wald test which distributed as χ^2 with one degree of freedom, to analyze short-run symmetric effect of trade balance with the null hypothesis $H_0: \sum \mu = \sum \sigma$. Thus, the trade balance has a short-run asymmetry impact on the spot exchange rate when $\sum \mu \neq \sum \sigma$. For the long-run symmetric effect, the null hypothesis is $H_0: -\delta_6/\delta_1 = -\delta_7/\delta_1$. If they are found to be the same, it indicates that the trade balance has a symmetry effect towards the spot exchange rate.

Finally, since we formed error correction term of the linear combination of variables in Equation (3), we also employed this term for the nonlinear model of Equation (7) and re-estimated using the same number of optimum lags derived from the ARDL($n_1, n_2, n_3, n_4, n_5, n_6, n_7, n_8, n_9$) as follows:

$$\Delta \text{Logs}_t = \alpha + \sum_{k=1}^{n_1} \varnothing_k \Delta s_{t-k} + \sum_{k=0}^{n_2} \beta_k \Delta \left(\log m_t - \log m_t^f\right)_{t-k} + \sum_{k=0}^{n_3} \varphi_k \Delta \left(\log y_t - \log y_t^f\right)_{t-k}$$
$$+ \sum_{k=0}^{n_4} \eta_k \Delta \left(i_t - i_t^f\right)_{t-k} + \sum_{k=0}^{n_5} \gamma_k \Delta \left(\pi_t - \pi_t^f\right)_{t-k} + \sum_{k=0}^{n_6} \mu_k \Delta \log \text{TBPos}_{t-k} \qquad (8)$$
$$+ \sum_{k=0}^{n_7} \sigma_k \Delta \log \text{TBNeg}_{t-k} + \sum_{k=0}^{n_8} \omega_k \Delta DU_{1,\,t-k} + \sum_{k=0}^{n_9} \partial_k \Delta DU_{2,t-k} + \rho \text{ECM}_{t-1} + \varepsilon_t.$$

4. Result and Discussion

4.1. Data Stationary Test Result

To ensure the data used were either stationery at level or first differences, we employed stationarity tests. The result of the tests revealed that integrated in order variables are either I(0) or I(1). To analyze the stationary of the data, this study used unit root tests namely Augmented Dickey-Fuller (ADF) developed by Dickey and Fuller (1979) and Kwiatkowski-Phillips Schmidt-Shin (KPSS) developed by Kwiatkowski et al. (1992). However, their test so far does not provide a structural break in the data generating process of the variable assessed. To fill the gap of this criticism, we applied the Lee-Straizicich (LS) unit roots test developed by Lee and Strazicich (2001, 2003).

The result of the unit root test is presented in Table 1. Due to the rule of the stationary test, the probability of the t-statistic should be lower than 1%, 5%, and 10% significance levels. The result of the ADF test showed that the log of spot exchange rates and differential money supply variables for all of the currency pairs were not stationary at the level, while the KPSS test showed inversely. However, all of the currency pairs are stationary at first difference by rejecting the null hypothesis at 10%. In particular, since the test conducted under first differences, it can be concluded that there are no unit roots, and so all of the series are either I(0) or I(1). These results are in line with Tawadros (2017) who criticized the failure finding of Cushman (2000) and Engel and West (2005) in the detecting of a long-run relationship between the exchange rate and macroeconomic fundamental variables.

We employed ADF and KPSS tests, however, these tests did not allow a structural break during the stationary test process. To criticize this methodological phenomenon, we employed the Lee-Strazicich unit root test. The result is also presented in Table 1, and the required test for the two endogenous structural breaks which were identified earlier are also included. The break model rejects the null hypothesis of the existence of a unit root under the structural breaks for relative money supply, output differential, and trade balance, for the IDR vis-á-vis CNY and JPY. For the IDR vis-á-vis USD, the break model rejects the null hypothesis for all macroeconomic variables. However, for the IDR vis-á-vis EUR, the break model rejects the null hypothesis for the spot exchange rate, relative output, and interest rate, while for the IDR vis-á-vis SGD, the break model rejects the null hypothesis for the relative money supply, output differential, and trade balance.

Table 1. Unit Root Testing Result.

Variable	ADF	KPSS	Lee-Strazicich Test (Break Model)	
			T-Stat	TB
		IDR vis-á-vis CNY		
$LogS_t$	−1.063 [1]	0.825 *** [6]	−4.626 [7]	2008Q1, 2012Q4
$(Logm_t - Logm_t^f)$	−0.407 [1]	0.926 *** [5]	−5.055 [5]	2008Q3, 2013Q4
$(Logy_t - Logy_t^f)$	−1.882 [1]	0.701 ** [5]	−6.650 ** [5]	2006Q2, 2008Q2
$(i_t - i_t^f)$	−3.478 ** [1]	0.595 ** [5]	−5.362 [3]	2009Q2, 2013Q2
$(\pi_t - \pi_t^f)$	−2.966 ** [1]	0.287 [5]	−6.593 ** [6]	2005Q2, 2011Q3
$(LogTB_t)$	−1.396 [1]	0.755 *** [6]	−18.009 *** [1]	2006Q4, 2008Q1
$\Delta LogS_t$	−5.432 *** [1]	0.093 [0]	−6.657 ** [5]	2008Q2, 2011Q1
$\Delta(Logm_t - Logm_t^f)$	−4.963 *** [0]	0.187 [0]	−6.492 ** [2]	2008Q2, 2010Q1
$\Delta(Logy_t - Logy_t^f)$	−7.217 *** [0]	0.170 [8]	−8.439 *** [6]	2008Q2, 2011Q1
$\Delta(i_t - i_t^f)$	−4.197 *** [0]	0.147 [3]	−5.505 [8]	2007Q1, 2010Q4
$\Delta(\pi_t - \pi_t^f)$	−5.132 *** [3]	0.043 [3]	−8.794 *** [7]	2005Q2, 2007Q3
$\Delta(LogTB_t)$	−4.781 *** [0]	0.108 [2]	−12.866 *** [5]	2007Q1, 2008Q1
		IDR vis-á-vis USD		
$LogS_t$	−0.490 [2]	0.602 ** [6]	−4.814 [5]	2009Q2, 2013Q1
$(Logm_t - Logm_t^f)$	−2.929 ** [0]	0.397 * [5]	−7.092 *** [3]	2007Q2, 2010Q3
$(Logy_t - Logy_t^f)$	−6.612 *** [0]	0.113 [4]	−7.703 *** [4]	2008Q2, 2009Q2
$(i_t - i_t^f)$	−3.842 *** [1]	0.138 [5]	−5.888 * [3]	2005Q3, 2008Q2
$(\pi_t - \pi_t^f)$	−2.938 ** [0]	0.220 [4]	−6.018 * [7]	2005Q2, 2011Q4
$(LogTB_t)$	−2.112 [9]	0.847 *** [6]	−8.893 *** [8]	2008Q3, 2010Q2
$\Delta LogS_t$	−5.818 *** [1]	0.141 [2]	−7.126 *** [1]	2008Q1, 2009Q1
$\Delta(Logm_t - Logm_t^f)$	−6.868 *** [3]	0.144 [4]	−7.948 *** [3]	2010Q2, 2011Q2
$\Delta(Logy_t - Logy_t^f)$	−11.573 *** [0]	0.189 [22]	−8.577 *** [7]	2008Q4, 2011Q2
$\Delta(i_t - i_t^f)$	−3.499 ** [0]	0.159 [4]	−5.846 * [3]	2008Q2, 2010Q3
$\Delta(\pi_t - \pi_t^f)$	−5.929 *** [3]	0.037 [0]	−9.077 *** [3]	2005Q2, 2007Q2
$\Delta(LogTB_t)$	−2.284 * [8]	0.153 [3]	−7.266 *** [3]	2007Q3, 2010Q3
		IDR vis-á-vis JPY		
$LogS_t$	−1.338 [2]	0.933 *** [5]	−5.447 [1]	2006Q2, 2009Q2
$(Logm_t - Logm_t^f)$	2.213 [1]	0.895 *** [6]	−5.544 [2]	2005Q4, 2011Q2
$(Logy_t - Logy_t^f)$	−6.612 *** [0]	0.1123 [4]	−7.703 *** [4]	2008Q2, 2009Q2
$(i_t - i_t^f)$	−3.787 *** [1]	0.758 ** [5]	−5.759 [5]	2005Q2, 2012Q2
$(\pi_t - \pi_t^f)$	−2.656 * [0]	0.562 ** [5]	−9.894 *** [8]	2005Q2, 2007Q2
$(LogTB_t)$	−2.115 [1]	0.351 * [5]	−9.683 *** [8]	2008Q3, 2011Q3
$\Delta LogS_t$	−7.320 *** [1]	0.066 [8]	−8.229 *** [1]	2008Q2, 2009Q3
$\Delta(Logm_t - Logm_t^f)$	−3.132 ** [0]	0.809 *** [5]	−5.655 [7]	2008Q2, 2011Q1
$\Delta(Logy_t - Logy_t^f)$	−11.573 *** [0]	0.189 [22]	−8.577 *** [7]	2008Q4, 2011Q2
$\Delta(i_t - i_t^f)$	−3.480 * [0]	0.122 [3]	−6.254 ** [8]	2010Q3, 2013Q4
$\Delta(\pi_t - \pi_t^f)$	−5.987 *** [3]	0.030 [1]	−7.783 *** [8]	2005Q2, 2007Q2
$\Delta(LogTB_t)$	−3.846 *** [0]	0.392 * [4]	−7.852 *** [3]	2007Q3, 2010Q3
		IDR vis-á-vis EUR		
$LogS_t$	−2.176 [1]	0.699 ** [5]	−5.983 * [7]	2009Q3, 2013Q1
$(Logm_t - Logm_t^f)$	0.111 [1]	0.893 *** [6]	−5.402 [7]	2007Q2, 2012Q3
$(Logy_t - Logy_t^f)$	−4.624 *** [0]	0.141 [4]	−8.480 *** [7]	2008Q2, 2013Q4
$(i_t - i_t^f)$	−5.152 *** [1]	0.149 [5]	−6.271 * [1]	2009Q2, 2012Q4
$(\pi_t - \pi_t^f)$	−2.639 * [0]	0.211 [5]	−5.043 [3]	2006Q2, 2013Q2
$(LogTB_t)$	−2.347 [9]	0.665 ** [6]	−5.376 [5]	2008Q2, 2010Q4
$\Delta LogS_t$	−5.129 *** [0]	0.150 [3]	−6.034 * [1]	2008Q4, 2013Q4
$\Delta(Logm_t - Logm_t^f)$	−3.771 *** [0]	0.370 ** [5]	−6.9422 *** [1]	2005Q4, 2010Q3
$\Delta(Logy_t - Logy_t^f)$	−10.554 *** [0]	0.327 [37]	−10.318 *** [8]	2008Q1, 2012Q1
$\Delta(i_t - i_t^f)$	−4.529 *** [1]	0.106 [3]	−6.771 *** [6]	2005Q2, 2007Q4
$\Delta(\pi_t - \pi_t^f)$	−5.491 *** [3]	0.036 [2]	−9.314 *** [3]	2005Q2, 2007Q2
$\Delta(LogTB_t)$	−1.398 * [8]	0.368 ** [4]	−7.062 *** [3]	2008Q3, 2011Q1

Table 1. Cont.

Variable	ADF	KPSS	Lee-Strazicich Test (Break Model)	
			T-Stat	TB
		IDR vis-á-vis SGD		
$LogS_t$	−0.578 [0]	0.871 *** [6]	−5.104196 [7]	2008Q3, 2013Q1
$(Logm_t - Logm_t^f)$	−2.278 [4]	0.413 * [4]	−6.623 ** [8]	2009Q3, 2014Q3
$(Logy_t - Logy_t^f)$	−1.713 [9]	0.302 [4]	−6.336 ** [7]	2007Q3, 2009Q2
$(i_t - i_t^f)$	−3.254 ** [1]	0.859 *** [5]	−5.730 [5]	2005Q2, 2011Q1
$(\pi_t - \pi_t^f)$	−2.339 [0]	0.302 [5]	−5.286 [6]	2005Q2, 2011Q4
$(LogTB_t)$	−1.879 [9]	0.697 ** [6]	−6.191 ** [8]	2008Q2, 2011Q3
$\Delta LogS_t$	−5.762 *** [0]	0.067 [0]	−6.879 *** [1]	2008Q1, 2009Q1
$\Delta(Logm_t - Logm_t^f)$	−6.142 *** [3]	0.046 [2]	−7.232 *** [3]	2006Q3, 2008Q3
$\Delta(Logy_t - Logy_t^f)$	−5.249 *** [7]	0.039 [3]	−6.387 ** [7]	2005Q2, 2006Q4
$\Delta(i_t - i_t^f)$	−3.561 *** [0]	0.114 [3]	−6.296 ** [8]	2010Q3, 2013Q4
$\Delta(\pi_t - \pi_t^f)$	−4.540 ** [3]	0.063 [4]	−8.228 *** [3]	2005Q2, 2007Q3
$\Delta(LogTB_t)$	−1.328 * [8]	0.333 [4]	−6.826 *** [7]	2006Q4, 2007Q3

The asterisk symbols showed the rejection of the null hypothesis at *** = 1%, ** = 5%, and * = 10% (Source: Author's Computation Using E-views 10).

4.2. The Analysis of Exchange Rate Determination Model

Exchange rates determination of the Indonesian Rupiahs (IDR) vis-á-vis Chinese Yuan (CNY), United States Dollar (USD), Japanese Yen (JPY), Euro (EUR), and Singapore Dollar (SGD) as transaction currency used among these trading partner countries mainly estimated using autoregressive distributed lag (ARDL). In order to compare the result of the ARDL model, we used the new extension of the ARDL model, the nonlinear autoregressive distributed lag (NARDL). The result of both estimations is discussed in the preceding section.

4.2.1. The Cointegration Analysis under the Linear ARDL Model

The cointegration of the Indonesian Rupiah (IDR) vis-á-vis currencies of primary trade partner countries, and macroeconomic fundamentals were mainly estimated through ARDL. We followed Bahmani-Oskooee et al. (2015) and Tawadros (2017) who examined the multivariate model between the exchange rate and macroeconomic fundamentals separately. The assessed null hypothesis that there is no correlation between the spot exchange rate and macroeconomic fundamentals are examined in accordance of the study of Devereux and Engel (2002). The estimation for each model used a maximum of four lags with Schwarz Info Criterion (SIC) model selection method. Panopoulou and Pittis (2004) argued that SIC worked better than another selection method.

The result of the bounds testing under the linear ARDL model is presented in Table 2 with the assumption that all of the macroeconomic fundamentals are diversified linearly. Panel (A) shows the short-run estimates of the ARDL model, including the F-statistic test and the adjusted R^2. Panel (A) also followed the diagnostic test for serial correlation, histogram normality, heteroskedasticity, and Ramsey-RESET for a functional form. The result of diagnostic test for each currency pair is well specified, with each equation having passed every test at a 5 percent level. Moreover, the adjusted R^2 shows that each estimation has a reasonable fit with the model, with the currency pair of the IDR vis-á-vis SGD having the highest goodness of fit. Finally, all the result of the error correction term that explains how long it takes for the system to revert to the equilibrium is negative and significant at 1 percent. It indicates that each model has a lower than 66.3 percent of the deviation in the short-run equilibrium which is corrected in a year.

The long-run estimated coefficients of the multivariate equation for each currency pairs is presented in panel (B). The result reveals a long-run equilibrium relationship between the exchange rate and macroeconomic fundamentals by rejecting the null hypothesis of no cointegration base on the existence of f-statistics of multivariate equations for each estimated currency pairs. This result refutes the previous study of Engel and West (2005) where all of their variables showed a small explanation to the floating exchange rate. However, it supports the study of Bahmani-Oskooee et al. (2015), Tawadros (2017). It is associated with the affirmation of money supply variable of Raza and Afshan's (2017) argument that an excess money supply cut down the interest rate by making money easier to acquire and devaluated the value of the home currency.

Moreover, the supply of money causes the availability of funds for buying goods and services. An increase in domestic money supply will depreciate the value of IDR vis-á-vis the CNY, USD, JPY, and SGD. However, in this study it has increased the value of IDR vis-á-vis the EUR. This finding has also confirmed the study of Lee-Lee and Hui-Boon (2007) who have reported a significant effect of money supply on the exchange rate movement in several Asian emerging economies.

The differential in output variable has no significant effect for the currency pair of the IDR vis-á-vis the USD and JPY. However, the value of other currency pairs namely the IDR vis-á-vis the CNY, EUR, and SGD have been affected by the movement of the relative output variable. In the case of a negative sign for the IDR vis-á-vis CNY and EUR, an increase in domestic output has reduced the value of IDR/CNY and IDR/EUR. This result had confirmed the study of Sarno and Schmeling (2014) who revealed a monotonic decline of the economic path when the exchange rate moved to the appreciation side (there is a moving phenomenon from G1 to G4 group countries).

Notably, the requirement of $\eta > |\gamma|$ as postulated by (Frankel 1979) cannot be met since the coefficient for the differential inflation rate is lower than the absolute value of the differential interest rate for each currency pair. In addition, the inflation rate differential provides a significant value at 1 percent for the IDR vis-á-vis the USD and SGD. This result confirmed that an increase of inflation rate in Indonesia depreciated the value of IDR/USD and IDR/SGD and was consistent with the study of Bilson (1978) and AbuDalu and Ahmed (2014) who provided the empirical result that the inflation differential and exchange rates have a positive correlation. However, this finding differs from Fitzgerald (2004), who stated that exchange rate volatility does not feedback to inflation since an increase in the interest rate in Indonesia caused by a tight monetary policy will attract a greater capital inflow, which will then appreciate the currency.

Likewise, the long-run coefficient of trade balance between Indonesia and its five biggest trading partner countries is strongly significant at 1 percent level to determine the exchange rate linearly. Although the study of Dekle et al. (2005) and Berman et al. (2012) used firm-level data, they showed a similar relationship between exchange rates and domestic export volume. The high depreciation as attached to the value of the spot rate especially to the exchange rates of IDR vis-á-vis the USD, EUR, and SGD, have correlated to the trading scenario in Indonesia with the United States, European countries, and Singapore. Respectively, China and Japan are the first and third largest trade partners of Indonesia, hence the finding of highly significant relationships is not very surprising. Following the previous big empirical finding, however, this result denies the explanation of Obstfeld and Rogoff (2001) about the international trade variable, they argued that the most traded goods market are not fully integrated into the exchange rates caused by the trade costs.

4.2.2. The Cointegration Analysis under the Nonlinear ARDL Model

Since the linear ARDL approach assumes that the trade balance is correlated with the spot exchange rate linearly, we modified this variable to become nonlinear. Following Shin et al. (2011), we estimated the Equation (7) of nonlinear ARDL by employing the same technique used in the linear ARDL model.

Table 3 presents the result of the bounds testing approach under the nonlinear ARDL model. The result of short-run estimates, as well as the diagnostic test, are presented in panel (A). The diagnostic test indicated that the model is quite stable, which there is no serial correlation among macroeconomic variables for each currency pair, except the IDR vis-á-vis CNY. It is proven by the F-statistic of Breusch-Godfrey Serial Correlation LM test. The Breusch–Pagan–Godfrey test for Heteroskedasticity, Ramsey-RESET for stability test, and the Jacque–Bera normality test report statistically significant F-statistics for each currency pair at a 5 percent significance level. Thus, the results indicated that each currency pair passed the diagnostic test for normality, heteroskedasticity, and the functional form.

Table 2. Result of Bounds Testing Approach under the Linear ARDL Model.

Variable	IDR vis-á-vis CNY	IDR vis-á-vis USD	IDR vis-á-vis JPY	IDR vis-á-vis EUR	IDR vis-á-vis SGD
		Panel A. Short-run Estimates			
$\Delta(\log m_t - \log m_t^f)$	0.001 (0.002)	0.003 ** (0.001)	0.053 ** (0.026)	0.001 (0.002)	0.00 (0.001)
$\Delta(\log m_{t-1} - \log m_{t-1}^f)$				−0.004 * (0.002)	0.003 *** (0.001)
$\Delta(\log y_t - \log y_t^f)$	0.001 (0.003)	0.007 (0.005)	−0.427 (0.897)	−0.037 (1.645)	0.002 *** (0.001)
$\Delta(\log y_{t-1} - \log y_{t-1}^f)$	0.013 *** (0.003)	−0.008 ** (0.004)		4.441 ** (2.044)	
$\Delta(\log y_{t-2} - \log y_{t-2}^f)$	0.011 *** (0.003)				
$\Delta(\log y_{t-3} - \log y_{t-3}^f)$	0.005 ** (0.002)				
$\Delta(i_t - i_t^f)$	0.023 *** (0.005)	0.046 *** (0.012)	−0.158 (0.588)	0.013 * (0.008)	−0.038 *** (0.010)
$\Delta(i_{t-1} - i_{t-1}^f)$		−0.082 *** (0.022)		0.001 (0.010)	−0.033 *** (0.010)
$\Delta(i_{t-2} - i_{t-2}^f)$		0.046 *** (0.013)		−0.016 ** (0.006)	
$\Delta(\pi_t - \pi_t^f)$	−0.007 *** (0.001)	−0.001 (0.002)	−0.043 (0.164)	0.002 (0.003)	0.006 *** (0.002)
$\Delta(\pi_{t-1} - \pi_{t-1}^f)$	0.007 *** (0.001)			−0.010 * (0.005)	0.005 *** (0.001)
$\Delta(\pi_{t-2} - \pi_{t-2}^f)$	0.010 *** (0.001)			0.007 * (0.004)	0.005 *** (0.001)
$\Delta(\pi_{t-3} - \pi_{t-3}^f)$	0.007 *** (0.002)				
$\Delta \log TB_t$	0.033 *** (0.005)	−0.226 *** (0.098)	4.042 *** (0.929)	0.659 *** (0.197)	0.133 ** (0.060)
$\Delta \log TB_{t-1}$	−0.071 *** (0.016)	0.335 *** (0.092)		0.946 *** (0.263)	0.178 *** (0.042)
$DU_{1,t}$	0.039 (0.069)	−0.079 *** (0.025)	−3.069 ** (1.402)	0.013 (0.025)	0.143 *** (0.022)
$DU_{1,t-1}$	−0.831 *** (0.156)		34.180 *** (2.517)	−0.093 *** (0.026)	0.079 ** (0.038)
$DU_{1,t-2}$	−0.143 *** (0.021)		−22.839 *** (3.930)		−0.024 (0.027)
$DU_{1,t-3}$			−13.348 * (7.521)		−0.104 *** (0.027)
$DU_{1,t-4}$			21.705 *** (3.855)		
$DU_{2,t}$	0.030 ** (0.016)	0.066 *** (0.020)	−9.943 *** (2.957)	0.050 ** (0.020)	0.005 (0.014)
$DU_{2,t-1}$	−0.120 *** (0.020)			0.076 *** (0.014)	0.019 ** (0.009)
$DU_{2,t-2}$	−0.065 *** (0.018)			0.071 *** (0.014)	0.091 *** (0.019)
Ecm_{t-1}	−0.024 *** (0.02)	−0.119 *** (0.021)	−0.426 *** (0.090)	−0.370 *** (0.034)	−0.663 *** (0.050)
F-Statistic	14.843 ***	3.597 **	2.407 **	11.481 ***	14.371 ***
Adjusted R^2	0.922	0.971	0.942	0.973	0.999
Serial Correlation	2.405 *** [0.1136]	1.480 *** [0.2397]	2.679 ** [0.0816]	3.012 ** [0.0681]	2.893 ** [0.0800]
Normality	0.244 *** [0.8850]	0.341 *** [0.8434]	1.640 *** [0.4405]	0.563 *** [0.7545]	1.475 *** [0.4782]
Heteroskedasticity	1.256 *** [0.2902]	1.277 *** [0.2674]	1.156 *** [0.3457]	0.572 *** [0.9206]	1.116 *** [0.4030]
Functional Form	0.114 *** [0.7392]	1.980 *** [0.1668]	4.048 *** [0.0512]	0.479 *** [0.4953]	1.390 *** [0.2523]

Table 2. Cont.

Variable	IDR vis-á-vis CNY	IDR vis-á-vis USD	IDR vis-á-vis JPY	IDR vis-á-vis EUR	IDR vis-á-vis SGD
		Panel B. Long-run Estimates			
$(Logm_t - Logm_t^f)$	0.406 ** (0.196)	0.024 ** (0.011)	0.125 *** (0.043)	−0.012 ** (0.005)	0.005 ** (0.002)
$(Logy_t - Logy_t^f)$	−0.442 * (0.231)	−0.002 (0.054)	−1.001 (2.231)	−1.157 *** (0.271)	0.003 *** (0.001)
$(i_t - i_t^f)$	−0.625 (0.411)	0.082 *** (0.021)	−0.370 (1.459)	−0.005 (0.024)	−0.087 *** (0.006)
$(\pi_t - \pi_t^f)$	−0.547 ** (0.207)	−0.012 (0.018)	−0.102 (0.386)	−0.002 (0.008)	0.030 *** (0.004)
$LogTB_t$	1.422 *** (0.474)	0.915 *** (0.030)	9.485 *** (1.938)	0.749 *** (0.055)	0.263 *** (0.025)
$DU_{1,t}$	20.431 *** (6.562)	−0.670 *** (0.186)	39.019 *** (6.540)	−0.217 *** (0.072)	0.026 (0.029)
$DU_{2,t}$	6.261 *** (2.153)	0.556 *** (0.156)	−23.33 *** (6.480)	0.394 *** (0.099)	0.174 *** (0.014)

Figures reported on the parenthesis ( ) are the standard error. An asterisk ***, **, and * indicates rejection of the null hypothesis at 1, 5, and 10 percent of significance level respectively (Source: Author's Computation Using E-views 10).

Table 3. The Result of Bounds Testing Approach under the Nonlinear ARDL Model.

Variable	IDR vis-á-vis CNY	IDR vis-á-vis USD	IDR vis-á-vis JPY	IDR vis-á-vis EUR	IDR vis-á-vis SGD
		Panel A. Short-run Estimates			
$\Delta(logm_t - logm_t^f)$	0.009 *** (0.002)	0.004 ** (0.001)	−0.500 *** (0.136)	0.004 (0.002)	−0.001 (0.001)
$\Delta(logm_{t-1} - logm_{t-1}^f)$	0.007 ** (0.002)			−0.003 (0.002)	0.001 (0.001)
$\Delta(logm_{t-1} - logm_{t-2}^f)$	0.005 * (0.002)			0.008 *** (0.002)	0.003 *** (0.001)
$\Delta(logy_t - logy_t^f)$	−0.025 *** (0.005)	0.005 (0.005)	0.565 (0.636)	1.257 * (0.676)	0.006 ** (0.002)
$\Delta(logy_{t-1} - logy_{t-1}^f)$		−0.009 (0.006)			
$\Delta(i_t - i_t^f)$	0.083 *** (0.008)	0.046 *** (0.013)	1.736 (1.895)	0.028 *** (0.007)	−0.065 ** (0.024)
$\Delta(i_{t-1} - i_{t-1}^f)$	0.012 (0.008)	−0.082 *** (0.0257)	−2.308 (1.693)	−0.043 *** (0.012)	−0.038 *** (0.009)
$\Delta(i_{t-2} - i_{t-2}^f)$	0.018 * (0.009)	0.052 *** (0.015)			
$\Delta(i_{t-3} - i_{t-3}^f)$	0.048 *** (0.009)				
$\Delta(\pi_t - \pi_t^f)$	−0.025 *** (0.003)	−0.002 (0.002)	−0.641 ** (0.25)	−0.007 * (0.004)	0.013 ** (0.005)
$\Delta(\pi_{t-1} - \pi_{t-1}^f)$	0.020 *** (0.003)			0.003 (0.003)	0.010 ** (0.003)
$\Delta(\pi_{t-2} - \pi_{t-2}^f)$	0.025 *** (0.003)			0.001 (0.001)	0.013 *** (0.002)
$\Delta(\pi_{t-3} - \pi_{t-3}^f)$	0.019 *** (0.003)			−0.011 *** (0.002)	
$\Delta logTBPos_t$	−0.064 * (0.032)	−0.186 * (0.109)	26.484 *** (7.261)	0.737 *** (0.149)	0.100 (0.111)
$\Delta logTBPos_{t-1}$	−0.219 *** (0.039)	0.326 *** (0.097)		0.539 * (0.271)	−0.287 ** (0.100)

Table 3. Cont.

Variable	IDR vis-á-vis CNY	IDR vis-á-vis USD	IDR vis-á-vis JPY	IDR vis-á-vis EUR	IDR vis-á-vis SGD
		Panel A. Short-run Estimates			
$\Delta \log TBPos_{t-2}$	−0.154 *** (0.034)			−1.676 *** (0.351)	
$\Delta \log TBNeg_t$	0.047 *** (0.006)	−0.269 (0.170)	−55.65 *** (15.34)	0.286 * (0.157)	0.035 (0.100)
$\Delta \log TBNeg_{t-1}$	−0.004 * (0.002)	0.767 *** (0.258)		−1.415 *** (0.178)	−0.099 (0.129)
$\Delta \log TBNeg_{t-2}$		−0.755 *** (0.194)			0.349 * (0.157)
$DU_{1,t}$	0.500 *** (0.088)	−0.206 *** (0.0381)	−1.793 (1.658)	−0.228 *** (0.060)	0.190 *** (0.038)
$DU_{1,t-1}$			27.082 *** (2.344)	−0.070 (0.431)	0.061 (0.038)
$DU_{1,t-2}$			−38.099 *** (4.003)	−0.201 *** (0.024)	0.170 ** (0.070)
$DU_{2,t}$	0.023 (0.018)	−0.003 (0.015)	−8.598 * (4.509)	0.049 *** (0.012)	−0.018 (0.009)
$DU_{2,t-1}$	−0.085 *** (0.022)	0.072 *** (0.008)		0.072 *** (0.010)	−0.010 (0.019)
$DU_{2,t-2}$	−0.005 (0.021)	0.008 (0.004)		0.091 *** (0.024)	0.037 * (0.018)
$DU_{2,t-3}$	0.103 *** (0.020)	−0.086 *** (0.010)			
Ecm_{t-1}	−0.041 *** (0.005)	−0.021 *** (0.004)	−0.241 *** (0.050)	−0.516 *** (0.029)	−0.896 *** (0.059)
F-Statistic	6.153 ***	2.788 ***	2.130 ***	20.066 ***	10.031 ***
Adjusted R^2	0.919	0.980	0.947	0.995	0.999
Serial Correlation	13.679 (0.0000)	0.096 (0.9086)	0.752 *** [0.4785]	3.002 *** [0.1003]	3.968 *** [0.0929]
Normality	10.958 ** (0.004)	0.690 *** (0.7084)	2.359 *** [0.3074]	7.707 *** [0.0212]	2.078 *** [0.3538]
Heteroskedasticity	1.554 *** (0.1560)	1.706 ** (0.0863)	1.041 *** [0.4364]	0.568 *** [0.9003]	0.627 *** [0.8379]
Functional Form	3.914 ** (0.061)	3.656 ** (0.0641)	1.202 *** [0.2797]	5.662 ** [0.0386]	1.881 *** [0.2193]
Wald S	4.133 **	16.489 ***	14.381 ***	3.601 *	6.003 **
Wald L	14.538 ***	3.134 *	9.446 ***	3.614 *	3.004 *
		Panel B. Long-run Estimates			
$(\log m_t - \log m_t^f)$	0.059 (0.045)	0.171 ** (0.084)	−2.077 *** (0.702)	0.037 *** (0.009)	−0.004 (0.003)
$(\log y_t - \log y_t^f)$	−0.802 *** (0.225)	−0.190 (0.301)	2.349 (2.857)	−3.923 *** (0.056)	0.005 ** (0.002)
$(i_t - i_t^f)$	−1.159 *** (0.313)	0.766 *** (0.073)	−2.379 (3.472)	0.037 *** (0.009)	−0.121 *** (0.012)
$(\pi_t - \pi_t^f)$	0.793 *** (0.086)	−0.108 (0.114)	−2.666 *** (0.925)	−0.034 *** (0.007)	0.050 *** (0.007)
$LogTBPos_t$	2.198 *** (0.509)	6.720 *** (1.634)	90.107 *** (6.198)	0.977 *** (0.056)	0.261 *** (0.028)
$LogTBNeg_t$	1.055 *** (0.337)	−12.321 ** (5.510)	−98.375 *** (7.027)	−2.295 *** (0.329)	0.388 *** (0.053)
$DU_{1,t}$	12.276 *** (4.024)	−9.870 *** (2.212)	−53.26 *** (21.598)	−1.196 *** (0.149)	0.166 *** (0.041)
$DU_{2,t}$	3.308 *** (0.859)	−0.415 * (0.739)	−35.746 *** (18.238)	0.410 *** (0.042)	0.132 *** (0.024)

Figures reported on the parenthesis ( ) are the standard error. An asterisk ***, **, and * indicates rejection of the null hypothesis at 1, 5, and 10 percent of significance level respectively (Source: Author's Computation Using E-views 10).

Additionally, the Adjusted R^2 explains that the multivariate equation for each currency pair has a good fit, with the IDR vis-á-vis SGD has the best fit. The panel (A) also reported that all the result of the error correction term is negative and significant at 1 percent. The coefficients of Ecm_{t-1} indicated that each model has less than 89.6 percent of the deviation in the short-run equilibrium, which is corrected in a year. Furthermore, the Wald test rejects the null hypothesis of $H_0: \sum \mu = \sum \sigma$. It implied that in the short-run, the sum of the coefficient $\Delta logTBPos$ is significantly different to the sum of the coefficient $\Delta logTBNeg$. Finally, the result of the Wald-L test reflects an evidence of long-run asymmetric effect of the trade balance.

Panel (B) of Table 3 presents the result of long-run estimates under the nonlinear ARDL. The result of F-statistic affirms the existence of cointegration between the exchange rate and macroeconomic fundamentals, hence rejecting the null hypothesis of no cointegration. The trade balance is then modified to become trade surplus and trade deficit due to the nonlinear ARDL model. The estimates of Equation (7) present an existence of asymmetry long-run impact on the spot exchange rate. Since we found that the coefficient of trade surplus and trade deficit in the $\delta_6 \neq \delta_7$ requirement been met, this supports the result of the long-run Wald test.

Compared to the linear ARDL for the IDR vis-á-vis CNY, the nonlinear ARDL for this currency pair has a higher cointegration, where most of the macroeconomic variables are significant at 1 percent. The modified variable, namely trade surplus and trade deficit, have a high significance for each currency pairs at 1 percent, except the trade deficit for IDR vis-á-vis the USD, which is significant at 5 percent. The positive significance of the trade surplus variable indicates that an improvement in the trade surplus between Indonesia and the trade partner countries lead to higher export revenue, increases the higher demand of the currency and boost the value of the Indonesian rupiah vis-á-vis the five currencies of the trading partner countries.

The coefficient of the trade deficit variable for the IDR vis-á-vis CNY and SGD showed a similar sign of the trade surplus variable. Following the fact of the trade deficit between Indonesia and China, the positive value of the spot exchange rate of IDR vis-á-vis CNY showed the higher trade deficit of goods and services towards China. The finding of the negatively significant of trade deficit entirely differs from the study of Chowdhury (1993) and Dekle et al. (2005). By using another level of data, they explained that the reduction of export volume correlates with an appreciation in the exchange rate. The deficit of trade balance has been responded by the increased of the value of the IDR/USD, IDR/JPY, and IDR/EUR.

Finally, the effect of the global shock to the exchange rate volatility between Indonesian rupiah vis-á-vis the currencies of trade partner countries are statistically significant. The implementation of dummy structural break for each currency pair successfully confirms the previous study of Tawadros (2017), who criticized the explanations of Cushman (2000) and Engel and West (2005) as failing to present a cointegration between the exchange rate and macroeconomic fundamentals. In Table 1, most of the structural break date correspond to the global crisis in 2008. The result of this study statistically confirms the significant effect of the first dummy variable (DU_1) as the most appropriate term reflecting when the crisis happened, rather than second dummy variable (DU_2) which represented the extended period of global shock.

5. Conclusions

The study of the relationship between exchange rate and macroeconomic fundamentals have matured in some developed economies. The innovations are widened to explore the exchange rate determinants such as analysis, statistical reform, and especially some theoretical variables. The study of this phenomenon has also implemented in several emerging economies, with the conclusion of cointegration between the exchange rate and the considered macroeconomic fundamentals. This study employed the currency of Indonesia vis-á-vis the five most significant trading partner currencies in order to prove the presence of cointegration in an emerging economy. The analysis compared the new econometric technique to prove the relationship of the exchange rate and macroeconomic fundamentals whether these economic variables are connected or disconnected. The result of the ARDL test showed that there is a high correlation between the exchange rate and its fundamental variables, both in the short-run and the long-run for each currency pair. Moreover, all five multivariate equations explain that almost all of the fundamental variables serve as a pass through to the exchange rates volatility. The modified variable, the trade balance, presents as the most statistically significant. Overall, in the long-run, the linear ARDL model produces twenty-one significances over twenty-eight fundamental variables.

The development of ARDL is also used to compare the result by including the asymmetric effect of the trade surplus and trade deficit in the nonlinear ARDL estimation. The trade balance including both the surplus and the deficit are significant for each currency pair. However, the trade deficit variable for the IDR vis-á-vis the CNY and SGD is negatively significant. The implementation of the dummy structural break has profoundly responded by the volatility of the exchange rate. Overall, the nonlinear manner provides a higher cointegration which has thirty-four significances over forty fundamental variables for determining the exchange rate of the IDR vis-á-vis the five currencies of trade partner countries in the long-run.

Author Contributions: Conceptualization, A.S. and K.S.; Methodology, A.S. and K.S.; Software, A.S.; Writing—Original Draft Preparation, A.S.; Writing—Review and Editing, A.S.; and Supervision, K.S.

Funding: This research was financially supported by the Ministry of Education Humanities & Social Science Fund under Grant No. 15YJC790086; Jilin Scientific Development Plan under Grant No. 20150418048FG and Jilin Education Department the 12th Five-year Plan Social Science Research Project 2015-555; National Social Scientific Funds 18VSJ045; and Fundamental Scientific Research Funds of Central University subordinate to the Ministry of Education.

Conflicts of Interest: The authors declare no conflict of interest.

Appendix A

The explanation of the data used to carry out the estimation is described as follows:

s	=	The spot exchange rate of the Indonesian rupiah, Chinese Yuan, Japanese Yen, Euro, and Singapore dollar (in terms of current US dollar). The data come from the official site of the International Financial Statistic of IMF;
$\overline{m}_t - \overline{m}_t^f$	=	Money supply differential is the difference between M2 in Indonesia and foreign countries (in terms of current US dollar). The data come from the official site of the International Financial Statistic of IMF;
$y_t - y_t^f$	=	Output differential is the difference between real GDP of Indonesia and foreign countries (in terms of current US dollar). The data come from the official site of the International Financial Statistic of IMF;
$i_t - i_t^f$	=	Nominal interest rate (in terms of percentage change). The data come from the official site of OECD, except Singapore, both home and foreign countries, the data come from the official site of International Financial Statistic of IMF;
$\pi_t - \pi_t^f$	=	Consumer price index. The data come from the official site of the International Financial Statistic of IMF; and
TB	=	Export and import differential between Indonesia and foreign countries (in terms of current US dollar). The data come from the official site of Indonesian Statistical Bureau

References

Abhyankar, Abhay, Lucio Sarno, and Giorgio Valente. 2005. Exchange Rates and Fundamentals: Evidence on the Economic Value of Predictability. *Journal of International Economics* 66: 325–48. [CrossRef]

AbuDalu, Abdalrahman, and Elsadig Musa Ahmed. 2014. The Determinants of ASEAN-5 Real Effective Exchange Rate *Vis-á-Vis* the UK Pound. *World Journal of Entrepreneurship, Management and Sustainable Development* 10: 98–118. [CrossRef]

Bahmani-Oskooee, Mohsen, and Hadise Fariditavana. 2015. Nonlinear ARDL approach, asymmetric effects and the j-curve. *Journal of Economic Studies* 42: 519–30. [CrossRef]

Bahmani-Oskooee, Mohsen, Amr Hosny, and N. Kundan Kishor. 2015. The Exchange rate disconnect puzzle revisited: The exchange rate puzzle. *International Journal of Finance & Economics* 20: 126–37. [CrossRef]

Bahmani-Oskooee, Mohsen, and Sujata Saha. 2017. Nonlinear autoregressive distributed lag approach and bilateral j-curve: India versus her trading partners: India's trade and J-curve. *Contemporary Economic Policy* 35: 472–83. [CrossRef]

Berman, Nicolas, Philippe Martin, and Thierry Mayer. 2012. How Do Different Exporters React to Exchange Rate Changes? *The Quarterly Journal of Economics* 127: 437–92. [CrossRef]

Bilson, John F. O. 1978. The Monetary Approach to the Exchange Rate: Some Empirical Evidence. *Staff Papers—International Monetary Fund* 25: 48–75. [CrossRef]

Bouraoui, Taoufik, and Archavin Phisuthtiwatcharavong. 2015. On the Determinants of the THB/USD Exchange Rate. *Procedia Economics and Finance* 30: 137–45. [CrossRef]

Charles, Amélie, and Olivier Darné. 2009. Testing for random walk behavior in euro exchange rates. *Économie internationale* 3: 24–45.

Chowdhury, Abdur R. 1993. Does Exchange Rate Volatility Depress Trade Flows? Evidence from Error-Correction Models. *The Review of Economics and Statistics* 75: 700. [CrossRef]

Cushman, David O. 2000. The Failure of the Monetary Exchange Rate Model for the Canadian-U.S. Dollar. *Canadian Journal of Economics* 33: 591–603. [CrossRef]

Dekle, Robert, Hyeok Jeong, and Heajin Ryoo. 2005. A Re-Examination of the Exchange Rate Disconnect Puzzle: Evidence from Japanese Firm Level Data. *SSRN Electronic Journal*. [CrossRef]

Devereux, Michael B., and Charles Engel. 2002. Exchange Rate Pass-through, Exchange Rate Volatility, and Exchange Rate Disconnect. *Journal of Monetary Economics* 49: 913–40. [CrossRef]

Dickey, David A., and Wayne A. Fuller. 1979. Distribution of the Estimators for Autoregressive Time Series with a Unit Root. *Journal of the American Statistical Association* 74: 427–31. [CrossRef]

Dornbusch, R. 1976. Expectations and Exchange Rate Dynamics. *The Journal of Political Economy* 84: 1161–76. [CrossRef]

Engel, Charles, and Kenneth D. West. 2005. Exchange Rates and Fundamentals. *Journal of Political Economy* 113: 485–517. [CrossRef]

Evans, Martin D. D., and Richard K. Lyons. 2005. Meese-RogoffRedux: Micro-Based Exchange-Rate Forecasting. *Financial Economics* 95: 10.

Fitzgerald, Doireann. 2004. A Gravity View of Exchange Rate Disconnect. *SSRN Electronic Journal*. [CrossRef]

Frankel, Jefrey A. 1979. On The Mark: A Theory of Floating Exchange Rate Based on The Real Interest Rate Differential. *American Economic Review* 69: 610–22.

Frenkel, Jacob A. 1976. A Monetary Approach to the Exchange Rate: Doctrinal Aspects and Empirical Evidence. *The Scandinavian Journal of Economics* 78: 200. [CrossRef]

Gente, Karine, and Miguel A. Leon-Ledesma. 2006. Does the World Real Interest Rate Affect the Real Exchange Rate? The South East Asian Experience. *The Journal of International Trade & Economic Development: An International and Comparative Review* 15: 441–67. [CrossRef]

Hooper, Peter, and John Morton. 1982. Fluctuations in the Dollar: A Model of Nominal and Real Exchange Rate Determination. *Journal of International Money and Finance* 1: 39–56. [CrossRef]

Kwiatkowski, Denis, Peter C. B. Phillips, Peter Schmidt, and Yongcheol Shin. 1992. Testing the Null Hypothesis of Stationarity against the Alternative of a Unit Root. *Journal of Econometrics* 54: 159–78. [CrossRef]

Laganà, Gianluca, and Pasquale M. Sgro. 2007. The Exchange Rate Disconnect Puzzle: A Resolution? *Asia-Pacific Journal of Accounting & Economics* 14: 43–68. [CrossRef]

Lee, Junsoo, and Mark C. Strazicich. 2001. Break Point Estimation and Spurious Rejections with Endogenous Unit Root Tests. *Oxford Bulletin of Economics and Statistics* 63: 535–58. [CrossRef]

Lee, Junsoo, and Mark C. Strazicich. 2003. Minimum Lagrange Multiplier Unit Root Test with Two Structural Breaks. *The Review of Economics and Statistics* 85: 1082–89. [CrossRef]

Lee-Lee, Chong, and Tan Hui-Boon. 2007. Macroeconomic Factors of Exchange Rate Volatility Evidence from Four Neighbouring ASEAN Economies. *Studies in Economics and Finance* 24: 266–85. [CrossRef]

Meese, Richard A., and Kenneth Rogoff. 1983. Empirical Exchange Rate Models of the Seventies. Do They Fit out of Sample? *Journal of International Economics* 14: 3–24. [CrossRef]

Obstfeld, Maurice, and Kenneth Rogoff. 2001. The six major puzzles in international macroeconomics: is there common cause? *NBER Macroeconomics Annual* 15: 339–90. [CrossRef]

Ouyang, Alice Y., and Ramkishen S. Rajan. 2016. Does Inflation Targeting in Asia Reduce Exchange Rate Volatility? *International Economic Journal* 30: 294–311. [CrossRef]

Panopoulou, Ekaterini, and Nikitas Pittis. 2004. A Comparison of Autoregressive Distributed Lag and Dynamic OLS Cointegration Estimators in the Case of a Serially Correlated Cointegration Error. *The Econometrics Journal* 7: 585–617. [CrossRef]

Pesaran, M. Hashem, Yongcheol Shin, and Richard J. Smith. 2001. Bounds Testing Approaches to the Analysis of Level Relationships. *Journal of Applied Econometrics* 16: 289–326. [CrossRef]

Raza, Syed Ali, and Sahar Afshan. 2017. Determinants of Exchange Rate in Pakistan: Revisited with Structural Break Testing. *Global Business Review* 18: 1–24. [CrossRef]

Sarno, Lucio, and Maik Schmeling. 2014. Which Fundamentals Drive Exchange Rates? A Cross-Sectional Perspective. *Journal of Money, Credit and Banking* 46: 267–92. [CrossRef]

Shin, Yongcheol, Byungchul Yu, and Matthew Greenwood-Nimmo. 2011. Modelling Asymmetric Cointegration and Dynamic Multipliers in a Nonlinear ARDL Framework. *SSRN Electronic Journal* 61. [CrossRef]

Tawadros, George B. 2017. Revisiting the Exchange Rate Disconnect Puzzle. *Applied Economics* 49: 3645–68. [CrossRef]

Turan, Taner, and Mesut Karakas. 2018. Asymmetries in Twin Deficit Hypothesis: Evidence from CEE Countries. *Ekonomický Časopis* 66: 580–97.

Umit, A. Oznur. 2016. Stationarity of Real Exchange Rates in the 'Fragile Five': Analysis with Structural Breaks. *International Journal of Economics and Finance* 8: 254. [CrossRef]

© 2019 by the authors. Licensee MDPI, Basel, Switzerland. This article is an open access article distributed under the terms and conditions of the Creative Commons Attribution (CC BY) license (http://creativecommons.org/licenses/by/4.0/).

Article

Money as an Institution: Rule versus Evolved Practice? Analysis of Multiple Currencies in Argentina

Georgina M. Gómez

International Institute of Social Studies, Erasmus University Rotterdam, Kortenaerkade 12, 2518AX The Hague, The Netherlands; gomez@iss.nl

Received: 6 March 2019; Accepted: 28 April 2019; Published: 8 May 2019

Abstract: Monetary policies and adjustments during a financial crisis depend on policy-makers' conceptions on what money is and how it works. There is sufficient consensus among scholars that money is an institution created within the economic system and is in line with other institutions that regulate economic action. However, there are different understandings of what institutions are and how they operate, and these understandings imply differences in terms of monetary enforcement, resilience, responsiveness and stability. This paper discusses the two main approaches that conceptualise institutions as rules and as practices presenting an empirically informed discussion of money as an institution drawing on these insights. It grounds the analysis on the empirical case of Argentina as a monetary laboratory and the plurality of currencies that circulate in its economy. The study argues that while the official currency of Argentina corresponds to the institutions as rules approach, the adoption of the U.S. dollar into a bimonetary economy evolved as equilibrium. In between, the massive community currency systems that rose and declined during the economic meltdown between 1998 and 2002 were a hybrid institution that combined rules and practice. All three of them show various degrees of resilience and stability.

Keywords: economic institutions; currency; monetary plurality; Argentina

---

1. Introduction

Every financial crisis poses the question of what sustains money and how it recovers from a downfall. In the last financial crisis, these questions were coupled with reflections on whether a different understanding of money should not imply another regulatory framework to prevent or ameliorate the toll that crisis takes on human beings. A discussion on the configuration of money and its stability hence seems timely.

There are two main narratives on the origin and meanings of money, one which corresponds to a spontaneous or evolutionary approach, and the other a centrally designed or rule oriented approach. Tymoigne and Wray (2006, p. 1) explain that in one view money is portrayed as a "cost-reducing innovation to replace barter" while in a rather unknown way individual utility maximizers settled on a single numeraire. This narrative translates in modern days into money being considered a given because it has happened an undefined long time ago and it is sustained by the expectation that it will continue to function. In contrast, heterodox approaches to money underline its social and political essence as the outcome of a historical process of negotiations and impositions by central authorities. The process is ongoing. Money is conceptualized as an institution which links individuals with each other and with the social world. Aglietta and Orlean (2002) offer a sophisticated argument on how money creates social bonds that support trade and social relations but clouds the specificity of relations and commodities. In this heterodox view, money is sustained by organisations, laws and rules that represent the institutions of the monetary system, and rests on the trust that money will deliver the usual monetary functions. Authorities, namely the state but also other agents such as banks and merchants' associations, participate in the process of structuring and imposing money over a sovereign territory, even by force if necessary (Cohen 1999; Wray 2004).

These two views leave us with a number of puzzles which are not specifically addressed. To start with, there are hardly any countries in the world in which the state's monopoly of one currency in the whole nation is complete. In the last three decades over 50 countries have hosted numerous local and complementary currencies that attempt to improve the responsiveness and inclusiveness of the monetary system (Blanc 2012, 2016; Michel and Hudon 2015; Seyfang and Longhurst 2013). These are often sustained by social agreements, with the occasional participation of state actors, and are considered "niches" (Seyfang and Longhurst 2013). They may be more than niches, as Greece and Italy, two EU member states, are exploring the introduction of local parallel currencies in the form of tax anticipation scripts which would allow them to retain the euro for national and international transactions (Bossone et al. 2015; Théret et al. 2015). Finally, at the global level the state's monopoly is being challenged by cryptocurrencies that facilitate counting and transferring value across borders and that enables an underground global economy. These trends suggest that the configuration of money, as a central economic institution, cannot be explained as the result of only central authority or practice. While money is normally established by states, it also circulates by simple practice, and sometimes these practices are contested or abandoned. How do economies go from these financial disruptions into new monetary practices?

An accepted definition of institutions, such as money, claims that they are "socially embedded systems of rules" that both constrain and enable social action (Hodgson 2006). In that sense, they bridge individuals with the social world because institutions exist in the minds as well as "out there" (Hodgson 2003; Gomez and Ritchie 2016). Institutional theory offers two main understandings on the construction of institutions and these have been intensely debated among institutionalists such as Kingston and Caballero (2009); Greif and Kingston (2011); Brousseau et al. (2011) and Hindriks and Guala (2015). The two competing accounts on institutional configuration conceptualise institutions as rules versus institutions as evolved equilibria.

This article engages with money as an institution and takes a step further to explore the implications of understanding money in this way. How do money (or moneys) get established among economic institutions, what factors sustain it and why does it change? The article aims at presenting an empirically informed discussion of money as an institution drawing on insights from the two main strands of institutional theory. This paper combines the two theoretical perspectives on institutional emergence to analyse different categories and configurations of money. The study avoids a discussion on which one of the two conceptualisations of institutions is more appropriate but considers that both views highlight different aspects of the various types of money. There are moneys that have been centrally designed while others have evolved rather spontaneously. A critical implication of conceptualizing money as an institution is that they are bound to be contextually diverse (Blanc 2016; Gómez and Dini 2016; Ingham 1998). The approach in this paper is different to the way other authors that have discussed money as an institution (for example, Aglietta and Orlean 2002; Wray 2004; Arestis and Sawyer 2006) in unveiling the varieties of money and exploring the fact that monies are institutions of various kinds.

The discussion is grounded in an empirical case in which there are different monies, a phenomenon termed plurality of money defined by the concurrent existence of more than one type of money in a particular space (Gómez 2018; Kuroda 2008). Such a setting was found in Argentina in the period of 1998–2002, in which there were five different types of money circulating in the country at the same time (Gómez and Dini 2016). In order to gain depth, the study will explain this scenario of monetary plurality in which sovereign money was centrally designed and other monetary practices came about spontaneously. It will later focus on the group of community currencies used by a total estimate of six million people around 2002. There were a few hundred of these currencies, created by grassroots organisations and generically known as *créditos*.

The study is based on both primary and secondary data, including previous research and reports. The primary data was gathered during several periods of fieldwork between 2004 and 2013 and is part of a larger database that includes a multimedia collection, survey data, focus groups, and expert interviews. Three periods of fieldwork were carried out in 2003, 2004 and 2006 to gather data at the level of participants and the coordinators of 45 modes across the country. The initiators, the three founders of the initiative, academic experts and regional leaders were interviewed at the same time and later on in 2009 and 2013. Interviews were held individually and collectively several times in order to reconstruct its evolution based on oral history. A survey with a semi-structured questionnaire was carried out among participants and it resulted in 386 responses. The next section will discuss the two approaches to institutions, namely the institutions as rules and the institutions as equilibria. The third section will focus on the emergence of the bimonetary system in Argentina (pesos and U.S. dollars) and the fourth section will analyse the complementary currency systems created at the grassroots. The last section offers some further reflection in terms of resilience, responsiveness and stability of currencies.

2. Institutions: Rules or Practices

Money is conceptualized as an institution, a term that has a number of definitions. Douglas North provided the definition that has probably become the most frequently quoted one in scholarly work: "Institutions are the rules of the game" (North 1990). Another Economics Nobel Prize winner, Elinor Ostrom, defined institutions in a similar way, as the prescriptions that are used to organize "all forms of repetitive and structured interactions" within communities, organisations, markets and so on (Ostrom 2005). Indeed, all social interaction is mediated or regulated by institutions that indicate "the way we do things around here" as phrased by Hall (1986).

The origin of the social structures that create stability and continuity in society is a point of contention. At the risk of simplification, there are two main accounts on how institutions originate and how they change or resist change, and have been discussed by scholars such as Kingston and Caballero (2009); Brousseau et al. (2011); Hindriks and Guala (2015); Hodgson (2015) and others. Despite some variation among authors, a first strand that sees institutions as rules that come out of purposeful design. Kingston and Caballero (2009) refer to this view as the "centralized" or "designed" version, while Hodgson (2015) and Greif and Kingston (2011) refer to "institutions as rules" and Brousseau et al. (2011) use the label of "constraining rules". In this strand, motivated agents express their preferences and negotiate, and exert pressure to push or block institutional changes according to their interests and benefit. The making of institutions is deliberate, centralized and assumes collective action because actors come together to bargain and make decisions or at times one exerts authority over others. In these negotiations, agents act according to their interests and in consideration of the existing rules. At the same time, negotiations are affected by authority and power asymmetries that favour the or voice or views of some decision-makers over the position of others. When it comes to institutional change, the focus is similarly placed on bargaining and consenting within the limits permitted or enabled by "rules of a higher order" (Ostrom 2005). Additionally, some actors, like judges, have special roles to play in the change of rules because they pass new legislation or mediate as rule makers. These special agents are rather "autonomous drivers of change" (Kingston and Caballero 2009, p. 158).

Critiquing this approach of institutions, Kingston and Caballero (2009) argue that rules may exist on paper but do not necessarily drive agents' behaviour. Then, to what extent are those to be considered institutions at all? Ostrom (2005) distinguishes between "rules in form" (on paper) and "rules in use" (effectively observed), and the rules in form do not actually steer people's behaviour. There are also rules that are observed but do not exist on paper, such as most informal rules which refer to culture. These are seen as adaptations to the context and to previous events, but without undergoing rational and consensual reform. They may become formalized, hence changing from rules in use, to rule in form.

A second strand of institutional theories underlines their evolutionary nature. Kingston and Caballero (2009) refer to them as "evolutionary", while Brousseau et al. (2011) opts for the label "self-enforcing expectations"; and Greif and Kingston (2011), Hindriks and Guala (2015) as well as Aoki and Hayami (2001) prefer the term "institutions as equilibria". According to this view, institutions appear in a decentralized and spontaneous manner out of repeated human interactions. Institutions depend and consist of repeated behaviour. There is no political process and no central instance that crafts the rules, but "uncoordinated choices of many individuals" (Kingston and Caballero 2009, p. 160). The expectation or belief that an institution guides the actions of others is enough to keep agents behaving in a given way and in that sense they are considered institutions as equilibria. If there are alternative courses of action for a given situation, it is conceivable that several agents may behave differently while institutions "compete" with each other to dominate the actions of agents. In the long run, one course of action will prevail and that will become the equilibrium institution that is sustained by repetition, replication and imitation. According to this view, only rules in use in the Olstromian terminology are proper institutions. Change is already embedded in the idea of evolutionary change, which is slow and endogenous. There is no explicit agent to coordinate the decision-making or the institutional reform process, and the selection of the institution that stands would happen spontaneously and signals the "most efficient" or superior solution (Williamson 2000). Aoki and Hayami (2001) explain that change occurs when a "general cognitive disequilibrium" happens, namely when an institution fails to obtain the expected results and when agents note a dissonance between the outcome obtained and the outcome expected.

Kingston and Caballero (2009) identify this aspect in their critique: little attention is paid to explaining how and why a particular institution prevails and what this process of institutional competition looks like before it is resolved. Williamson (2000) claims that the prevailing institution is the most efficient one in reducing transaction costs and its survival can be taken as sufficient proof that this particular institution is the best alternative. Other authors, instead, resort to an explanation by partial or local equilibria that result when institutions are not placed in the same geography or time, so they would not be exposed to institutional competition but to geographical segmentation. Additionally, an institution may start locally and be adopted elsewhere but this assumes there is contact between groups. Other authors (for example, Hayek (1973) or Greif and Tadelis (2010)) link the selection process to competition among rival groups or leaders in which each group promotes its own solution to a certain problem or resists the institutions of another, among other reasons because those institutions are inconsistent with cultural norms or because of its distributional impact. In short, the account tells "an empirical success story" (Williamson 2000, p. 607; quoted in Kingston and Caballero 2009, p. 161). Once equilibrium has been established, there is little further theorization on what pushes agents to change the institution as equilibrium.

Money has been analysed as an institution by several authors (Ingham 1998; Gómez 2018; Aglietta and Orléan 2006; Blanc et al. 2016; Dodd 2014; Gilbert and Helleiner 1999; Goodhart 2005; Wray and Forstater 2006). However, such analysis has been done following strictly one of the two institutional perspectives presented in this section. There are a number of scholars that underlined the essence of money as an institution in which institutions are understood as rules (see for example, Wray and Forstater 2006; Aglietta and Orléan 2006; Goodhart 2005). At the same time, there are a number of studies that highlight the nature of money as an institution which evolved as the belief that a certain thing has the capacity to perform the known monetary functions (for example, Banerjee and Maskin 1996; Kiyotaki and Wright 1989; Selgin 2001). In both cases, there are empirical puzzles that remain unexplained. This paper proposes to analyse money as an institution which results from both centralised rules and as evolved beliefs. In the last years, there have been attempts by institutional scholars to combine both strands of institutional theory into a hybrid approach that conceptualizes "rules in equilibrium" (Hindriks and Guala 2015). This means that as several solutions are available, eventually one appears as the satisfactory one and can be codified, i.e. summarized as symbolic representation. The authors follow John Searle, who distinguished regulatory from constitutive rules

(Searle 2005, p. 10), in which constitutive rules define status. Subsequent institutional change occurs by negotiation and centralized design, and includes the possibility that formal rules are nothing but endorsements of prevalent informal rules. In turn, Brousseau et al. (2011) focus on different temporal dimensions: institutions as rules concern the shorter term in which political negotiation and agreements are possible with a top-down approach, while the self-enforcing or equilibria account of institutions deals with the long term implied in social evolution and bottom-up approaches. In the meantime, Hodgson (2015) argues that rules include norms of behaviour and social conventions as dispositions to act in a certain way but with no certainty that behaviour will effectively and invariably follow. Effective behaviour is secondary to the existence of institutions, which are mainly a disposition to act.

Among scholars that study money as an institution, such combination has also been initiated. Aglietta and Orlean (2002, p. 35), for example, underline that money is an abstraction that depends on trust in the "supposition that money will always be accepted in trade by third parties". Trust, the authors continue, is a relationship between each private agent and the community that uses a certain money. According to them, trust is not a contract, so "trust cannot dispense with regulation, or regulation with public authority". So, "maintaining trust must be regarded as a regulatory problem of the utmost importance". They further elaborate on this point by distinguishing three types of trust. The first one is methodical trust, founded on routine and repetition of actions. Methodical trust, they claim, "pales into insignificance before the furious rivalries unleashed by the power of money" and hence they distinguish a second type of trust, which is hierarchical trust. The latter is imparted by the political authority and they consider hierarchical trust superior to methodical trust because "the political authority over money has the power to change the rules". The third one is ethical trust, which is an ethical attitude that reconciles conflicts and develops at the social level. It ascertains that a certain monetary order will maintain the value of private contracts over time. Aglietta and Orléan (2006) touch upon the distinction of money as an equilibrium sustained by methodical trust and regularity and consider that this type of money is inferior to money as rules that stems from centralized political authority and generates hierarchical trust. If there is any conflict between the two, it will be resolved at the loose level of ethical trust to protect social welfare and order. The authors hence incline themselves in favour of the state as the final decision maker on monetary matters. As it will be argued in the case of Argentina, the conviction that the state can induce such an ethical trust over methodical trust proves exaggerated. The next section will explore money as an institution from both approaches through the empirical case of Argentina.

3. Peso by Rule, Dollar by Practice

Argentina is often mentioned as a "laboratory" in terms of monetary and financial systems (for example, Della Paolera et al. 2003; Ginieniewicz and Castiglione 2011; Mogliani et al. 2009; North 2008). Since its origins the country has been prone to inflation and monetary instability, in combination with particularly deep and long downturns of the economic cycle (Gerchunoff and Llach 2005). Among the historians, Cortes Conde (1989) traces Argentine monetary instability already to the period 1880–1914, when there was a Currency Conversion Board and free banking system based on a gold standard (Bozzoli and Paolera 2014; Della Paolera et al. 2003).

Simultaneous deficits in the external current account and the fiscal accounts were often met with policies that attempted to control both government spending and exchange rates at the same time (Cortés Conde and Harriague 2006). But this could not prevent two-digit inflation rates from becoming normal. Some of these policies involved changes in the regulations on commercial and state-owned banks alike, as well as restrictions on the use of reserves and deposits, which undermined the credibility of the banking system in general. The combination of controls over the exchange rates, national inflation and low trust in the banking system created a parallel "black market" for foreign currency in which U.S. dollars were sold for more pesos than the restricted official exchange rate. Arbitration between the official and the black market dollar became a profitable business, while the U.S. dollar became the preferred currency to reserve value.

From an institutional point of view, the attempts of the central bank and other monetary authorities to control the key financial variables represent centralised and deliberate efforts to configure rules that organise economic life. The emphasis among the Argentine monetary authorities was placed on making the national currency a reliable unit of account, means of payment and reserve of value, while retaining control of the main financial variables in the hands of the state. However, institutions as rules depend on the capacities of the state or other authorities to enforce these rules. Inflation and instability undermined these capacities and actors such as the central bank and the Treasury, that were supposed to mediate the link between rules and effective behaviour, saw their capacities eroded by the poor performance of the Argentine money. In turn, this undermined other agents in the monetary system such as commercial banks.

By the end of the 1950s, high inflation and unstable business cycles introduced the practice of buying dollars as reserve of value and keeping them out of the banking system (Canitrot 1981). Argentines gradually adopted the dollar as a second currency. Initially it was only a reserve of value but around the 1970s dollar-denominated prices gradually became common practice. The U.S. dollar became accepted in the transfers of goods such as houses and cars and long term contracts (Gaggero and Nemiña 2016). By the 1980s, U.S. dollars were accepted as means of payment to trade most goods and services. In other words, the U.S. dollar was performing functions that national currencies do. The use of the U.S. dollar as second currency was not designed by any central authority but happened gradually, uncoordinated, spontaneously. Muir (2015) considers this behaviour especially prevalent among Argentine middle classes and contributed to the symbolic construction of the "small saver".

The inflationary problem eventually derived in three hyperinflation periods between May 1989 and the end of 1990. Following that serious financial crisis, a monetary policy was launched that aimed at rebuilding the institutions regulating the relationship between Argentines and their money. It was introduced in March 1991 under the name of convertibility plan because the core policy was a currency board that pegged the peso to the U.S. dollar at a rate of 1 to 1. Equally important from an institutional point of view, the new plan allowed economic agents to open bank accounts, denominate prices or trade in U.S. dollars. In other words, the rule in use of adopting the U.S. dollar as unit of account and means of payment together with the official Argentine currency was formally adopted as a rule by the government. From currency in practice, the dollar became a currency as rule.

In the long run, inflation and a series of failed monetary policies contributed to form a peculiar understanding of money among many Argentines as a flexible social construction. Indeed, experience showed them that it can be transformed. In 1969 a new currency was introduced by law, changing 100 of the old circulating units for one unit of a new one. The measure did not work to stop inflation and was repeated in 1983, when 10,000 units of the circulating currency were changed for one unit of the new Argentine peso. That second reduction in the amount of digits was not effective either to regain trust and inflation eroded the value of the currency even faster. A third change occurred in 1985, when 1000 units of circulating Argentine pesos were changed for one unit of the new currency, named Austral. That currency vanished with hyperinflation, and it was replaced again in 1992 at a rate of 10,000 Australes for one new peso. In total, four changes of currency denominations scrapped thirteen digits off the unit of account between 1969 and 1992 (Billetes Argentinos 2008).

The reforms in the currency reflect the difference between institutions as rules and actual behaviour. According to Hodgson (2006), rules are dispositions or injunctions to act in a certain way but do not establish behaviour per se. Indeed, the Argentine currency did not maintain its stability to serve as reserve of value, means of payment and unit of account. In the Ostromian terminology, the peso was partially performing as a currency in form and lost ground as currency in use. The U.S. dollar, instead, evolved as a currency in use, in the line of the approach of institutions as equilibria. It became accepted by the pervasive expectation that others would accept it too.

However, the official monetary authorities did not surrender their powers over the monetary system. As soon as the central bank regained some capacity to enforce rules, they tried to affect the bimonetary equilibrium and regain space for the official currency. Following another financial crisis with capital outflows, the Argentine government imposed a series of restrictions on the currency exchange in force between 2011 and 2015. The regulations restricted the rights to buy foreign currency and were difficult to impose because it implied the government could effectively distinguish who wanted foreign currency as reserve of value and for other purposes. The measures recreated a black market for foreign currency and were gradually relaxed until the new government abandoned them completely in December 2015.

Luzzi and Wilkis (2018) discussed the implications of this attempt of the official monetary authorities to regain their sovereignty over the currency in Argentina. Despite the regulations to "domesticate" it, bimonetary practices presented a remarkable resistance to change. Resilience is a key element of the conceptualisation of institutions as equilibria. In the terminology proposed by Brousseau et al. (2011), bimonetarism evolved as an institution and was not only resistant to change but also self-enforcing by mutual expectations. However, the restrictions cannot be considered a complete failure, highlighting that this competition between two currencies is not a normal monetary practice in other countries and has social costs.

4. A Hybrid Institution: Community Complementary Currencies

It was mentioned above that in 1995 the currency board system was challenged by an international financial crisis that started when Mexico devalued its currency. The Argentine economy adjusted by deflation and recession which in turn translated into a loss of jobs and income. Unemployment had risen gradually throughout the 1990s, but in 1995 the unemployment rate hit 18.8 per cent. Used to the term "hyper-inflation", Argentines were introduced to the term "hyper-unemployment" when media and experts used the word to describe the new situation. The purchasing power of wages in 1995 fell to 68 per cent of their 1986 level and 62 per cent of their 1975 level. Another term that became common around that time was that of the "new poor" to describe households that had fallen under the poverty line for the first time. Only a decade earlier, 70 per cent of the Argentine population had declared itself to be part of the middle class (Minujín and Kessler 1995). The new poor were the shopkeepers, public servants, skilled workers, graduates, blue-collar workers, bank clerks, teachers and small-firm owners, among others whose basic needs were covered who could no longer afford their lifestyle.

Amidst this environment of economic demise, civil society organisations launched a number of small-scale bottom-up initiatives to reorganise social life at the community level (Gomez 2009; Gómez and Dini 2016). Among them was the Club de *Trueque*, a circle of neighbours that exchanged goods and services with each other and was launched in May 1995. The informal exchange of goods within a closed network of impoverished middle-class members was initially carried out in one organiser's garage. Participants offered care services, home-made foods, handmade toiletries, organically-grown vegetables in their gardens, and all sorts of handicrafts. After six months of testing different methods with 25 to 50 participants meeting every Saturday, the group developed an exchange system that they found to be effective and practical. Participants came into the garage and placed their products on a table. The value was calculated at the formal market prices and was recorded on individual cards carried by the participants and on a computer worksheet. When the value of everyone's products had been recorded, participants turned to the role of consumers to choose what they wanted to take. The value of their acquisitions was deducted from the amount on their cards. Thus, the higher the value of the products brought, the more the producer would get of other people's products. Any producer who did not agree with the price given to a product was free to withdraw it, but that hardly ever happened. When people thought the price was low, they viewed it as a partial gift to others, which they would recover some other time when they obtained something below the regular price. When they left, their sales and purchases were entered as debits and credits on a computer worksheet. The overall balance roughly returned to zero every week. The remaining credits and debits were transferred to the following meeting. The system emulated a closed market in which exchanges were multireciprocal, so two individuals did not need to coincide with each other directly. The payment system was a novelty- it was not based on bartering or making payments through a basic commodity but was based on mutual credit/debts in an accountancy system.

It quickly became clear to the organisers that book-keeping on the basis of individual cards and computer records was hitting a limit. The organisers felt that entering transactions into the computer file was too burdensome and time consuming. Besides, they did not like the centralisation inherent in the system. "I was at the centre and we didn't like the idea of centres. As ecologists, we believed in autonomous self-regulation, like the environment is. The cards were blocking the potential of the scheme" (Interview with an initiator, Bernal, 13 June 2004). The successful propagation of two more nodes made the limitations of the individual card accountancy system more evident. Moreover, participants often travelled considerable distances to participate in the *Trueque* market, which means a waste of time and money. One of the organisers then got an innovative idea to facilitate the payments. He recalled, "One day I was walking by a print shop and saw their business cards. Then I thought, 'Why don't we just make vouchers that can circulate among the members to pay each other?' We could just print them, right? So we went into the shop and asked the shopkeeper to make us some notes". The others liked the idea of using vouchers as means of payment because of its practicality and because it removed them from the centre.

The scheme was so successful that it grew and the original organisers replicated it in the locations of friends and contacts across the city of Buenos Aires, at first, and the rest of the country, later on. Surrogate currencies were instituted in each *Trueque* node. Every new participant received a credit of fifty créditos so they could start trading, but they were committed to giving them back if they left the group. In comparison with the card system, physical notes were easier to handle. Organisers and participants alike assure that nobody perceived the vouchers as money but as the system grew, it slowly dawned on them that the vouchers were a social type of money. Anyone in the *Trueque* would accept the notes, but they were normally not convertible to pesos. By all means, *Trueque* created an institutional equivalent of what is considered money in modern economies. It was an abstract means of payment, depersonalised, dematerialised, transferable promise to pay (Gomez 2010; Gonzalez Bombal 2002; North and Huber 2004). The créditos were printed in denominations following those of the formal economy. Not surprisingly, the money was called *crédito*, indicating that members "gave credit to each other because we trust everyone here" (Interview with initiator, Bernal, 6 September 2004).

In the middle run, complementary currency systems (CCS) printed by grassroots organisations emerged at the local, regional and national levels. The initiative kept replicating, hence forming regional and national networks, together with umbrella organisations that kept them interconnected or steered replication rather hierarchically. The *Redes de Trueque* turned out to be the largest experiment with a complementary currency system in the world in modern times. According to unofficial figures, by the beginning of 2002, with the regular economy melting down, the *Redes de Trueque* reached a peak of 2.5 million participants in 4700 centres across the country (Ovalles 2002). There are no official statistics that would allow a more accurate estimation of how large they were and what their exact impact as an anti-cyclical device was. An indicative estimation is presented in Figure 1, which combines data from several sources and is meant only as an indication of their scale. Colacelli and Blackburn (2009) have a small and partial dataset that would corroborate these figures in the location where they gathered data.

In terms of the modern monetary practice of 'one country, one currency', the creation of a currency system of the scale of the Trueque is a real anomaly. It is clear that an economic demise that chopped 20 per cent of the GDP contributed greatly to the phenomenon. However, other countries in recent decades have had similarly severe economic downturns and their monetary system stuck to one currency. The *Trueque* calls for a broader explanation to bring new insights into the origins and meanings of money. In relation to the extended complementary currency systems in the U.S.A. and Europe in the 1920s and 1930s, the main difference was organisational: the *Trueque* was structured in regional and national networks articulating local markets. Each one issued its own currency, which was normally accepted in other neighbourhoods and networks too, so it was possible to pay for goods and services with the same scrip across the whole country. For some time, there was an umbrella organisation checking each other's currency systems; before and after its existence, scrip was accepted simply out of trust in the system. Similar integration has been attempted less successfully on a regional level in places like Manchester, UK, but with limited success (North 2006). Nowhere has an attempt been made to create a national, private, yet not-for-profit monetary system as the *Trueque*.

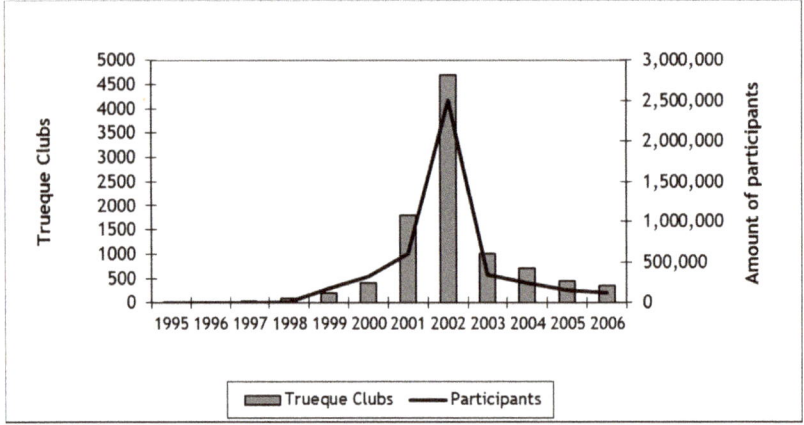

Figure 1. Size of Trueque in terms of participants and centres or clubs. Sources: Ovalles (2002) for 1995–2002; La Nación for 2003; author's estimation for 2004–2006 based on RT groups visited and information given by participants. Estimations refer to the beginning of each year.

In the longer run, the use of community currencies promoted the launch of new small businesses that could learn their trade in a protected market, and helped the unemployed to survive their disenfranchisement and return to regular jobs when the economy recovered. Thus, the institutions of the community currency systems were clearly responsive, but they proved not to be resilient. With several million participants, it had grown beyond the scale in which it was appropriate to "trust everyone here"; shirking and opportunistic behaviour became rampant. The institutional weaknesses of the *Trueque* became evident at exactly the same time as the regular economy started a period of vigorous recovery, and within a year, by 2003, they collapsed to about a fifth of their peak size. Still, the fieldwork done in 2013 proved that the *Trueque* did not disappear completely but became much smaller.

Are complimentary currency systems institutions as rules or institutions as equilibria? On the one hand, the *Trueque* had been established by deliberation, negotiation and agreement along the lines described in the institution as rules approach. The leaders and organisers performed the role of "autonomous drivers of change" as described by Kingston and Caballero (2009, p. 158). They discussed and made a myriad of decisions at different levels, including the design and name of the currency, the amounts to print, the methods to distribute it among existing and new members, and the participants that would be allowed to join and would be required to follow these procedures. The leaders kept reframing and improving the scheme, while the number of participants soared. They had to decide on the institutions to guide the behaviour of participants, setting rules for who was allowed to join, what was acceptable and what was not. The collective action process by which institutions as rules were made proved to be complex and exhausting, yet rules were made. The outcomes of these negotiations were institutions as rules that regulated the actions of members who had voluntarily accepted to abide by them. There was a clear and open commitment in the community to abide by the rules, which is an additional factor theorized by Gilbert (1992, p. 197) as the common understanding that under certain conditions people are jointly bound to pursue a certain action as long as they all do the same action. At the same time, the leaders had insufficient means to enforce the rules and sanction trespassers. They could not prevent massive forgery of the currency, abusive behaviour with prices and widespread speculation. They had created institutions as rules that did not always translate into effective action in the long run, as it happens with so many other institutions as rules created at the grassroots level. Eventually, the collapse of the *Redes de Trueque* does not undermine the significance of these complementary currencies that performed as units of account and means of payment among thousands of Argentines for about a decade (Gomez 2010; Plasencia and Gutiérrez 2006).

On the other hand, the complementary currency systems show traits of evolved institutions. The growth from one small and local *Club de Trueque* to a complementary currency system of over 2.5 million members took place without centralised and deliberate design. Groups across the country spontaneously imitated and replicated the initiative across the country. There was no coordinated planning such as, for example, where to locate them, but barely copying and replicating what other groups were doing nearby. Participants in one *Club de Trueque* would often learn the rules and get the idea to launch one in their neighbourhood. They obtained information and know-how on how to run one informally by word of mouth, through the media, by contacting an organiser in their own personal networks or simply learning by doing. The expansion of the *Redes de Trueque* around every corner is mainly a tale of evolved institutions that spontaneously disseminated the initiative by gaining ground from the failing official currency. Since there were no legal regulations supporting them, they were primarily self-enforcing institutions, according to the terminology suggested by Brousseau et al. (2011).

In terms of institutional theory, the complementary currency systems present a puzzle: they cannot be conceptualised as either institutions as rules or institutions as equilibria. It would be easy to dismiss them because they were relatively small and collapsed in the end but they existed long enough and reached a scale that merits a more elaborate explanation. The Argentine complementary currency systems show characteristics corresponding to both institutional narratives. However, they did not prove their resilience in the longer run and collapsed quickly. A note should be added about their responsiveness, and that is that they continue to exist in some locations, away from the public attention and the media. Moreover, they tend to reappear as soon as recession or a new financial crisis dawns in the horizon

5. Reflections

This paper has analysed the plurality of money in Argentina arguing for the use of plurals to refer to institutions and moneys. To move forward and analyse the implications of understanding moneys as institutions in the event of a new financial crisis, the discussion required a clear conceptualization of money as an institution. At the risk of overgeneralizing, there are two prevalent approaches to institutions, namely as rules and as equilibria. The first one focuses on centralized design, bargaining and authority to establish rules of use and form. The second one defines institutions as equilibria and underlines their evolutionary nature with a period of competition after which one outcome prevails and remains in equilibrium. Is money an institution as rule or an institution as equilibrium?

Research discussing these two narratives on institutions has not resorted to empirical explorations. This article presents an empirically informed discussion of money as an institution drawing on insights from the two main strands of institutional theory, while it avoids an evaluation of which one is more correct. It has discussed the issues of resilience and responsiveness of the currencies, the role of centralised monetary authority and the means of enforcement or self-enforcement that make the monetary institutions stable in the longer run. In a nutshell, the national sovereign currency of Argentina, the peso, emerged within the formation process of the nation state in the 19th century. Throughout the 20th century the imbalances in the Argentine economy undermined the performance of the monetary system, including episodes of hyper-inflation, poor performance of the functions of money, low trust in the central bank and other monetary authorities, and a generalized weakness of the banking system. The formal institution of money as a rule did not perform in reality all the functions that are expected of money. Gradually, the population adopted the U.S. dollar as unit of account and reserve of value, and later on also as means of payment, so Argentina became a bimonetary economy.

The emergence of the U.S. dollar as an alternative further undermined the long-term credibility of the peso as the national currency sustained by the state, i.e. the currency as rule. In turn, various failed efforts to rescue the functionality of the national currency diluted the legitimacy of the monetary authorities to impose a national currency.

Contrary to the claim by Aglietta and Orlean (2002) that hierarchical trust (by state regulation) is superior to methodical trust (by evolved regularity), the Argentine case suggests that use of the U.S. dollar as an institution in equilibrium has proved self-enforcing, extremely resistant to change and defiant of the state's authority. Methodical trust has resisted the monetary authorities' determination to win the wrestle between its centrally designed currency (the peso) and the spontaneously adopted currency (the U.S. dollar). At the same time, the phenomenon of bimonetarism has not been responsive to the demands for social change and inclusiveness of some sectors of the Argentine population.

A third type of currency was widespread between 1995 and 2005. The *Redes de Trueque* were born small, and spread fast across the country. These community currency systems were launched during a financial crisis and had their greatest expansion during the economic meltdown around the turn of the millennium. They represented a hybrid category between institutions as rules and institutions as equilibria and exhibit traits of both approaches. That is, they were centrally designed and sustained by grassroots organisations while they expanded rather autonomously across the country by the copying, imitation and replication of local initiatives. The case of the *Redes de Trueque* also suggest that the centralised design of institutions as rules is time consuming and requires a myriad of decisions and agreements to make them work, even if this is partial and lacking the means to sanction trespasses. As there are various types of money, the article refers to money as institutions, in its plural forms, because spontaneous evolution and centralized design do appear together in different combinations to generate money. Monies such as complementary currencies are hybrids between institutions as equilibria and institutions as rules.

The expansion of the complementary currencies was sustained by need and the crisis of the regular economy, so they were clearly responsive but did not prove to be resilient and collapsed after a few years. They could not resist the combination of opportunistic behaviour and the recovery of the regular economy and these institutions fell into demise. In a nutshell, they expanded rather autonomously in a decentralized manner, and they collapsed in competition with the regular economy and its money as rule. These institutions as rules had been agreed at the central level of the *Redes de Trueque*, so they expanded by belief and expectations and collapsed by disbelief and negative expectations. In comparison with the use of the U.S. dollar as evolved institution, the complementary currency systems could not be seen as having reached long term equilibrium. While the Argentine state failed to regain the exclusivity of the national currency in the monetary system against the U.S. dollar, in the case of the complementary currency systems the state did not need to take exceptional measures to reduce them. The question which begs to be asked is how long does an institution need to be in equilibrium to become a rule, or viceversa, how long does a rule need to be enforced until it becomes self-enforcing?

This discussion offers tools to rethink bimonetarism, not by continuing what seems a lost battle against the endogenously adopted currency (U.S. dollar) but by designing additional features on this institution as equilibrium in order to move towards a hybrid. Such policies would have higher chances of success because they would not be fighting against what is already a resilient and established practice. At the same time, it suggests working on strengthening the institution as a rule, the peso, in search of a hybrid that would keep both currencies but with more elements of the centrally designed institution that exist at present.

Funding: This research was partially funded by WOTRO/NWO grant number WB 46-494.

Conflicts of Interest: The authors declare no conflict of interest.

References

Aglietta, Michel, and André Orlean. 2002. *Whence and Whither Money? The Future of Money*. Paris: OECD, pp. 123–45.

Aglietta, Michel, and André Orléan. 2006. *Money between Violence and Trust*. Moscow: Publishing House HSE.

Aoki, Masahiko, and Yujiro Hayami, eds. 2001. *Communities and Markets in Economic Development*. Oxford: Oxford University Press.

Arestis, Philip, and Malcolm C. Sawyer. 2006. *A Handbook of Alternative Monetary Economics*. Cheltenham: Edward Elgar Publishing.

Banerjee, Abhijit V., and Eric S. Maskin. 1996. A Walrasian theory of money and barter. *Quarterly Journal of Economics* 111: 955–1005. [CrossRef]

Billetes Argentinos, Fundación. 2008. Modelos de Billetes de la Republica Argentina. Available online: www.billetesargentinos.com.ar (accessed on 1 November 2017).

Blanc, Jérôme. 2012. Thirty years of community and Complementary currencies: A review of Impacts, potential and challenges. *International Journal of Community Currency Research* 16: 1–4.

Blanc, Jérôme. 2016. Unpacking monetary complementarity and competition: A conceptual framework. *Cambridge Journal of Economics* 41: 239–57. [CrossRef]

Blanc, Jérôme, Bruno Théret, Ludovic Desmedt, and Pierre Alary. 2016. *Théories Françaises de la Monnaie*. Business & Economics. Paris: Presses Universitaires de France.

Bossone, B., Marco Cattaneo, Enrico Grazzini, and Stefano Sylos Labini. 2015. *Per una Moneta Fiscale Gratuita. Come Uscire Dall'austerità Senza Saccare L'euro*. Rome: MicroMega.

Bozzoli, Guillermo, and Gerardo della Paolera. 2014. Evolución monetaria, regímenes de Banca Central y la teoría cuantitativa del dinero en Argentina (1880–2010). In *Historia de las Instituciones Monetarias Argentinas*. Edited by Roberto Cortés Conde, Laura D'Amato and Javier Ortiz Batalla. Buenos Aires: Asociación Argentina de Economía Política & Temas, pp. 193–228.

Brousseau, Eric, Pierre Garrouste, and Emmanuel Raynaud. 2011. Institutional changes: Alternative theories and consequences for institutional design. *Journal of Economic Behavior and Organization* 79: 3–19. [CrossRef]

Canitrot, Adolfo. 1981. Teoría y práctica del liberalismo: Política antiinflacionaria y apertura económica en la Argentina. *Desarrollo Económico* 21: 1–73. [CrossRef]

Cohen, Benjamin J. 1999. The New Geography of Money. In *Nations-States and Money. The Past, Present and Future of National Currencies*. Edited by Emily Gilbert and Eric Helleiner. New York and London: Routledge, pp. 121–38.

Colacelli, Mariana, and David J. H. Blackburn. 2009. Secondary currency: An Empirical Analysis. *Journal of Monetary Economics* 56: 295–308. [CrossRef]

Cortes Conde, R. 1989. *Dinero Deuda y Crisis; Evolución Fiscal y Monetaria en la Argentina 1862–1890*. Instituto Torcuato Di Tella. Buenos Aires: Sudamericana.

Cortés Conde, Roberto, and Marcela Harriague. 2006. *Finanzas Públicas y Moneda en América Latina en Los Siglos XIX y XX: Argentina, Brasil, Chile, Colombia y México*. Edited by Academia Nacional de la Historia. Buenos Aires: Dunken.

Della Paolera, Gerardo, Maria Alejandra Irigoin, and Carlos G. Bozzoli. 2003. Passing the buck: Monetary and fiscal policies. In *A New Economic History of Argentina*. Edited by Gerardo Della Paolera and Alan M. Taylor. Cambridge: Cambridge University Press, pp. 46–86.

Dodd, Nigel. 2014. *The Social Life of Money*. Princeton: Princeton University Press.

Gaggero, Alejandro, and Pablo Nemiña. 2016. La vivienda como inversión: El origen de la dolarización del mercado inmobiliario durante la última dictadura cívico-militar. In *De Militares y Empresarios a Políticos y CEOS: Reflexioines a 40 Años del Golpe*. Edited by Guillermo Levy. Buenos Aires: Gorla, pp. 175–93.

Gerchunoff, Guillermo, and Lucas Llach. 2005. *El Ciclo de la Ilusión y el Desencanto; un Siglo de Políticas Económicas Argentinas*, 2nd ed. Buenos Aires: Ariel.

Gilbert, Margaret. 1992. *On Social Facts*. Princeton: Princeton University Press.

Gilbert, Emily, and Eric Helleiner, eds. 1999. *Nation-States and Money. The Past, Present and Future of National Currencies*. London and New York: Routledge.

Ginieniewicz, Jorge, and Celeste Castiglione. 2011. State response to transnational asset accumulation: The case of Argentina. *Bulletin of Latin American Research* 30: 133–47. [CrossRef]

Gomez, Georgina M. 2009. *Argentina's Parallel Currency: The Economy of the Poor*. Edited by Robert E. Wright. Volume 11, Financial History. London: Pickering & Chatto.

Gomez, Georgina M. 2010. What was the deal for the participants of the Argentine local currency systems, the Redes de Trueque? *Environment and Planning A* 42: 1669–85. [CrossRef]

Gómez, Georgina M., ed. 2018. *Monetary Plurality in Local, Regional and Global Economies*. London: Routledge.

Gómez, Georgina M., and Paolo Dini. 2016. Making sense of a crank case: Monetary diversity in Argentina (1999–2003). *Cambridge Journal of Economics* 40: 1421–37. [CrossRef]

Gomez, Georgina M., and Holly A. Ritchie. 2016. The Institutional Foundations of Civic Innovation. In *Exploring Civic Innovation for Social and Economic Transformation (Routledge Studies in Development Economics)*. Edited by Kees Biekart, Wendy Harcourt and Peter Knorringa. Abington and New York: Routledge, pp. 20–40.

Gonzalez Bombal, Inés. 2002. Sociabilidad en las clases medias en descenso: Experiencias en el trueque. In *Sociedad y Sociabilidad en la Argentina de los 90*. Edited by Luis Beccaria, Silvio Feldman, Ines González Bombal, Gabriel Kessler, Miguel Murmis and Maristella Svampa. Buenos Aires: Universidad Nacional de General Sarmiento and Editorial Biblos, pp. 97–136.

Goodhart, Charles A. E. 2005. What is the essence of money? *Cambridge Journal of Economics* 29: 817–25. [CrossRef]

Greif, Avner, and Christopher Kingston. 2011. Institutions: Rules or Equilibria? In *Political Economy of Institutions, Democracy and Voting*. Edited by Norman Schofield, Gonzalo Caballero, Avner Greif and Christopher Kingston. Berlin/Heidelberg: Springer, pp. 13–43.

Greif, Avner, and Steven Tadelis. 2010. A theory of moral persistence: Crypto-morality and political legitimacy. *Journal of Comparative Economics* 38: 229–44. [CrossRef]

Hall, Peter. 1986. *Governing the Economy: The Politics of Stated Intervention in Britain and France*. Oxford and New York: Oxford University Press.

Hayek, Friedrich August. 1973. *Rules and Order, Book 1 of Law, Legislation and Liberty: A New Statement of the Liberal Principles of Justice and Political Economy*. London: Routledge & Kegan Paul.

Hindriks, Frank, and Francesco Guala. 2015. Institutions, rules, and equilibria: A unified theory. *Journal of Institutional Economics* 11: 459–80. [CrossRef]

Hodgson, Geoffrey Martin. 2003. The hidden persuaders: Institutions and individuals in economic theory. *Cambridge Journal of Economics* 27: 159–75. [CrossRef]

Hodgson, Geoffrey M. 2006. What are institutions? *Journal of Economic Issues* 40: 1–25. [CrossRef]

Hodgson, Geoffrey M. 2015. On defining institutions: Rules versus equilibria. *Journal of Institutional Economics* 11: 497–505. [CrossRef]

Ingham, Geoffrey. 1998. On the underdevelopment of the sociology of money. *Acta Sociologica* 41: 1–17. [CrossRef]

Kingston, Christopher, and Gonzalo Caballero. 2009. Comparing theories of institutional change. *Cambridge Journals Online* 15: 151–80. [CrossRef]

Kiyotaki, Nobuhiro, and Randall Wright. 1989. On money as a medium of exchange. *Journal of Political Economy* 97: 927–55. [CrossRef]

Kuroda, Akinobu. 2008. What is the complementarity among monies? An introductory note. *Financial History Review* 15: 7–15. [CrossRef]

Luzzi, Mariana, and Ariel Wilkis. 2018. Soybean, bricks, dollars, and the reality of money: Multiple monies during currency exchange restrictions in Argentina (2011–15). *Journal of Ethnographic Theory* 8: 252–64. [CrossRef]

Michel, Arnaud, and Marek Hudon. 2015. Community currencies and sustainable development: A systematic review. *Ecological Economics* 116: 160–71. [CrossRef]

Minujín, Alberto, and Gabriel Kessler. 1995. *La Nueva Pobreza en Argentina*. Buenos Aires: Planeta.

Mogliani, Matteo, Giovanni Urga, and Carlos Winograd. 2009. *Monetary Disorder and Financial Regimes: The Money Demand in Argentina, 1900–2006*. PSE Working Papers. Available online: https://halshs.archives-ouvertes.fr/halshs-00575107/ (accessed on 1 March 2019).

Muir, Sarah. 2015. The currency of failure: Money and middle-class critique in post-crisis Buenos Aires. *Cultural Anthropology* 30: 310–35. [CrossRef]

North, Douglass. 1990. *Institutions, Institutional Change and Economic Performance*. Cambridge: Cambridge University Press.

North, Peter. 2006. *Alternative Currency Movements as a Challenge to Globalisation? A Case Study of Manchester's Local Currency Networks. Economic Geography*. Aldershot: Ashgate.

North, Peter. 2008. Voices from the Trueque: Argentina's Barter Networks Resisting Neoliberalisation. In *Social Justice and Neoliberalism: Global Perspectives*. Edited by Adrian Smith, Alison Stenning and Katie Willis. London: Zed.

North, Peter, and Ulli Huber. 2004. Alternative Spaces of the "Argentinazo". *Antipode* 36: 963–84. [CrossRef]

Ostrom, Elinor. 2005. *Understanding Institutional Diversity*. Princeton: Princeton University Press.

Ovalles, Elinor. 2002. *Argentina es el País del Mundo en el Cual el Fenómeno del Trueque Tiene Mayor Dimensión Social*. Buenos Aires: Carta Económica, Centro de Estudios Nueva Mayoría, pp. 42–45.

Plasencia, Adela, and Cristina Gutiérrez. 2006. 10 años del trueque en la Argentina: ¿éxito o fracaso? In *Moneda Social y Mercados solidarios. Potencial Pedagógico y Emancipador de Los Sistemas Monetarios Alternativos*. Edited by Adela Plasencia and Ricardo Orzi. Buenos Aires: Ciccus.

Searle, John R. 2005. What is an institution? *Journal of Institutional Economics* 1: 1–22. [CrossRef]

Selgin, George. 2001. *Adaptive Learning and the Transition to Fiat Money*. Athens: University of Georgia.

Seyfang, Gill, and Noel Longhurst. 2013. Growing Green Money? Mapping Community Currencies for Sustainable Development. *Ecological Economics* 86: 65–77. [CrossRef]

Théret, Bruno, Thomas Coutrot, and Wojtek Kalinowski. 2015. The Euro-Drachma, a monetary lifeline for Greece. *Libération*, March 16.

Tymoigne, Éric, and Randall Wray. 2006. Money: An Alternative Story. In *A Handbook of Alternative Monetary Economics*. Edited by Philip Arestis and Malcolm Sawyer. Cheltenham: Edward Elgar Publisher, pp. 1–16.

Williamson, Oliver. 2000. The New Institutional Economics: Taking Stock, Looking Ahead. *Journal of Economic Literature* 38: 595–613. [CrossRef]

Wray, Randall. 2004. *Credit and State Theories of Money: The Contributions of A. Mitchell Innes*. Cheltenham: Edward Elgar.

Wray, Randall, and Mathew Forstater, eds. 2006. *Money, Financial Instability and Stabilization Policy*. Cheltenham: Edward Elgar.

© 2019 by the author. Licensee MDPI, Basel, Switzerland. This article is an open access article distributed under the terms and conditions of the Creative Commons Attribution (CC BY) license (http://creativecommons.org/licenses/by/4.0/).

Article

Simulation of the Grondona System of Conditional Currency Convertibility Based on Primary Commodities, Considered as a Means to Resist Currency Crises

Patrick Collins [1,*,†], **Jameel Ahmed** [2] **and Ahamed Kameel Meera** [3]

1. Azabu University, Sagamihara City 252-5201, Japan
2. Institute of Management Sciences, University of Baluchistan, Quetta 87300, Pakistan; jamil.ahmed@um.uob.edu.pk
3. Department of Finance, International Islamic University of Malaysia, Kuala Lumpur 68100, Malaysia; akameel@gmail.com
* Correspondence: collins@azabu-u.ac.jp
† Retired from the Azabu University.

Received: 28 February 2019; Accepted: 22 April 2019; Published: 29 April 2019

Abstract: Currency crises are a significant feature of the present-day world economy, in which financial transactions are many times larger than monetary flows in the "real economy", so that defending a currency's exchange-rate is a major challenge for the governments of countries which may be smaller than a single large corporation. It is made even more difficult due to the United States government and its agents openly using economic pressures to try to force other countries to obey its orders, even including regime change. Guaranteed convertibility of a currency, such as maintaining a gold standard, can in principle help to stabilise its value, but this has been absent since the end of US dollar convertibility in 1971. The Grondona system of conditional currency convertibility was not planned as a counter-measure for currency crises. However the simulation of its operation demonstrated in this paper shows clearly how its automatic counter-cyclical stock-holding in response to movements in commodity prices—and so to exchange-rate movements that alter domestic commodity prices—causes monetary flows that would resist large exchange-rate movements (among other effects), and thereby tend to ameliorate a currency crisis. Moreover, it would achieve this without the need for international negotiations, agreements or other geopolitical trade-offs.

Keywords: Grondona system; currency convertibility; commodity price stabilisation; currency crisis

1. Introduction: The Challenge of Currency Crises

Perhaps the most visible and best-known aspect of a currency crisis is a sharp fall in a currency's exchange-rate, which may be either the result or the cause of crisis. In today's world of countries of very different sizes linked by trade and financial markets, a fall in the exchange-rate may be caused either wittingly or unwittingly by the actions of a single large organisation, whether a country's government or a large corporation, as well as by loss of international confidence in the government's monetary policy.

A large and/or sudden drop in the exchange-rate puts a burden on domestic importers, leads to imported inflation, and makes foreign debt repayments heavier. Government's counter-measures may also impose severe costs on a country. For example, a government may sell foreign exchange reserves, or may raise interest-rates to strengthen the currency and resist inflation, thereby causing a severe deceleration in domestic economic activity. The risk of currency crisis increases as international financial markets widen and deepen, thereby becoming more complex, including due to international derivative market operations, of which the scale dwarfs the real economy today.

The problem is well exemplified by the South-East Asian currency crisis of 1997–1998 which exhibited many of the features that make a currency crisis so challenging for policy makers: contagion from one country to another, high speed of events, high cost of policy-mistakes, limited capabilities of policy instruments, vulnerability to external pressure—all aggravated by a high level of uncertainty. The importance of high uncertainty is well shown by the case of Malaysia during that crisis: in the face of a tidal wave of severe criticism from Wall Street, the US government and US news media, Prime Minister Mahathir stood his ground and adopted a policy that was recognised, several years later, to have been by far the most successful! This event was a profound—though largely ignored—demonstration of the very limited value of "mainstream economics" for policy-making: if the advice offered at such a critical time by an overwhelming majority of "respected" economists, policy-makers and economic commentators in the mainstream media, dominated by the USA, is so poor, what is these peoples' function? And it raises the age-old question: "Do they know that what they are saying is wrong? That is, that their advice would actually aggravate the problem?" If they do not know, then they are incompetent, and should not be in the influential position they have; but if they do know, then they are dishonest—literally enemies pretending to be friends.

Much the same criticism can be made concerning the 2008 financial crisis spreading from Wall Street and causing recession around the world, nominally triggered by the collapse of Lehman Brothers Inc. Did the thousands of well-paid economics professors in American universities not know how extremely fragile the US financial system was? Or did they know but kept silent? Is it actually a condition of economists' employment that they must not discuss the fundamental instability—and dishonesty—of the US fractional-reserve banking system? Solving this ever-worsening problem is the central goal of the work of the Public Banking Institute (PBI) and American Monetary Institute in the USA, among other organisations.

There is an extensive literature on currency crises, including various generations of currency crisis models which discuss the causes of crises and political remedies. In parallel, a range of strategies have evolved over recent years to mitigate the risk of currency crisis: building up foreign exchange reserves commensurate to a country's holdings of foreign debt, making currency swap arrangements with allied countries, use of "derivatives" such as currency futures, and others.

An additional aspect that must be considered is political risk. Although a country's government and corporations may be following normally adequate prudential policies, it may be targeted for destabilisation for political reasons by the US government. As of 2019, this is being done openly against Iran, Russia, Syria, North Korea and Venezuela, among other countries which are the target of publicly announced economic attack by the US government, often intended to achieve "regime change". Defence against such politically motivated economic pressure is more complex and needs a stronger basis than defence against purely economic risks. That is, while the US government continues to use its dominant role in dollar-based economic activities to try to force other countries to follow its orders, relatively smaller countries in particular need to try to insulate themselves from such political pressures, in addition to the risks and problems caused by major market fluctuations.

A counter-measure that has been spreading in recent years is for countries to avoid using the US dollar in their trade. This is implemented through bilateral agreements between pairs of countries to make arrangements to pay for mutual imports and exports in their own currencies. In order for such agreements to be successful, it is necessary to achieve a satisfactory level of stability in the relative value of their respective currencies. However, due to the absence of any component of convertibility of currencies into real commodities today, the value of a country's currency is defined solely by activity in foreign exchange markets. This dependence on foreign exchange markets makes the currency of all but the largest countries subject to manipulation by large operators, both commercial and governmental.

The present paper takes a different approach: it is concerned neither with the causes of crises, nor with the politics of counter-measures. It considers the extent to which an "automatic stabilizer" (i.e., driven by market prices), which operates predictably, regardless of the causes of a crisis, whether political or economic, can reliably exert a stabilizing influence on various economic parameters relevant to overcoming a currency crisis. Unemployment insurance has been called a macro-economic "automatic stabilizer", since it automatically reduces the extent to which consumption falls as a result of rising unemployment, analogous to the stabilisers on a ship: whatever the cause of turbulence in the sea, whether wind, earthquake, typhoon or another cause, they automatically reduce the extent to which the ship rolls from side-to-side. Likewise, unemployment insurance acts dependably, on a scale decided in advance by the government, to prevent the vicious circle by which recession worsens into depression, without giving rise to suspicion of political misjudgement or nepotism, nor being vulnerable to distortion or failure caused by speculative attack.

Another example, which has been known for centuries but is not widely discussed today, is the "automatic" macro-economic stabilizing effects of a system of currency convertibility based on primary commodities. Because of inadequacies in the operation of gold convertibility, even during the 19th century heyday of the gold standard, convertibility based on a range of basic commodities was recommended by the first of a long list of influential economists, including (Jevons 1877; Marshall 1887; Fisher 1913; Fisher 1928; Graham 1937; Keynes 1938; Hayek 1943; Hart et al. 1964; Riboud 1981; Kaldor 1976; Luke 1975; Kaldor 1983; Borsodi 1989; Greco 1990; Lietaer 2001; Ussher 2011; Ussher 2012) and others from across the political spectrum. None of these plans for commodity convertibility have been implemented, because they were either impractical (that is they would not be able to achieve their stated objective, such as to keep commodity prices between fixed limits), or would have required detailed international negotiations among multiple countries for their possible implementation for which there has not been the required political will. Further, most of these commodity-backed currency-systems were described only conceptually without providing detailed guidelines for implementation, nor for how to perform simulations of their operation in order to analyse their possible effects.

This long-term and widespread support has not attracted the attention that might be expected. As a single striking example, the recent book "Keynes Hayek: The Clash that Defined Modern Economics" (Wapshott 2012), of which the theme is representative of present-day "mainstream" economic thinking, *does not even mention* the fact that, far from being entirely opposed in their thinking, both Keynes and Hayek wrote strongly in favour of the macro-economic stabilizing benefits of a system of currency convertibility based on primary commodities, due to its automatic counter-cyclical stock-holding function. Their strikingly similar views are epitomised in the following short excerpts from their writings on the subject:

> "At present a falling off in effective demand in the industrial consuming countries causes a price collapse ... But if ... "Commodity Controls" are in a position to take up at stable prices the slack caused by the initial falling off in consuming demand ... the vicious cycle may be inhibited at the start; and, again, by releasing stocks when consumption recovers ... prevent the inflation of raw material prices.". (Keynes 1938)

> "With this system in operation an increase in the demand for liquid assets would lead to the accumulation of stocks of raw materials of the most general usefulness ... And as the hoarded currency was again returned to circulation and demand for commodities increased, these stocks would be released to satisfy the new demand.". (Hayek 1943)

These two short excerpts do not discuss another inherent aspect of the operation of such a system, namely that it would also cause a limited, counter-cyclical variation in the supply of the currency in which it operated. As a result, the system would also act indirectly to resist changes in the exchange-rate and both inflation and deflation, like an "automatic stabiliser". However, despite this endorsement at literally the highest level of the mainstream "western" economics establishment, such a system has never been implemented, and indeed, devising a practical plan is not easy, although the difficulty is rather different from that of resuming gold convertibility.

In the case of gold, proposals to revive an international gold standard face such problems as the need to revalue gold by a factor of approximately 10× in order to provide cover for world currencies, which would cause gross economic injustice due to the very uneven ownership of gold. In addition, the system would be vulnerable to speculative attack, not least by geopolitical competitors, who have essentially unlimited "fiat" funds at their disposal. Consequently, a realistic attempt to implement a modern gold standard would require international agreement—which removes it from consideration as a "practical" measure such as a sovereign national government can implement independently.

Instead, the key problem faced in trying to implement currency convertibility based on primary commodities is that it must accommodate continuing wide movements in their market prices, which are essential for markets to balance demand and supply. This problem is much less significant for gold, since its industrial uses are far less than its use as a store of value. By contrast, most primary commodities are important components of international trade and industry, and their market prices are notoriously unstable, swinging widely over the business cycle by as much as −50% and +100% or more. Trying to use commodities with such widely moving prices as the basis of currency convertibility seems, prima facie, self-contradictory. However, if it were possible, even partially stabilising primary commodity prices would have a beneficial stabilizing effect on world trade and economic growth, for which reason both Keynes and Hayek strongly supported the principle, rather than trying to revive a gold standard, which would have no direct stabilising influence on world commodity trade and markets.

However, the various international plans that have been proposed to implement the concept of commodity convertibility have unfortunately all been demonstrably impractical—requiring an unrealistic degree of international cooperation, an unacceptable level of interference with market forces, excessive dependence on experts' discretionary judgement, lack of transparency, or other critical problems, as discussed further in (Collins 1985).

The main contribution of the present paper is to provide evidence to justify further attention to the system described in the following section, which the authors propose is a genuinely practical means of implementing currency convertibility based on primary commodities, able to be safely implemented by individual countries, and thereby offering a useful, incremental step towards strengthening them against currency crises. An additional strength of the system is that its operation can be simulated reliably. The current paper illustrates this in the following sections by describing the Grondona system, simulating its operation in Indonesia, a D-8 member country, and thereby showing its resulting economic effects. Finally, it discusses their economic implications, and the potential value of wider implementation by D-8 countries.

2. Grondona System of *Conditional* Currency Convertibility

In contrast to the various international systems proposed over more than a century, the Australian writer Leo St. Clare Grondona (1890–1982) developed a less ambitious system of conditional currency convertibility during the 1950s, comprising a multi-polar system which enables individual countries to partially stabilise their currencies in real terms, independently, on a scale determined in advance. Most importantly, Grondona prepared a detailed plan of how to implement this form of partial price stabilisation of durable, essential, basic, imported commodities, which is also a system of conditional currency convertibility based on these primary commodities (Grondona 1975).

NB Grondona stipulated that only durable, essential, basic, imported commodities should be included, and handled only in large units of quantity, in order to minimise operating costs and avoid problems of deterioration, as well as political issues of subsidising domestic primary production, which might arise with products for which the country did not depend on imports.

Studies which evaluated the Grondona system from Shariah perspective, and which concluded that its operations are indeed Shariah-compliant, have been published in (Ahmed et al. 2014; Ahmed 2015; Ahmed et al. 2018b), and on-line at https://emeraldinsight.com/doi/abs/10.1108/JIABR-05-2015-0018?journalCode=jiabr. In outline, the Grondona system of currency convertibility is based on the fundamental principle of economic planning of Prophet Yusuf (AS), accumulating reserves of primary commodities during times of abundance and releasing those reserves during periods of scarcity, as described in Holy Quran (Ahmed 2015). Briefly, the currency that is "created" to pay for the CRD's reserves is backed by the real commodity reserves which it is used to purchase. As the quantity of reserves falls (when market prices rise) the currency is retired from circulation (at a pre-announced premium). Hence, even under an existing fiat money system, the CRD's role cannot be criticized as "riba", neither for issuing "fiat" money, nor for being debt-based, like all currencies which are largely supplied via the fractional-reserve banking system. This is a very encouraging result, since it means that implementing the Grondona system in terms of their domestic currencies could be a way for D-8 countries to improve their macro-economic stability in the face of destabilising external influences.

Grondona described his system of partial price stabilisation of primary commodities in detail in many speeches, articles and papers, starting from 1950 (Grondona 1950), and in a series of books (Grondona 1958; Grondona 1962; Grondona 1964; Grondona 1972; Grondona 1975). It is not possible to summarise all of this information in a single paper. However, the underlying idea is very simple, but in critical points it is different from related proposals, and so the effects of its operation are very different. In particular, the financial liability involved in implementing the system is limited in advance by the government establishing it, thereby avoiding the open-ended liability involved in commodity "buffer-stock" schemes, which attempt to limit the movement of commodity prices. This has the important implication that, in contrast to other proposals for commodity-backed currency, individual countries are able to implement the Grondona system independently in terms of their own currencies, legitimately paying for purchases of reserves through monetary expansion rather than taxation, as was done under the gold standard. Grondona envisaged that, in the long term, many countries would adopt the system, thereby leading to greater stability of primary commodity prices, and also indirectly to gradual stabilisation of exchange-rates, in addition to smoothing the trade cycle. In this way, the Grondona system avoids the extremely difficult and unpredictable process of trying to negotiate different countries' shares of an international system, while preserving each country's sovereignty and ensuring mutual benefits from implementation. This is a particularly important advantage from the perspective of political feasibility or "practicality".

A second critical difference from other related proposals is that the guarantee to provide commodities in exchange for monetary units on demand at specified prices would apply only as long as the system was holding reserves of those commodities (the exact levels of which would be publicised at all times). Thus, on occasions, reserves of one or more commodities might fall to zero, making the system's guarantee of a minimal value of the currency in terms of those commodities temporarily ineffective. However, the system would continue to provide support to the commodities' market prices, and reserves of the commodity would be likely to subsequently accumulate as market prices fell once again, making the system's maximum prices effective once more. This and other important details of Grondona's proposals are described at length in (Grondona 1958; Grondona 1975; Collins 1985; Ahmed 2015), and on-line at https://link.springer.com/book/10.1007/978-1-349-07058-9.

A notable advantage of the Grondona system over the gold standard is that it is fully counter-cyclical: that is, it is automatically stimulatory as well as contractionary over the business cycle. It was a major weakness of the gold standard that it obliged countries with a trade deficit and/or inflation to contract demand, but did not oblige surplus countries to expand demand. As a result, it had a net deflationary tendency, leading to unnecessarily high unemployment and slow economic growth. This is a serious weakness also of the operation of the IMF which remains from the Bretton Woods gold exchange standard system, as discussed at length by (Stiglitz 2002) and (Pettifor 2003). By contrast, under the Grondona system a fall in commodity prices in the domestic currency, and/or a rise in the exchange-rate, would automatically expand the money supply and the flow of currency abroad, thereby stimulating economic activity automatically in response to deflationary market pressure as advocated (as noted above) by both (Keynes 1938; Hayek 1943).

Institutionally, the Grondona system would be implemented by a "Commodities Reserve Department" (CRD) which would stand ready to purchase or sell reserves of specified commodities at prices in its official "price schedules" on demand (as illustrated below). It would not actively enter the market but would respond predictably to market participants who wished to sell or purchase commodities from its reserves on its published terms. Being passive it would not try to alter market prices, but its predictability would provide a valuable link between the monetary world and the real economy, while being compatible with a country's existing monetary system, using the national currency.

2.1. Details of Implementation

For each of the durable, essential, basic, imported commodities involved, the CRD would publish a "price schedule", according to which the prices paid or accepted by the CRD in exchange for specified (large) units of that commodity would adjust in proportion to the CRD's current level of reserves of the commodity, as illustrated in Table 1 for the case of Aluminium, in Indonesian Rupiah. This is not a plan: it merely shows that, having initially offered to pay 83,389,528 Rupiah per ton of Aluminium (of a standard grade used in world markets), if the CRD's reserves reach a level of 6900 tons, then the price which the CRD will subsequently offer will fall to 79,220,056 Rupiah per ton. The CRD's offer price and sale price (which Grondona called its "low point" and "high point" would continue to adjust according to this "price-schedule" as the quantity of its reserves rose or fell.

Table 1. Illustrative Rupiah Price-Schedule for Aluminium.

Current CRD Buying Price (Low Point) Rp/Tonne	Current CRD Selling Price (High Point) Rp/Tonne	Max. Quantity in Indonesian CRD's Reserves	Number of Blocks
83,389,528	101,920,536	6900	1
79,220,056	96,824,512	13,800	2
75,050,576	91,728,480	20,700	3
70,881,096	86,632,456	27,600	4
66,711,624	81,536,432	34,500	5
62,542,148	76,440,400	41,400	6
58,372,672	71,344,376	48,300	7
54,203,192	66,248,348	55,200	8
50,033,716	61,152,320	62,100	9
45,864,240	56,056,296	69,000	10
41,694,764	50,960,268	75,900	11
37,525,288	45,864,240	82,800	12
33,355,812	40,768,216	89,700	13
29,186,336	35,672,188	96,600	14
25,016,858	30,576,160	103,500	15

More generally, with a CRD in operation, when a commodity's market price in terms of that country's currency was falling (that is, when the value of that country's monetary unit in terms of a particular commodity was rising), market participants would sell commodities to the CRD in exchange for monetary units once the CRD's current buying price became attractive relative to current market prices. When the quantity of reserves of the commodity rose to a pre-specified quantity (which Grondona termed a "Block"), the CRD's official buying and selling prices for that commodity (known as its "points") would fall by a pre-specified amount. If the value of the monetary unit in terms of this commodity continued to rise, so that market prices fell to this new, lower "point" and reserves continued to accumulate, the process would repeat, and the cycle would continue until the CRD's buying price (lower "point") fell low enough to be unattractive to sellers. Later, when the value of the monetary unit in terms of that commodity declined as market prices recovered, buyers would repurchase reserves from the CRD at the successively higher selling prices (upper "points") in its published reserve price schedule, as each in turn became attractive relative to the current market price.

In the following it is assumed that an Indonesian CRD is established following Grondona's guidelines (Grondona 1975). As described above, the Indonesian Rupiah would thereby become convertible into a range of durable, essential, basic, imported commodities, at prices which would adjust according to the level of reserves held by the CRD, following each commodity's published "price schedule".

The simplicity of the Grondona system also enables detailed simulations of its operation in order to examine its potential effects under different conditions, without the need to use a macro-economic model to evaluate its impact (although such could be used in more advanced simulations). Collins simulated the timing and scale of changes in the national money supply that would have occurred in Japan during the 1990s, on the assumption that CRDs were established on representative terms (Collins 1996a, 1996b). Ahmed performed simulations of the Grondona system in the four D-8 countries Pakistan, Malaysia, Turkey and Indonesia in (Ahmed 2015). Recently, Ahmed, Collins and Meera performed more up-to-date simulations of the Grondona system for Turkey and examined its monetary effects (Ahmed et al. 2018a).

Because of its "automatic" operation, activated by market forces rather than by political or "expert" judgement, the Grondona system can be realistically simulated with a high degree of confidence. Consequently, these simulations of its potential operation in different countries have helped to illustrate the counter-cyclical timing of its automatic functioning (Ahmed 2015).

The development of these simulations has also created an essential tool for the government of any country either considering or planning to implement the system: in order to decide the optimal initial conditions (including which commodities and grade(s) to include, the maximum quantity of reserves to hold at each price level, the initial price-levels and the steps in the price-schedule, for each commodity), being able to run numerous simulations based on a range of different initial conditions is clearly very valuable.

2.2. Costs and Risks

The main cost of implementing the Grondona system comprises the cost of preparing and maintaining the warehousing needed for the commodities that will be accumulated by the CRD. Grondona discussed this in detail, including such details as that CRD warehouses should be sited near ports and/or major users within the host country (Grondona 1975). This cost is determined by the scale on which the system is set up, and so will be chosen not to be an excessive burden on the government budget.

A second "cost" is that of permitting the money supply to increase and decrease in proportion to the CRD's reserves (within predetermined limits). That is, as under the gold standard, it is an important aspect of the CRD's operation that the funds used to pay for the reserves should not be raised from taxation or government borrowing but should comprise "new money" released into the economy. Likewise, the proceeds of sales of the CRD's reserves should not be treated as government revenues but should leave circulation. This makes the reserves "costless" (subject to the obvious condition that the scale of implementation is not excessively large, thereby causing severe distortion of the money supply). As discussed in detail in (Collins 1985), counter-cyclical variation in the money supply will in general be beneficial: however, it can be countered by the monetary authorities, if desired, without cancelling the beneficial stabilising influence on each commodity trade and industry, due to the different route by which monetary policy acts on the economy (such as through government bond market operations). A priori it is equally likely that the monetary authorities would wish to accentuate the monetary effects of the CRD operations, due to their counter-cyclical timing, as discussed in (Collins 1985).

Considering the potential risks of "political economy" that are involved in all government activities, decisions on the siting of the CRD's warehousing may be used for political purposes of regional development, use of favoured contractors, and/or other political purposes, as is common with public works projects. Deciding the scale of the system's operation in respect to different commodities may also be distorted in favour of some commodities. However, provided that the central principle of the CRD's automatically adjusting support-prices is preserved, there are no complex macro-economic or geo-political issues, such as politically controversial trade-offs typical of international negotiations that need to be resolved. Due to this, the authors consider it appropriate to describe the system as "politically practical".

Among other risks, the Grondona system is not vulnerable to attack by speculators, due to the predictable conditionality of its stabilizing operations. For example, a "speculative attack" on a CRD might involve buying all its reserves of one or more commodities, or conversely selling large quantities of commodities to it. But in either case the CRD would benefit—either by selling all its reserves at some 20% above the prices which it paid (as per its price-schedules), or by accumulating reserves of essential imports at ever-lower prices. Hence, except in case of actual fraud, the CRD is literally immune to speculative attack—while at the same time acting to strengthen the currency against speculative attack in the foreign exchange markets, due to its counter-cyclical response to major changes in commodity market prices (i.e., in its national currency) that may be caused by large exchange-rate movements.

Nor would a CRD be vulnerable to harm from "competition" from another country's CRD. Any "competition" between different countries' CRDs would comprise their setting higher prices in order to attract reserves. However, provided that they use the central feature of the Grondona system, namely the market price-driven adjustment of its support prices in its price-schedules, their buying prices would adjust downwards after accumulating a certain quantity of reserves, thereby making the price offered by other countries' CRDs more attractive (allowing for considerations of exchange-rate risk). Hence, there would be no need for coordination between different countries establishing CRDs, and any "competition" between different countries' CRDs would act to improve the stability of commodity prices and trade by increasing the quantity of counter-cyclical stock-holding capacity in the world economy.

3. Simulation of Grondona System Operation in Indonesia

The following case study of Indonesia, selected in view of its role as a member of the "D-8" group of leading Islamic countries, illustrates how the automatic adjustment mechanism of the Grondona system exerts a stabilising influence on the real value of the currency of a country which implements the system. This stabilising influence comprises direct stabilisation in terms of the commodities handled, and indirect stabilisation through counter-cyclical changes in the money supply. The simulations are based on the principles and guidelines suggested in (Grondona 1975) and use past data on the annual quantities and values of Indonesia's imports of primary commodities, and their monthly market prices, found in World Integrated Trade Solution (WITS) on the IndexMundi website. The simulation results show how the Indonesian money supply changes in parallel with changes in the levels of reserves of the different primary commodities stockpiled by the Indonesian CRD. By this, the simulation results show how the automatic price adjustment mechanism of the Grondona System, by partially stabilizing the real value of the Rupiah, would thereby help to insulate the Indonesian economy from fluctuations of the business cycle and other external shocks.

Grondona suggested that, in practice, each country should decide the details of the initial conditions of implementation to suit their own conditions, but he himself offered some preliminary guidelines. For simplicity, in the following we use the uniform guidelines suggested in (Grondona 1975):

i. The CRD would make only Indonesian Rupiah transactions and would operate without national discrimination.
ii. It would handle only selected commodities of specified standard grades, in specified, large units of quantity. The CRD would have no dealings with commodity futures, currency or financial markets.
iii. It is also assumed that Indonesian imports would continue to come from the same supplying countries as before the CRD was established, and that domestic users of the commodities in question would continue to use approximately the same quantities as they did before the CRD was established.

3.1. Simulation Methodology

The simulation of an Indonesian CRD was performed by using past data on the annual quantities and values of Indonesia's imports of primary commodities, and their monthly average market prices, using a program developed in C++ to perform the simulations. The outputs of the simulations were further analysed in Microsoft Excel to generate relevant graphs.

3.2. Data Description

Indonesian primary imported commodities were selected based on the attributes recommended in (Grondona 1975), namely durable, essential and basic. Based on these attributes, the authors used the Harmonized System (HS) 6-digit codes to select a list of primary commodities imported by Indonesia, and used the 6-digit HS codes to retrieve their annual quantities and trade values from the World Integrated Trade Solution (WITS) developed by the World Bank (World Bank 2013). The HS 6-digit codes provide more detailed information about trade statistics than other nomenclatures, and they have been used since 1988. Table 2 shows the HS 6-digit codes for Indonesian primary commodity imports. The HS codes of imported primary commodities of Indonesia listed in Table 2 were used to identify the required primary commodities from the full list of imported commodities.

Table 2. Country-Wise List of Primary Commodities with HS Codes.

S. No	Product Description	HS Product Codes
1.	COFFEE NOT ROAST, NOT DECAFEINATED	090111
2.	DURUM WHEAT	100110
3.	BARLEY	100300
4.	SOYA BEANS, WHETHER OR NOT BROKEN	120100
5.	COCOA BEANS, WHOLE, BROKEN, RAW OR ROAST	180100
6.	RAW SUGAR, NOT CONTAINING ADDED FLAVOURING OR COLOURING MATTER: CANE SUGAR	170111
7.	COTTON, NOT CARDED OR COMBED	520100
8.	RICE IN HUSK (PADDY OR ROUGH)	100610
9.	JUTE AND OTHER TEXTILE BAST FIBRES, RAW OR RETTED	530310
10.	NATURAL RUBBER LATEX, WHETHER OR NOT PRE-VULCANISED	400110
11.	REFINED COPPER, CATHODES & SECTIONS	740311
12.	NICKEL, NOT ALLOYED	750210
13.	ALUMINIUM, NOT ALLOYED	760110
14.	REFINED LEAD	780110
15.	ZINC CONTAINED BY WT>99.99% NOT ALLOYED	790111
16.	ZINC CONTAINED BY WT<99.99% NOT ALLOYED	790112
17.	TIN, NOT ALLOYED	800110

The annual quantities and trade values, obtained from WITS for Indonesia, were given in kilograms and U.S. dollars respectively. Thus, the authors converted the annual quantities into tonnes, and trade values into the domestic currency of Indonesia i.e., Indonesian Rupiah. For conversion of trade values, the annual exchange-rates were obtained from the World Bank website. Annual data on Indonesia's Consumer Price Index (CPI) were also retrieved from the database of the World Bank, in order to adjust the prices of primary imported commodities for inflation as suggested in (Grondona 1975).

Table 2 shows the complete list of candidates among Indonesia's primary imported commodities. After initial examination of these data, the authors found that some of the commodities are imported either in small quantities or have missing values for a few years. Thus, such commodities were excluded from the simulation. Table 3 represents the final list of primary imported commodities which were included in the simulation.

The monthly market prices of the above listed Indonesian primary commodities were retrieved from the IndexMundi website. This monthly data was available in the domestic currency of Indonesia (IDR) on the given website. Since the data about a few commodities, namely Cocoa Beans, Sugar,

Cotton, Coffee and Rubber were given in IDR/KG, the authors converted them into IDR/Tonne by multiplying each month's price by 1000.

There are five parameters (which Grondona called the "gearing" of the system), which determine the extent of the system's monetary and economic influence, and the government's financial commitment involved in implementing this system. These parameters are the range of commodities, the initial price level for each commodity, the size of "Blocks", the width of the price-band for each commodity, and the price steps between successive price-bands.

Table 3. List of Primary Imported Commodities Selected for Simulation.

Country	Agricultural Commodities	Metals	Total Primary Commodities
Indonesia	Soybean; Coffee; Cocoa Beans; Sugar; Cotton; Rice in Husk; Natural Rubber Latex	Copper; Nickel; Lead; Tin; Zinc; Aluminium	13

Table 4 provides a brief description of these parameters and their values as proposed in (Grondona 1975). The authors used Grondona's proposed values of these parameters for the purpose of performing the simulation, which was simplified in several ways and based on the following assumptions:

- It considers only one grade of each commodity and is based on monthly data.
- It assumes that the CRD would have no stabilizing influence on commodity prices, and therefore overestimates the CRD's turnover, and so its direct effect on the money supply. (In reality, it can be expected that the CRD would have a significant stabilizing influence on some commodity prices at some times.)
- In addition, the CRD's overall scale is selected somewhat arbitrarily, and could readily be increased.

Table 4. Description of Parameters of Price Schedule.

S. No	Parameters of Price Schedule	Description of Parameters	Grondona Suggested Values of Parameters
1.	Range of Commodities	Only imported commodities should be included which are durable, essential and basic. Domestically produced commodities and fuel minerals are therefore not part of the system.	List of commodities depends on the country's primary imported commodities.
2.	Initial Price index	The initial "Index" for each commodity is based on the average trend of previous years' average c.i.f.[1] price, (adjusted for inflation).	Average c.i.f. prices of each commodity of the country.
3.	Width of Price Band	This is the difference between the CRD's lower and upper "points" for each commodity. This should depend on the normal range of fluctuations in each commodity's market price.	For initial simulation, the price band is set 10% below and above the initial "Index".
4.	Block Size	10% of average annual imports is used as a guideline to calculate the quantity in the "Block" of each commodity.	10% of the country's average annual imports (in terms of quantity).
5.	Size of Price Step between Successive Price Bands	This ratio should be fixed so that the upper and lower points in each price-band maintain a constant ratio.	The upper and lower points adjust by 5% of their initial levels, on withdrawal or receipt of each full Block.

---

[1] c.i.f. stands for Cost, Insurance and Freight.

4. Simulation Results

Initially, the authors computed the average inflation rate as the average of 2005–2008 annual Consumer Price Indices (CPI) to adjust Indonesia's annual primary imported commodity prices for inflation. Based on these average inflation-adjusted prices for the period of 2005–2008, the authors developed price schedules for all the primary commodities selected for simulation. After development of the price schedules, the authors performed simulations for each individual primary commodity for the period 2009–2018. The results of the simulations show that, on these assumptions, the Indonesian CRD would have accumulated reserves of Copper, Nickel, Lead, Zinc > 99%, Zinc < 99%, Aluminium, Coffee, Cotton, Sugar and Rice during the 10-year period. However it was found that the CRD's prices for some primary commodities (namely Tin, Cocoa beans and Rubber) were too low, so that the CRD purchased no reserves throughout the simulation period: consequently the initial Index of each of these commodities should have been set at a higher price (i.e., based on a different calculation than the other commodities).

The overall pattern of financial flows resulting from the Indonesian CRD's operations is to disburse Indonesian Rupiah abroad at times of falling commodity prices, and to withdraw Indonesian Rupiah from the domestic economy (which would otherwise flow abroad) at times of rising commodity prices. Such patterns are shown by the graphs in Figures 1 and 2 These flows would tend to reduce fluctuations in the prices paid by domestic users of commodities, in the prices received by foreign commodity producers, and secondarily in the demand for exports from Indonesia.

The financial effect of sales of reserves to the Indonesian CRD, (as shown in Figures 1 and 2) will be similar to an increase in government payments to the private sector. The Indonesian CRD's payments will appear first as an increase in banks' deposits at the Bank of Indonesia, which will influence the "reserve progress ratio of reserve deposits" and, if not counter-acted by the monetary authorities, the call rate. In this case it could lead to a further expansion of bank deposits by some multiple of the CRD's payments over following months.

Sales to the CRD will be made mainly by primary commodity exporters in foreign countries, and so the increase in the money supply will comprise first an increase in Rupiah bank accounts held by foreigners. Foreign-held Rupiah bank deposits may be used in various ways:

- They may be exchanged for national currency, in which case there could be some downward influence on the Rupiah exchange rate in relation to the currency in question, which is generally appropriate when commodity prices are falling (and so the value of the Rupiah in terms of those commodities is rising).
- They may be used to invest in Indonesian securities; and
- They may be used to purchase goods and services from Indonesia, in which case they could increase Indonesian exports.

Since the initial recipients of the CRD's Rupiah payments will be usual sellers of raw materials to Indonesia, the relative amounts of these three possibilities could be estimated to some extent from past statistics. In addition, to the extent that the Indonesian CRD's operations had the effect of maintaining Rupiah-denominated import prices of the commodities involved higher than the level to which they would have fallen in the CRD's absence, this will maintain the flow of commercial payments abroad above the level to which it would otherwise have fallen. Thus, the flow of Rupiah abroad resulting from the CRD's operations, and the commercial activities which this supports, can be expected to be larger than the amount disbursed by the CRD itself.

The financial flows resulting from purchases of reserves from the CRD will reduce bank deposits at the Bank of Indonesia, equivalent to receipts by the public sector. The fall in bank deposits at the Bank of Indonesia will alter the "reserve progress ratio of reserve deposits" and, if not counter-acted, the call-rate. In this case it could lead to a further reduction in bank deposits to some multiple of the CRD's transactions, which is generally appropriate when commodity prices are rising (and so the value of the Rupiah in terms of those commodities is falling).

Purchases from the CRD will generally be made by domestic users of the commodities concerned. That is, although the CRD will operate without national discrimination, Grondona proposed that the sites of its reserves should be chosen to be convenient for domestic users, who will as a result generally find the CRD's selling prices somewhat more attractive than foreign buyers, by the difference in cost of transport (Grondona 1975).

Purchases from the CRD will lead to a reduction in the flow of Rupiah abroad below what it would have been in its absence. In addition, imports by domestic users will be purchased at prices lower than they would have been in the CRD's absence, due to its influence in resisting rises in Rupiah-denominated import prices. Consequently, the reduction in the flow of Rupiah abroad resulting from the CRD's activities, and the commercial activities which this supports, will be larger than the value of purchases from the CRD itself.

Such effects, i.e., the increase/fall in the Indonesian CRD's reserves in response to a fall/rise in the market prices of the respective commodities, are evident from the graphs shown in Figure 1, and their corresponding effects on the financial flows of the Bank of Indonesia are also depicted in the graphs of Figure 2. For instance, in the graphs of Nickel in Figures 1 and 2, the Indonesian CRD accumulated reserves of Nickel during the first few months of 2009 due to a fall in Nickel prices, causing Rp 39,079 million expansion in the Indonesian money supply. And as a result of the rise in Nickel market prices during June–July 2009, it released the accumulated reserves of Nickel which caused a contraction of Rp 47,745 million in the Indonesian money supply.

It is important to note that the expansion of the Rupiah money supply was slightly less than the subsequent contraction, due to the sales premium, namely the difference between the buying and selling prices offered by the CRD. In the present case, Rp 8666 million is the sales premium earned by the Indonesian CRD during that period of the simulation. Grondona proposed that a portion of the sales premium should be used to cover the administrative and maintenance costs of the warehouses of the CRD, while any remainder could be transferred to a specified account which could be used for poverty alleviation or other programs for enhancing the welfare of the public within the country. However, continuing inflation in the host country will lead to loss of reserves again, even if world market prices are not rising. This can be partially compensated by Grondona's proposed remedy (described below). However, rapid inflation of about 10% per year or more would considerably reduce a CRD's beneficial influence, by preventing it obtaining reserves of some or all commodities.

Grondona suggested a solution to address this issue, namely that if the CRD obtains no reserves of a commodity for a certain specified period of time, say, two years (or more or less), then the initial index, and the upper and lower points for that particular commodity should automatically be increased by a certain stipulated percentage, say 5 percent (or other specified percentage) of the original initial levels. And the initial index and points should automatically be increased by the same percentage after each year until the CRD accumulates reserves of that commodity, the then index and points at which the CRD accumulated reserves becoming the new initial index and points. Grondona argued that such an adjustment to the initial index is required to tailor the CRD's gearing to the inflation prevailing in the country (Grondona 1975). Once again, the most appropriate pace of adjustment should probably not be uniform but should vary according to different commodities' conditions.

The Indonesian CRD stockpiles reserves of Zinc < 99% due to its initial gearing. Such an increase in Indonesian CRD reserves expands the Indonesian money supply by an amount equivalent to Rp 641,786 million (see the graphs in Figure 2). On the other hand, the purchase of Zinc < 99% Blocks by traders during August–December 2009 contracts the Indonesian money supply by Rp 70,849 million. Likewise, the Indonesian CRD had an expansionary effect on the money supply when Sugar market prices fell in January 2009, and the money supply contracted again in July 2009 due to a rise in Sugar market prices. Similar patterns were observed in the study described in (Ahmed 2015) of shorter simulations of four D-8 member states, which showed how each D-8 country's CRD stockpiled reserves of primary imported commodities (as a result of a drop in market prices of primary commodities), and released those reserves during subsequent periods of price hikes. Consequently, the transactions of each CRD caused corresponding changes in each country's domestic money supply. That is, the national money supply of each D-8 country changed with the change in level of reserves of primary commodities stockpiled by their respective CRDs in response to an increase or decrease in market prices of the primary commodities. Such a mechanism helps to stabilise the prices and trade quantities of primary commodities and lessen the fluctuations in primary commodity markets during both slump and boom periods. As a result, the system would have exerted a corresponding stabilising influence on the real value of the Indonesian Rupiah.

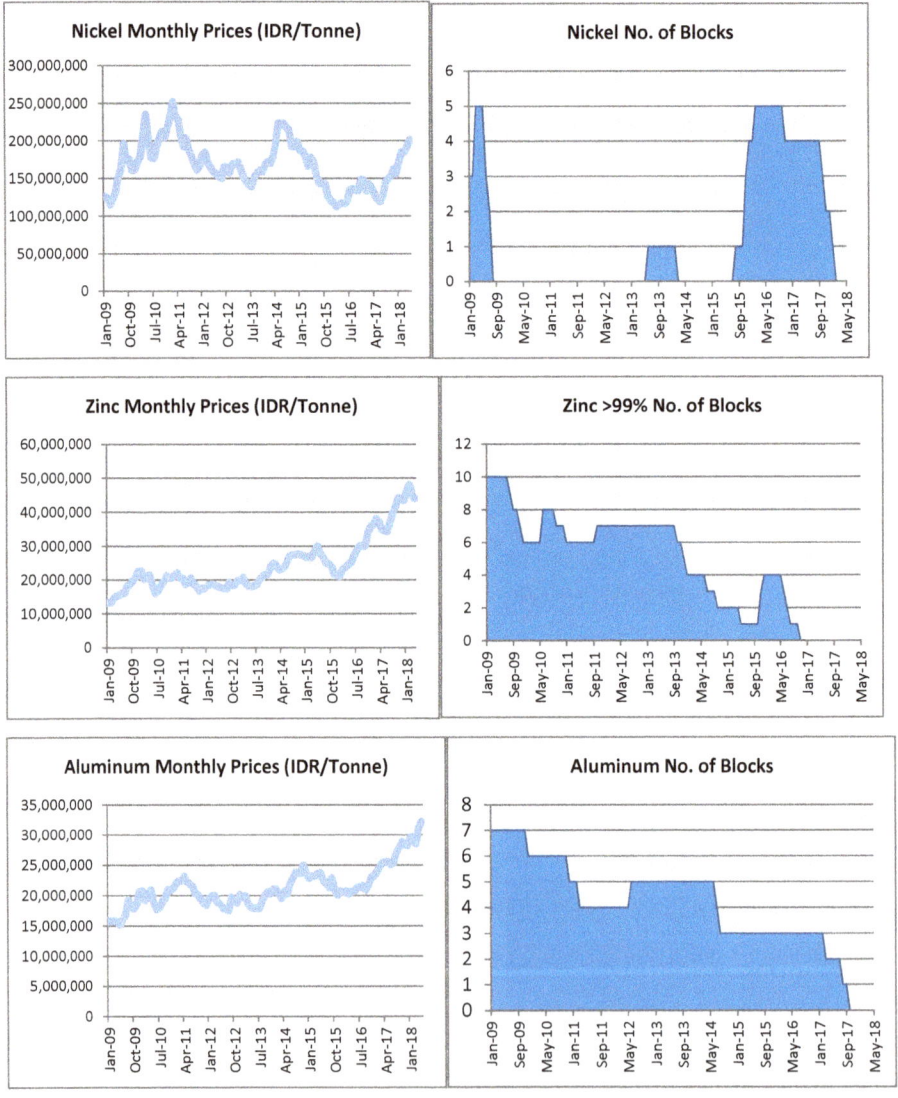

Figure 1. *Cont.*

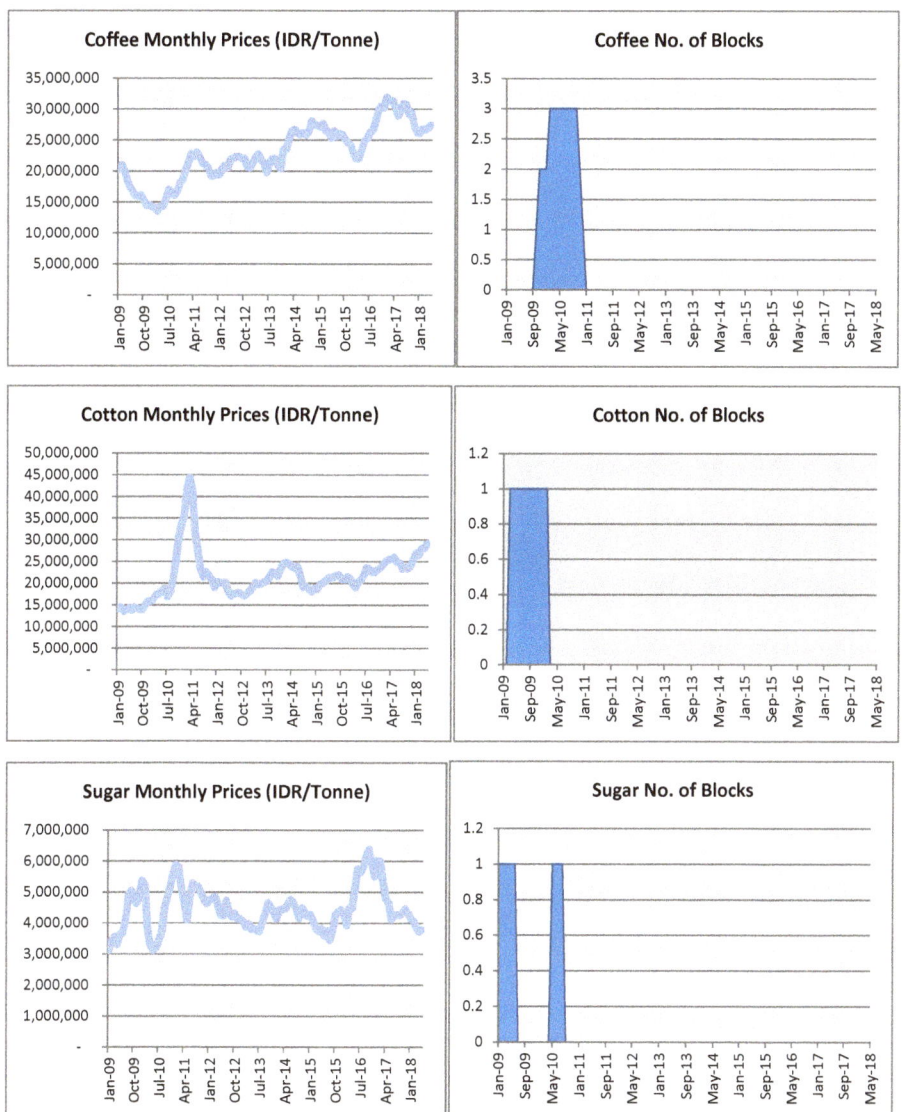

Figure 1. Changes in CRD Reserves of Various Commodities by the Indonesian CRD over the Period of 2009–2018.

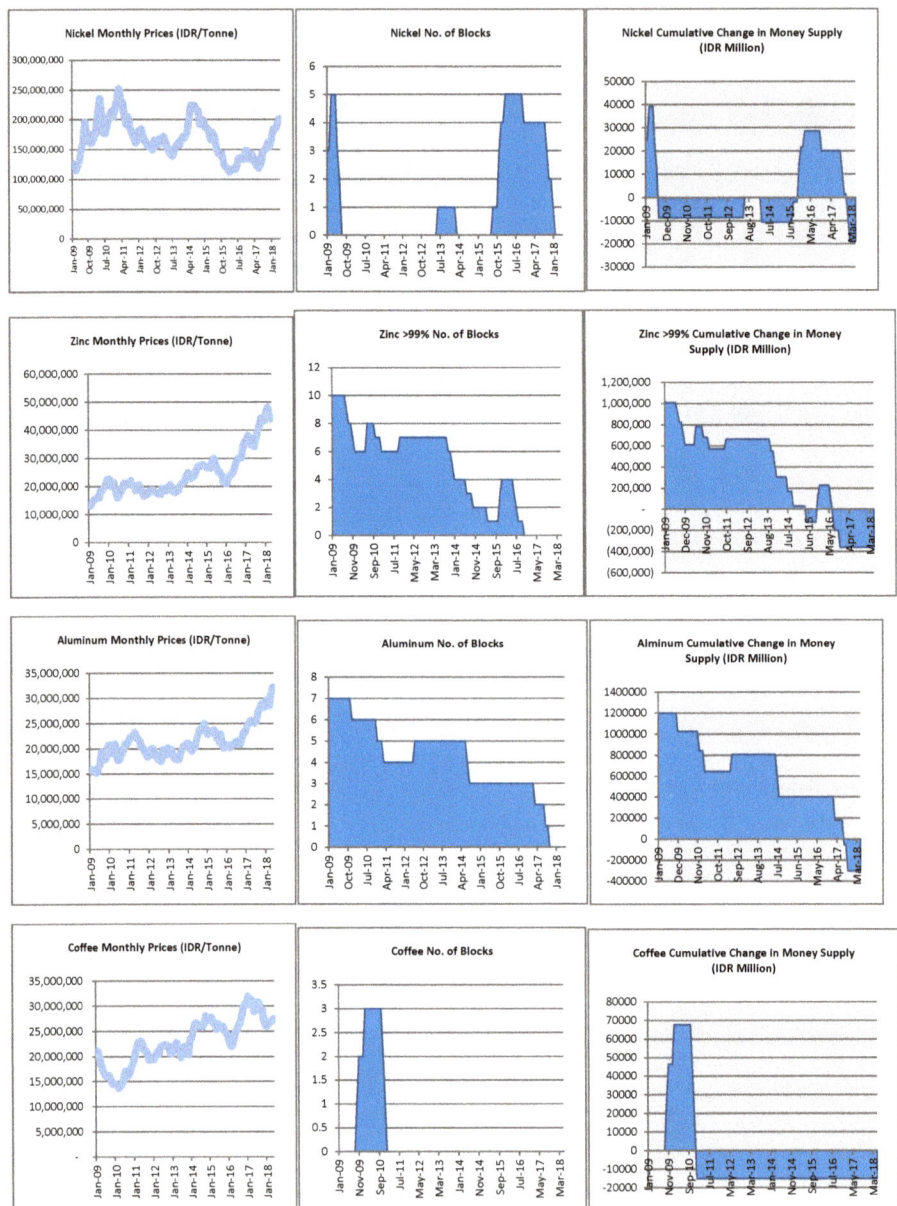

Figure 2. *Cont.*

Figure 2. Financial flows caused by the Indonesian CRD Operations.

5. Discussion of Simulation

This simulation of the operation of an Indonesian CRD has shown the simplicity of simulating the operation of the Grondona system, under real (past) market conditions with high reliability. This is primarily due to its "automatic" (i.e., market price-driven) price-adjustment mechanism. This simplicity enabled this paper to analyze the probable result of its implementation in Indonesia in considerable detail, and with considerable confidence. That is, the results of the simulations clearly show the CRD's ability to stockpile reserves of primary imported commodities as a result of a drop in their market prices, and/or in response to a rise in the exchange-rate that reduces import prices, and to release those reserves during the following period of domestic price rises, whether due to market price rises or a fall in the exchange-rate (see graphs in Figure 1). Such a mechanism would help to stabilise Indonesia's trade quantities and Rupiah prices of primary commodities, and to lessen fluctuations in Indonesia's primary commodity trade over business cycles.

The simplicity of performing such useful simulations also shows how easy it would be to perform repeated runs with different initial values, in order to determine optimal conditions. This is one aspect of how this system is more practical than various proposals for international commodity-backed currency systems which unavoidably leave many important aspects to be decided by unpredictable negotiations, and/or unpredictable discretionary decisions during operation.

The simulation also demonstrated the impact of an Indonesian CRD's operations on the national money supply: the graphs in Figure 2 show the transactions of the Indonesian CRD causing corresponding changes in the domestic money supply. That is, the Indonesian CRD expanded the supply of Rupiah when there was a fall in the prices of primary commodities (and/or a rise in the exchange-rate) and contracted the supply of Rupiah when the prices of imported primary commodities rose (including in response to a fall in the exchange-rate). This pattern of financial flows clearly illustrates the counter-cyclical influence of the Grondona system, which improves the regularity and dependability of stock-holding of primary commodities over their price cycles.

The simulations also show that the uniform rule used to determine the initial conditions for all commodities was not optimal: the prices of some commodities never fell low enough for the CRD to accumulate reserves, thereby limiting the CRD's stabilizing influence. In practice, the different conditions of each commodity would need to be considered in deciding the most appropriate details of the system's gearing for each. These include longer-term trends in each commodity's price, the quantities imported and used annually, relative inflation, and future prospects, including technological changes and other countries' imports.

Uncertainties

It is important also to consider three remaining uncertainties about the above simulations. First, the simulation is a "worst case", in that it was assumed that the CRD had no stabilising influence on world commodity market prices. In practice, the CRD might well have a stabilizing influence on prices of some commodities, particularly after a few years of operation, as discussed in (Collins 1985). The effect of this would be to reduce the quantities of purchases and sales by the CRD to some extent, thereby also reducing the size of changes in the Rupiah money supply. In one sense, this can be thought of as reducing "risk" to the Indonesian economy. However, since the timing of the movements will be strictly counter-cyclical for each commodity, larger movements are generally desirable, acting as an "automatic stabilizer" for the economy. Hence, to the extent that the CRD had a stabilising influence on world market prices, the government might decide to further increase the scale of the CRD.

It is also possible to simulate CRD operations on the assumption that it would have some significant stabilizing influence, although this introduces some uncertainty into the results. Nevertheless, the present "worst" case, which is the simplest and least uncertain to simulate, is useful for planning purposes. NB in practice it may not be "worst", since wide price fluctuations would generally be beneficial for the CRD, exerting a greater counter-cyclical stabilizing influence on the economy, while providing opportunities for greater profits from resale of greater quantities of reserves bought at lower prices. (NB Grondona recommended that the CRD should maintain a uniform margin between its buying and selling prices, rather than acting pro-cyclically in order to maximize its profits.)

A second uncertainty about establishing a CRD is the unavoidable uncertainty of future movements in commodity market prices. Remembering that market prices of many primary commodities show movements of −50% or more during recession and +100% or more during economic boom, the government would need to make arrangements that, in the event of a severe market "crash", it would be able to lease commercial storage space at short notice if reserves increased beyond the scale of normal price fluctuations for which it had prepared its own dedicated storage facilities.

Until implemented, a third uncertainty will remain about markets' likely reaction to the actions of a CRD during a currency crisis, in the form of extreme exchange-rate movements (including to unprecedented levels or at unprecedented speed). This is because, as the CRD's reserves increase, the money supply increases proportionately—which might be expected (on theoretical grounds) to reduce the value of the currency through markets' loss of confidence. However, at the same time, the real value of the currency, in terms of the commodities stored by the CRD, would be increasing proportionately as their prices fell, and reserves of the country's essential imports would be growing, thereby clearly improving the prospects for the economy in the future—as a result of which, by contrast, the currency might be expected to strengthen, thereby leading to even lower commodity prices. In advance of implementation it is not possible to know which of these sentiments will have the stronger influence on markets.

6. Conclusions: Contribution of a CRD to Preventing and Ameliorating Currency Crises

In summary, the most important result of the simulation described in this paper is to demonstrate a "practical" means of implementing a system of currency convertibility based on primary commodities. As discussed above, by making the terms of convertibility conditional, the maximum possible liability is limited to what the government of the implementing country can support independently. Moreover, by making the conditions of convertibility inversely dependent on the quantity of commodity reserves held, according to an openly published table, the system's operation is made "automatic" and so both dependable and predictable, by both government itself and by market participants. By avoiding dependence on discretionary decisions which are essentially unpredictable, the operation of the system is made transparent, dependable, predictable and easy to simulate.

As described above, this concept was developed by Grondona, and is implemented in the above simulation by a "Commodities Reserve Department", or CRD. The simulation shows how the direct effects of a CRD's operations are exerted on commodity trade, by adding some reliably counter-cyclical stock-holding capacity to existing market conditions (any stabilizing effect that is achieved on commodity trade flows and prices being generally beneficial). In addition, the continuous operation of a CRD as a direct damping influence on fluctuations in commodity markets would introduce a counter-cyclical component into the growth of the money supply, and would have an indirect stabilizing influence on a range of other economic parameters, including the balance of payments, inflation, exchange-rate and interest-rates. As a consequence, in relation to currency crises, a CRD would play at least three roles of value to policy-makers.

6.1. Underlying Stabilising Influence

The CRD's continuous, underlying, stabilising influence could be expected to grow over the years following its implementation, as its role became familiar to market participants. Gradual recognition of the CRD's function as a modern equivalent of the gold standard would make a sudden major loss of confidence, as is needed to precipitate a currency crisis, progressively less likely as its successful operation continued.

6.2. Clear Guidance to Monetary Authorities

Movements in the CRD's reserves will provide a clear and undeniable, objective, public measure of changes in the real value of the currency in terms of the commodities handled, trends therein, and the effect of government policies. This will be of great help to governments in resisting pressure to distort monetary policy by expanding or contracting the money supply excessively. It will also be valuable for members of the general public trying to judge government policy. For example, inflationary policies would lead to steady reduction in the CRD's reserves of all commodities. A fortiori, permitting the reserves of all commodities to fall to zero, which would temporarily end the CRD's role of providing a measure of the minimum real value of the currency, would be widely seen as putting the currency and the economy at risk.

6.3. Concrete Step Towards Revival of Real Currency Convertibility

As a CRD's successful operation continued, there are numerous ways in which its stabilizing influence could be strengthened and extended to wider scale, for example by adjusting its "gearing", including other commodities or grades thereof, and in other ways. In addition, by initiating conditional currency convertibility, it will serve as a demonstration to other countries of the feasibility and potential benefits of following suit. Growing experience of the cumulative stabilising influence of several countries' CRDs could in turn lead to wider resumption of real convertibility.

6.3.1. Further Work

For further work, it will be valuable to continue simulations of a CRD in Indonesia and other countries, using a variety of initial conditions different from the uniform rule used to date, so that the CRD accumulates reserves of all commodities. It will also be valuable to simulate the CRD with different values for the sizes of Blocks and other aspects of the "gearing" for different commodities in order to determine initial conditions for each country's CRD that are as nearly optimal as possible.

Simulations of several different countries' CRDs over the same time-scale are also potentially very valuable. This was performed for the first time for four D-8 member-states in (Ahmed 2015). Simulating how the combined monetary impact of several countries' CRDs' transactions, each in its own domestic currency, in response to changes in primary commodity market prices, could exert a cumulative stabilizing effect over the business cycle, and in response to other external shocks is a promising extension of that work. Depending on the extent of overlap in the commodities handled, even without any formal coordination, the different CRDs' operations would tend to expand and contract the supply of the different CRDs' currencies in synchrony, thereby having a mutually stabilizing influence on their exchange-rates. This is a highly desirable outcome, and hence could be an important topic for joint investigation by D-8 countries. In particular, because the influence of each country's CRD acting alone would be relatively small relative to world commodity markets, the simultaneous operation of several different CRDs would have much greater influence. In addition, any effect of synchronising changes in the different countries' money supplies would exert some influence towards creating an informal currency "bloc".

6.3.2. Potential for D-8 Countries' Initiative

Considering the ongoing risk of financial crises around the globe, both "natural" due to the instability in world financial markets, and politically induced by US government policies, this study has potentially important implications for policy makers in the D-8 member-states. As discussed elsewhere, the Grondona system has been recognised as Shariah-compliant, and the above simulation shows that it could contribute to improving D-8 member-states' macro-economic stability. Consequently, implementation of the Grondona system by the leading D-8 member-states could be a preliminary step towards insulating themselves from economic instability, and thereby spreading their monetary and trade stabilising influence on other OIC member-states and beyond. In this case the potential benefits of such an initiative for the implementing countries include the following:

- It would partially stabilise the real value of the participating currencies, albeit within a flexible range of approximately ±10%.
- Its operations would lead to counter-cyclical changes in each currency's money supply, tending to maintain a constant real value of each.
- It would have direct stabilising effects on domestic prices of primary commodities. By this, it not only helps to preserve economic stability but also to reduce the economic dependence of developing OIC countries on developed countries for financial assistance.
- It will help governments to resist external political pressures. As an example, deliberate destabilisation of the exchange-rate would lead to wider movements in domestic commodity prices, which would increase the premiums earned by the CRD over the full cycle, while making stronger stabilising changes in the money supply. Hence, for example, a country targeted for destabilisation, as during the South East Asian currency crisis, would be better able to withstand such political pressure with a CRD in operation than without.

Author Contributions: Conceptualization, P.C.; Methodology and computation, J.A.; Drafting, P.C. & J.A.; Supervision, A.K.M.

Funding: This research received no external funding.

Acknowledgments: We thank Saba Raja for invaluable assistance in performing the simulations for Indonesia.

Conflicts of Interest: The authors declare no conflict of interest.

References

Ahmed, Jameel. 2015. *Application of the Grondona System in Selected OIC Countries: Justification, Simulation, Feasibility and Evaluation from Shariah Perspective.* Selangor: International Islamic University Malaysia, Available online: https://lib.iium.edu.my/mom/services/mom/document/getFile/oneh1gXujxSsPD2dCErExSuLFshT4VDy20160309163205756 (accessed on 26 April 2019).

Ahmed, Jameel, Akamed Kameel Meera, and Patrick Collins. 2014. An Analysis of Yusuf (AS)'s Counter-Cyclical Principle and its Implementation in the Modern World. *Journal Tazkia Islamic Finance and Business Review* 7. [CrossRef]

Ahmed, Jameel, Patrick Collins, and Ahamed Kameel Meera. 2018. Simulation of Shariah Compliant Commodity Backed Currency System: A Turkish Case-Study. *Turkish Journal of Islamic Economics* 5: 95–128. [CrossRef]

Ahmed, Jameel, Patrick Collins, and Ahamed Kameel Meera. 2018. Analysis of Commodity Reserve Currency System from *Siyasah Shariyyah* Perspective. *Journal of Islamic Accounting and Business Research* 9: 222–50. [CrossRef]

Borsodi, Ralph. 1989. *Inflation and the Coming Keynesian Catastrophe: The Story of the Exeter Experiment with Constants*. Cochranville: E. F. Schumacher Society (Great Barrington, Mass.). Cochranville: The School of Living.

Collins, Patrick. 1985. *Currency Convertibility: The Return to Sound Money*. London: Macmillan, New York: St. Martin's Press, Available online: https://link.springer.com/book/10.1007/978-1-349-07058-9 (accessed on 26 April 2019).

Collins, Patrick. 1996a. Conditional Currency Convertibility and its Application to Japan. Paper Presented at the Japanese Monetary Society Autumn Conference, Japan, September.

Collins, Patrick. 1996b. Implications for Japanese Monetary Policy and its Simulation of the Implementation of Conditional Currency Convertibility (the Grondona System). Unpublished.

Fisher, Irving. 1913. Compensated Dollar. *Quarterly Journal of Economics* 27: 213–35. [CrossRef]

Fisher, Irving. 1928. *The Money Illusion*. New York: Adelphi Company.

Graham, Benjamin. 1937. *Storage and Stability*. New York: McGraw-Hill.

Greco, Thomas. 1990. *Money and Debts: A Solution to the Global Crisis*. Tucson: Thomas Greco, Jr.

Grondona, Leo. 1950. Insurance against Slumps: A Way to Price Stability. *The Manchester Guardian*, July 21.

Grondona, Leo. 1958. *Utilising World Abundance*. London: George Allen and Unwin.

Grondona, Leo. 1962. *A Firm Foundation for Economy*. London: Anthony Blond.

Grondona, Leo. 1964. *A Built-in Stabiliser for Commodities*. London: Westminster Bank Review.

Grondona, Leo. 1972. *A Built-in Basic-Economy Stabiliser*. London: Economic Research Council.

Grondona, Leo. 1975. *Economic Stability Is Attainable*. London: Hutchinson-Benham.

Hart, Albert, Nicholas Kaldor, and Jan Tinbergen. 1964. *The Case for an International Commodity Reserve Currency*. Geneva: United Nations Conference on Trade and Development.

Hayek, Friedrich. 1943. A Commodity reserve currency. *Economic Journal* 53: 176–84. [CrossRef]

Jevons, William. 1877. *Money and the Mechanism of Exchange*. New York: Appleton & Co.

Kaldor, Nicholas. 1976. Inflation and Recession in the World Economy. *Economic Journal* 86: 703–14. [CrossRef]

Kaldor, Nicholas. 1983. The Role of Commodity Prices in Economic Recovery. *Lloyds Bank Review*, July.

Keynes, John. 1938. The Policy of Government Storage of Foodstuffs and Raw Materials. *Economic Journal* 48: 449–60. [CrossRef]

Lietaer, Bernard. 2001. *The Future of Money: Creating New Wealth, Work and a Wiser World*. London: Century.

Luke, Jon. 1975. Inflation-Free Pricing Rules for a Generalized Commodity Reserve Currency. *Journal of Political Economy* 83: 786. [CrossRef]

Marshall, Alfred. 1887. Remedies for Fluctuations of General Prices. *Contemporary Review*, March. 1925. *Memorials of Alfred Marshall*. London: Macmillan. Reprinted in Arthur Pigou, ed.

Pettifor, Ann. 2003. *Real World Economic Outlook. The Legacy of Globalization: Debt and Deflation*. London: New Economics Foundation.

Riboud, Jacques. 1981. *The Mechanics of Money*. London: Macmillan.

Stiglitz, Joseph. 2002. *Globalization and Its Discontents*. England: Penguin.

Ussher, Leanne. 2011. *Kaldor's Commodity Reserve Currency*. Available online: www.qc-econ-bba.org/seminarpapers/leanne_figss.pdf (accessed on 30 May 2013).

Ussher, Leanne. 2012. *Combining International Monetary Reform with Commodity Buffer Stocks: Keynes, Graham and Kaldor*. Available online: blog.global-systems-science.eu/wp.../11/ussher_Bancor_19Dec12.pdf (accessed on 30 May 2013).

Wapshott, Nicholas. 2012. *Keynes Hayek: The Clash that Defined Modern Economics*. New York: W.W. Norton & Co.

World Bank. 2013. Gross Domestic Product 2012. Available online: databank.worldbank.org/data/download/GDP.pdf (accessed on 26 April 2019).

© 2019 by the authors. Licensee MDPI, Basel, Switzerland. This article is an open access article distributed under the terms and conditions of the Creative Commons Attribution (CC BY) license (http://creativecommons.org/licenses/by/4.0/).

Article

Monetary Policy, Cash Flow and Corporate Investment: Empirical Evidence from Vietnam

Linh My Tran [1,*], Chi Hong Mai [1], Phuoc Huu Le [2], Chi Linh Vu Bui [3], Linh Viet Phuong Nguyen [4] and Toan Luu Duc Huynh [5]

[1] Faculty of Accounting and Auditing, Banking University of Ho Chi Minh City, Ho Chi Minh City 700000, Vietnam; chimh@buh.edu.vn
[2] English Faculty, Foreign Trade University, Ho Chi Minh City 700000, Vietnam; lehuuphuoc.cs2@ftu.edu.vn
[3] Faculty of Business Administration, Banking University of Ho Chi Minh City, Ho Chi Minh City 700000, Vietnam; linhchinh179@gmail.com
[4] Faculty of Finance, Banking University of Ho Chi Minh City, Ho Chi Minh City 700000, Vietnam; linhngo2998@gmail.com
[5] School of Banking, University of Economics Ho Chi Minh City, Ho Chi Minh City 700000, Vietnam; toanhld@ueh.edu.vn
* Correspondence: linhtm0909@gmail.com

Received: 7 February 2019; Accepted: 13 March 2019; Published: 19 March 2019

Abstract: This paper examines the relationships between macroscopic determinants (typically, monetary policies) and microscopic factors (mainly, cash flows and other controlling variables) on corporate investment. By employing system-GMM estimation for the 250 Vietnamese non-financial firms, the authors find that the expansionary monetary policy not only encourages the borrowing activities but also results in more corporate investment activities over the period from 2006 to 2016. Noticeably, the internal cash flow is also significant factor, which enhances the activities of corporate investment. Finally, there are differences between internal cash flow effects on corporate investments between two groups, divided by three theoretical criteria. To recapitulate, our implications highlight the importance of monetary policy stability for sustainable growth in corporate investment in Vietnam.

Keywords: monetary policy; cash flow; investment; GMM

JEL Classification: E52; M21; D92

1. Introduction

Monetary policy (MP) is one of the most significant macroeconomic policies in the market economy, which directly affects monetary circulation, contributing to promoting activities in the economy, in which investment is the most important. These policies, which are controlled by the State Bank of Vietnam (SBV), are measures to influence money supply, thereby impacting the market interest. Monetary policies are supposed to have substantial impacts on corporate lending (Kashyap et al. 1993) and corporate investment (Morck et al. 2013).

According to money supply statistics from World Bank, the money supply in Vietnam has increased continuously in recent years, which is the result of Central Bank's expansionary money policy. Our question is whether the level of investment in Vietnam is proportional to the level of the money supply of SBV—in other words—whether it increases as SBV applies expansionary monetary policy. In this research, the authors focus on measuring the impacts of monetary policy on corporate investment decisions in Vietnam, comparing the impacts of macroeconomic policies with the impacts of internal factors (amount of holdings, cash flow, business scale, financial leverage, etc.). Especially, one of main reasons to choose Vietnam as country research is that Vietnam is becoming the standing-out element among emerging markets (Bloomberg 2016). Moreover, Batten and Vo (2014, 2015) also emphasized that Vietnamese stock markets have typical characteristics such as (i) the significant participant of foreign ownership (ii) liquidity and (iii) institutional control.

The sensitivity of the corporate investment to the change in monetary policy depends on the financial capacities of the business and its dependence on internal funds. According to Gertler and Gilchrist (1994), tightening monetary policy puts pressure on business investment decisions, now that the importance of money holdings which can timely 'rescue' companies from difficulties in external borrowing is more critical than ever. Moreover, this does not necessarily mean that, with expansionary monetary policy, the investment of the business depends only on external borrowing since the practice is bound to legal conditions. Especially, when the investment is not sufficient, the interest expense to be covered will increase the probability of bankruptcy. For this reason, the authors decided to study the sensitivity of investment to the internal cash flows of enterprises in Vietnam, comparing the differences in the sensitivity of enterprises with low and high financial constraints.

The State Bank of Vietnam is a unit of the state management apparatus. It is entitled to a monopoly in money issuing, performing the task of stabilizing the monetary value, establishing order, ensuring safe, stable, and effective operations with the aim of achieving the macroeconomic objectives of the state. To govern monetary policies, SBV must formulate and use its system of instruments, whose characteristics are to enable SBV to influence the predetermined factors for credit institutions to tailor their activities under the direction of SBV but still ensure their autonomy in business as well as the equality in the competitive environment among banks. There are four objectives of monetary policy: (i) to ensure economic growth, which is the most important and overarching purpose; (ii) to stabilize price and currency; (iii) to create employment and reduce the unemployment rate; (iv) to control the balance of payment. Therefore, the roles of the State Bank of Vietnam is significant in the transmission mechanism to corporates.

This paper will be conducted based on the following structure: Section 2 acknowledges the theoretical framework of monetary policies as well as internal cash flow on corporate investment. Then, Section 3 will briefly summarize the literature and empirical studies, which are relevant to the authors' research. In Section 4, methodology and research data will provide readers with the insights which the authors conducted. Afterwards, the authors discussed research findings and results in Section 5. Finally, the paper ends with conclusions and implications in Section 6.

2. Theoretical Framework

When it comes to the effect of monetary policies, we refer to Friedman (1978) theory about the crowd out theory. This theory means that the unsustainable and unclear in macroscopic policies can adversely trigger consequences such as higher inflation, or an increase of the interest rate in capital markets and vice versa. In brief, this phenomenon will be considered as a 'crowd out effect' of private sector borrowing as the study of Terjesen et al. (2016), Ayturk (2017). In addition, we also refer to Miller (1977) and Myers (1984) about the theoretical framework in two aspects (i) debt and taxes (ii) capital structure in corporates.

Originally initiated by Donaldson (1961), Pecking order theory was later developed by Myers and Majluf (1984), the theory starts with information asymmetry. When making investment decisions, corporations will always choose either the use of private capital or external financing. As a result, asymmetric information influences the choice between these two sources. According to the pecking order theory, private capital will be the priority in the investment decision, in which first comes the reinvested profits, then comes mobilized capitals through borrowings or debt-issuing (bonds). Issuance of new shares (stocks) is regarded as a last resort by this theory.

Before Q theory of (Grunfeld and Griliches 1960) is supposed to be the pioneer in using the market value of enterprises which represents the ability to generate expected returns and investment depends on the corporate's market value. Brainard and Tobin (1968), and Tobin (1969) had an idea to use Q index which stands for investment. The Q index is calculated using either the ratio of market value of capital and replacement cost of capital or the ratio of market value and book value. According to Q theory, when the Q index is higher than one, corporate investment should be encouraged because if this is the case, the returns on investment are higher than the cost of buying corporate's assets. Conversely, corporate's investment should be discouraged if the Q index is lower than one due to the fact that the cost of buying assets is higher than the project's expected returns. According to Keynes (1936), investment can be determined by either aggregate demand or aggregate supply. This theory holds that the investor multiplier explains the relationship between an increase in investment and an increase in quantity, or, in other words, how an increase in investment affects quantity. From this perspective, investment appears to be a component of aggregate demand. From the perspective of aggregate supply, investment increases the quantity, which increases capital volumes, and promotes investment. This means that changes in quantity affect investment. As the demand for materials and labor increases, it is necessary to increase the number of products produced, leading to the need for more capital to invest in fixed assets in order to produce the number of products according to demand.

In brief, our study is mainly based on these essentially theoretical frameworks, which are mentioned carefully in this part. In Section 3, the authors will summarize the existing studies which are relevant to this research.

3. Literature and Empirical Studies

To begin, Tobias and Chiluwe (2012) used a number of classicist studies to explore how monetary policy impacts corporate investment. This research also refers to the enormous studies from Majumder (2007), Mishkin (2009), Kahn (2010), Bernanke and Gertler (1995). By employing macroeconomic data from 1996 to 2005, Tobias and Chiluwe (2012) concluded that the proportion of domestic debts and interest rates of the Ministry of Finance (MOF) was negatively related to the investment of private firms. Meanwhile, the money supply and savings do not show any statistical evidence on corporate investment. These studies provided fundamental concepts that microscopic factors are significant factors for corporate investment. Additionally, the expansion of monetary policies will positively influence corporate investment. To sum up, when money supply increases, interest rates fall. Finally, many companies are likely to attempt to finance their investments using external cashflows. That is the reason why Li and Liu (2017) and Morck et al. (2013) emphasized that the role of monetary policies on corporate financing sources is irreplaceble.

Recently, Yang et al. (2017) figured out that the tightened money supply from 2003 to 2013 made a corporate investment in China decrease. This policy also leads to the increase of cash holdings in Chinese firms. Interestingly, this study explicitly investigates the roles of institutional quality, ownership structure and financial development on the level of cash holding. There are many previous works done in terms of the efficiency of monetary policies such as Brandt and Li (2003), Carlino and DeFina (1998), as well as Devereux and Schiantarelli (1990). To be more precise, although the tightened monetary policy reduces investment, thanks to the use of cash holdings, corporates are still likely to be more active in their investments. Therefore, the role of cash holdings also supports the corporate activities in the context of tightened monetary policies. This motivates the authors to carry out further investigation into cash holdings as one of the controlling variables in this research.

When it comes to the internal cash flows, Fazzari et al. (1988) employed the dividend payout ratio as the identification variable for financial constraints. The study suggests that the dividend payout ratio is the measure of the availability of one of internal financing sources. Firms having the low dividend payouts are financially constrained while the ones with high dividend payouts are less financially constrained. In the research model, Fazzari et al. (1988) pointed out that firms which experience "financial constraints" are heavily dependent on internal cash flow. Therefore, it might lead to a decrease of investment in the future. In contrast, non-financially-constrained firms tend to expand their investments due to indifference between the externally and internally financing cost of capital. Therefore, these corporates are less dependent on cash flows. Once again, this empirical research encourages the authors to raise a question whether internal cash flows impact on investment decisions or corporate investments in Vietnam. Contradictorily, there are some studies which provide the opposite results with the work of Fazzari et al. (1988). For example, Kaplan and Zingales (1997) employed the sample having 49 firms over the period from 1970 to 1984 to test the investment activities in terms of cash-flow sensitivity. These authors combined relevant information and qualitative data to determine the availability of internal and external financial capital of the firms. Based on this, this research ranked the financial constraint level of each company per year. In conclusion, the results indicated that firms having less financially constrained features have higher investment cash flows than those in the counterparty group. Moreover, Kadapakkam et al. (1998) contributed an empirical result to the existing literature that internal cash flows and liquidity will forecast the future investment. These findings also pointed out that the sensitivity of investment activities is high in large firm group rather than the small ones. The following theoretical research from Almeida et al. (2004) also confirms these findings. Meanwhile, Richardson (2006) criticized that the dependence on internal cash flows might cause over-investment. Therefore, the authors inherited the previous studies to examine the role of internal cash flows in corporate investments in Vietnam. The authors acknowledge the various theoretical and empirical studies, which were conducted before such as Lamont (1997), Chen et al. (2016), Ahiadorme et al. (2018), etc. Furthermore, Devereux and Schiantarelli (1990) introduced how to classify the group of firms for testing the internal cash flow effects on firm investments. This study applied the method of market value of equity shares. Thus, the findings suggest that cash flows plays an important role in large companies than in small companies. Explaining this result, these authors asserted that large companies tend to have a relatively low cash balance and that these companies often have a large capital structure that increases representation costs. In addition, Athey and Laumas (1994) divided the sample of Indian firms by the book value of equity. These authors examined the importance of accelerated investment, internal funds, and depreciation for investment by manufacturing companies. The results indicate that internal funds and depreciation are significant in the accelerated investment model, but the relationship between internal and investment funds is not uniform among firms. In particular, internal funds and investment have a closer relationship in large companies and high-end manufacturing companies. Lastly, Vogt (1994) classified the US firms on the 'price-to-book ratio'. This classification shows that the companies having higher ratio experience the higher level of sensitivity, and vice versa. These empirical studies prove that internal financing sources have strong impacts on investment activities, regardless of firm size. Therefore, the authors would prefer to find out if the situation is different when it comes to Vietnam by measuring the levels of impact from the firm size perspective.

In brief, previous studies have explained the relationship between internal cash flow and firm investment through evidence of the existence of financial constraints. These studies explored inconclusive insights on the sensitivity of investment cash flows between low and high financially constrained groups. Noticeably, most studies also confirmed that there is an impact of internal cash flows on corporate investments with different signs and levels. Therefore, testing this phenomenon on Vietnamese equity market, which is considered as one of emerging markets in the world, is necessary to contribute to the existing studies. Our paper attempts to answer three main research questions: (i) Does the monetary policy influence on corporate investment in Vietnam? (ii) Is internal cash flow a factor which impacts on corporate investment in Vietnam? and (iii) Are there any differences between small and large groups in three main criteria regarding the influence of internal cash flows on corporate investments? These research questions will be answered in the Sections 5.1–5.3, respectively.

Hence, this paper will contribute to the existing literature in three main ways as follows. Firstly, this paper will provide the insights about the macroscopic determinant such as monetary policies on corporate investments. The purpose of this research is similar to the studies of Chang et al. (2018), Chen et al. (2018) and Zhao et al. (2018), which are up-to-date. Secondly, our paper offers the further novel and additional evidence on the relationship between microscopic factors such as internal cash flows and corporate investments. Thirdly, to complement to current studies, the authors classify the effects of internal cash flows according to three different sub-samples, namely (i) price-to-book ratio,

(ii) net revenue, and (iii) total assets. Proposed by Devereux and Schiantarelli (1990), Vogt (1994), Allen et al. (2005), as well as Athey and Laumas (1994), respectively.

4. Data and Methodology

This research uses a sample of 250 Vietnamese firms with ten years from 2006 to 2016. The authors eliminate the firms, which have insufficient data as well as been delisted during their operation. Therefore, our sample can generalize the Vietnamese stock market. The chosen firms are all listed in the stock market, except financial firms, primary companies (banks and insurance companies), which had many values missing in the years to chosen to observe, individual firms, and particular transfer companies. The sample firms' financial information is collected from their financial reports, a reliable source.

Basically, Bond and Meghir (1994), Dickinson and Jia (2007) and Yang et al. (2017) introduced their research models, which explain the impact of supply of money on the corporate investment. Their models are rewritten as follows:

$$Invest_{i,t} = \beta_0 + \beta_1 MP_{i,t} + \beta_2 CF_{i,t} + \beta_{3n} \sum_{1}^{t} \vec{Z}_{n,i,t-1} + \varepsilon_{i,t}$$

In which, i refers to sample firms and t for a year, and $\varepsilon_{i,t}$ is the error term; β stands for coefficients; $Invest_{i,t}$ is investment of ith firm in year t; $MP_{i,t}$ is referred to as money supply in year t; $CF_{i,t}$ is referred to as ith firm's cash flow in year t. The authors denote the vector of Z as a group of controlling variables such as S (firm size), Q (price-to-book ratio), LEV (financial leverage), ROA (return on asset), T (tangible asset over total asset), Growth (growth rate of revenue from business activities), NR (net revenue), and Cash (net cash holding).

Kadapakkam et al. (1998) also represented the research model hereinafter.

$$\frac{Invest_{i,t}}{Net\ fixed\ asset_{i,t-1}} = \frac{\beta_1 CF_{i,t}}{Net\ fixed\ asset_{i,t-1}} + \frac{\beta_2 Cash_{i,t-1}}{Net\ fixed\ asset_{i,t-1}} + \beta_3 Q_{i,t-1} + \frac{\beta_4 NetRevenue_{i,t-1}}{Net\ fixed\ asset_{i,t-1}} + \varepsilon_{i,t}$$

In which, $\frac{Invest_{i,t}}{Net\ fixed\ asset_{i,t-1}}$ stands for corporate investment, which is the ratio of investment in fixed asset in the year to the company's net fixed asset value, referred to as 'investment variable'. $\frac{CF_{i,t}}{Net\ fixed\ asset_{i,t-1}}$ means the ability of the company to generate cash flow in a year, which is the ratio of cash flow in a year to the net fixed asset value at the beginning of that year, referred as 'cash flow variable'.

$\frac{Cash_{i,t-1}}{Net\ fixed\ asset_{i,t-1}}$ is the ratio of cash and cash equivalents at the beginning of the year to net fixed asset at the beginning of the year, referred to as 'cash holding variable'.

$Q_{i,t-1}$ is the value of q variable of Tobin at the beginning of the year, which is referred to as Q variable.

$\frac{NetRevenue_{i,t-1}}{Net\ fixed\ asset_{i,t-1}}$ is the ratio of net revenue of the previous year to the net fixed asset at the beginning of the year, which is referred to as revenue variable.

Finally, $\varepsilon_{i,t}$ is standard error.

The Table 1 demonstrates our variables, expected sign, explanation, calculation as well as literature review for using them.

This research used three indicators (i) price-to-book ratio, (ii) net revenue, and (iii) total assets to classify companies into two group: (a) large and (b) small by median of the total sample. Finally, the authors also construct to test our three main hypotheses as follows:

Hypothesis 1: *The investments of Vietnamese firms increase when the State Bank of Vietnam promulgates the expansionary monetary policy.*

Hypothesis 2: *Internal cash flow affects the investment of Vietnamese firms.*

Hypothesis 3: *The impacts of internal cash flows on investment vary according to business scale.*

Table 1. Variables summary.

Variables	Expected Sign	Explanation	Calculation	Literature Review
Invest (Investment)	Dependent variable	The additional investment of facilities in the company's fiscal year	Invest = Net end-of-year fixed assets (−) Net worth of fixed assets at the beginning of the year.	Duchin et al. (2010) and Kadapakkam et al. (1998)
MP (Monetary Policy)	(+)	The amount of central bank supply money under the expansionary monetary policy	The value of M2 supply money	Li and Liu (2017)
LEV (Leverage)	(+)	Corporate financial leverage	Total liabilities/total assets	Kaplan and Zingales (1997), De Jong et al. (2008)
SIZE (Size)	(−)	The scale of the business since listing on the stock market	The natural logarithm of total assets	Kaplan and Zingales (1997)
ROA (Return-on-Asset)	(+/−)	Return on asset	Net profits/total assets	Yang et al. (2017)
Q (Tobin-Q)	(+)	Q represents the growth opportunities of company.	Tobin Q = market value/book value	Yang et al. (2017) and Kadapakkam et al. (1998)
T (Tangible Asset over Total Asset)	(+/−)	Asset structure	Fixed assets/total assets	Yang et al. (2017)
Growth	(+/−)	Growth rate of operating income	Sale Ggrowth in year N/ sale growth in year (N − 1)	Yang et al. (2017)
CF (Cash Flow)	(+)	Internal cash flow of company	CF is earning after tax (+) fixed asset depreciation in the year (+) corporate income tax (−) dividend payment.	Kadapakkam et al. (1998)
Cash	(+)	Cash holding	Cash, deposits at banks, and cash equivalents.	Kadapakkam et al. (1998)
NR (Net Revenue)	(+)	Revenue from the sale of goods and provision of services minus (−) sales	Revenue from sales and service provision—revenue deductions	Kadapakkam et al. (1998)

In order to test these hypotheses, the authors briefly introduced the following regression models:

The first model is to test the presence of monetary policy on firm investment (Hypothesis 1). This model is theoretically referred to Bond and Meghir (1994).

$$\text{Invest}_{i,t} = \hat{\beta}_0 + \hat{\beta}_1 \text{MP}_{i,t} + \hat{\beta}_2 \text{LEV}_{i,t} + \hat{\beta}_3 S + \hat{\beta}_4 \text{ROA} + \hat{\beta}_5 Q + \hat{\beta}_6 T + \hat{\beta}_7 \text{Growth} + \varepsilon_{i,t} \quad \text{(Model 1)}$$

The second model is to test whether the internal cash flows influence the firm investment (Hypothesis 2). This model is theoretically referred to Kadapakkam et al. (1998).

$$\text{Invest}_{i,t} = \hat{\beta}_0 + \hat{\beta}_1 \text{CF}_{i,t} + \hat{\beta}_2 \text{Cash}_{i,t} + \hat{\beta}_3 Q + \hat{\beta}_4 \text{NR} + \varepsilon_{i,t} \quad \text{(Model 2)}$$

The third model is to test the differences in the impacts of internal cash flows on firm investment between two groups with three criteria (Hypothesis 3). The authors also employed model 2 but divided our sample into three sub-samples based on (i) price-to-book ratio, (ii) net revenue, and (iii) total assets. Afterward, the authors perform the individual regression for each group.

The authors employed the rich set of quantitative techniques namely pooled-ordinary least squares (pooled-OLS), fixed effect model, random effect model, and system-generalized method of moments (system-GMM) for this estimations. In order to enhance this paper methodological approach, the authors will briefly introduce the system-GMM procedure from Arellano and Bover (1995), and

Blundell and Bond (1998, 2000). The econometric method of system-GMM introduces the pedagogic approach to linear regression for 'small-T and large-N' (our samples have 10 years and 250 firms). Therefore, this methodology also confirms the use of instrumental variables to correct the endogeneity, which causes the biased and inconsistent results. Especially, system-GMM requires two-step robust estimation, which generates covariance matrix derived by Windmeijer (2005). Therefore, according to Maddala and Lahiri (1992) the results of system-GMM are robust for interpretation.

5. Findings and Results

This research is carried out by adopting the two main models:

Model 1: A study on the impacts of expansionary monetary policy on corporate investments.
Model 2: A study on the impacts of internal cash flows on corporate investments.

Firstly, the authors attempt to employ the statistical description for interpreting the data characteristics before performing regression.

As presented in Table 2, it is seen that the variables have the skewed and fat-tail distribution. This phenomenon might lead to the homogeneous characteristics, which probably causes endogeneity in these econometric models. Therefore, the authors bear in mind to adopt quantitative techniques, particularly system-GMM for correcting the bias and ensuring consistency.

Table 2. Statistical description of variables used for validation in the study.

Variables	Mean	Standard Deviation	Percentile q10	Percentile q90	Skewness	Kurtosis
Invest	73.275574	2828.286	0.0092945	0.406804	43.69604	2011.846
MP	112.1366	19.59663	93.65717	137.6491	0.4071207	2.540372
S	26.53337	5.002883	25.7329	29.111	−4.737473	25.37874
Q	547.7386	20115.94	0.3380425	1.849735	37.41705	1410.435
LEV	0.4728379	0.2499534	0.112023	0.784358	−0.1535366	2.201218
ROA	0.0665066	0.1375101	−0.5436	0.1609	13.53076	336.1934
T	0.2551115	0.5036074	0.0116105	0.562433	35.59383	1611.327
Growth	0.7006606	26.70394	−0.383467	0.987084	15.66164	1344.683
NR	180	0.496	105	342	8.22054	89.17907
Cash	406	0.952	254	372	51.50165	2682.775
CF	−162	0.947	−814	180	48.79517	2504.257

(Note that NR, Cash, and CF are million Vietnam dong).

5.1. First Hypothesis

Table 3 presents the results of the regression model of the impacts of expansionary monetary policy on corporate investment (Model 1) by dependent variable (Invest) through four methodological approaches: pooled-OLS, FEM, REM, and GMM. The independent variables used to explain Invest (the investment variable) are MP (monetary policy), LEV (financial leverage), S (firm size), ROA (return on asset), Q (price-to-book ratio), T (tangible asset over total asset), Growth (growth rate of revenue from business activities), where MP is the primary explanatory variable and the most crucial one for this study.

Firstly, based on the pooled-OLS model, only the Q (price-to-book ratio) influences corporate investment at 1% significance level whereas there is no evidence about the relationship between monetary policies (the first hypothesis) on corporate investments. The remaining variables are insignificant. The authors suspect that there are endogeneous errors in this model. By employing the further quantitative techniques, namely fixed effect model and random effect model, the authors investigate that the results are not better. Once again, only Q (price-to-book ratio) is significant at 1% significance level while all explanatory variables fail to explain corporate investments. Hence, the authors implement the system-GMM for estimating Model 1 equation and afterwards, the results are documented in the last column in Table 2 above.

Table 3. Results of the regression model of the impact of monetary expansion policy on corporate investment (Model 1).

Invest	$Invest_{i,t}=\hat{\beta}_0+\hat{\beta}_1 MP_{i,t}+\hat{\beta}_2 LEV_{i,t}+\hat{\beta}_3 S+\hat{\beta}_4 ROA+\hat{\beta}_5 ROA+\hat{\beta}_6 Q+\hat{\beta}_7 T+\hat{\beta}_8 Growth+\hat{\varepsilon}_{i,t}$			
	Pooled OLS	FEM (Fixed Effects Model)	REM (Random Effects Model)	System GMM (Generalized Method of Moments)
MP	−0.5711737	−0.6836043	−0.5711737	0.8546331 *
	[−0.67]	[0.451]	[0.504]	[0.058]
Lev	−34.25557	−110.0149	−34.25557	49.69802 *
	[0.625]	[0.348]	[0.625]	[0.087]
S	1.699131	3.657795	1.699131	−13.69331 **
	[0.645]	[0.419]	[0.645]	[0.018]
ROA	−0.7834284	6.300236	−0.7834284	51.8322
	[0.995]	[0.964]	[0.995]	[0.385]
Q	0.1345481 ***	0.1353923 ***	0.1345481 ***	0.1687338 ***
	[0.000]	[0.000]	[0.000]	[0.000]
T	−1.27182	−2.928004	−1.27182	−17.29324
	[0.968]	[0.936]	[0.968]	[0.352]
Growth	−0.0058518	−0.2729514	−0.0058518	−0.3502424
	[0.992]	[0.675]	[0.992]	[0.198]
Cons	0.748	0.791	0.748	0.044
AR(1)				0.000
AR(2)				0.231
Sargan test				0.376

The symbols *, **, and *** denote the significance at the 10, 5, and 1% levels, respectively whereas t-statistics of the corresponding coefficients are reflected in square brackets. The Sargan test is a Sargan–Hansen test of over-identifying restrictions. AR(1) and AR(2) are tests for first and second-order serial correlation in the first-differenced residuals.

Secondly, the findings are similar to the previous studies of Tobias and Chiluwe (2012), Majumder (2007), Mishkin (2009), Kahn (2010), and Bernanke and Gertler (1995) in many different countries. The monetary policies have positive influences corporate investments. However, this is weak evidence because its coefficient is significant at 10% significance level. In other words, when SBV promulgates expansionary monetary policy, corporate investment will increase. Thus, the result fails to reject the first hypothesis.

When it comes to the other variables, Lev (financial leverage) also shows a weak evidence of its impacts on corporate investments. When Vietnamese companies choose to increase their financial leverage, they tend to obtain new investment at 10% significance level. To be more specific, the stronger the financial leverage, the higher the investment. Interestingly, the S (firm size) has a negative coefficient, which means that the larger firms might have fewer investments. In addition, the Q (price-to-book ratio) significantly affects the firm investments. This means that the market value has a strong impact on corporate investment. As companies have greater market value, they will increasingly promote their investments. The other variables, namely ROA (return on asset), T (tangible asset over total asset), Growth (growth rate of revenue from business activities) have no statistical evidence to come into conclusion.

Finally, the authors also need to confirm that the findings and results are unbiased and robust. The further tests of AR(1), AR(2), as well as Sargan test are appropriate. To be more specific, the authors fail to reject the null of hypothesis that instrumental variables have no correlation with the residuals. Moreover, the errors in the first-differenced regression do not demonstrate the second-order serial correlation. To sum up, the results and findings are worth to interpret. These results are appropriately used to answer the first research question that monetary policy influences corporate investment.

However, to be sure whether the multicollinearity errors among the variables exists, the authors perform the Variance Inflation Factor (VIF) test for the model, see Table 4.

The result of the VIF test shows that all the VIF coefficients are less than 10. This explains that the multi-collinear phenomenon did not occur in the research set (Kennedy 1992).

Table 4. Multicollinearity verification in model 2.

Variable	VIF	1/VIF
Net	1.01	0.986199
CF	1.01	0.988369
Cash	1.00	0.997063
Q	1.00	0.999537

5.2. Second Hypothesis

When it comes to Model 2, the results of regression on the impacts of cash flow on investment with the dependent variable investment (Invest) through four models: pooled-OLS, FEM, REM, and system-GMM. The independent variables that are used to explain the investing variable are CF (cash flow), Cash (cash holding), Q (price-to-book ratio), and NR (net revenue). There is no evidence of model errors such as multicollinearity, autocorrelation as well as heteroscedasticity. Therefore, the model with pooled-OLS, FEM, REM, and GMM are statistically employed to test the second hypothesis. Firstly, based on the pooled-OLS model, the Q (price-to-book ratio) is only determinant of corporate investments at 1% significance level. However, the remaining variables show no statistical evidence at any significance level. The findings are the same for fixed effect model and random effect model. To be more specific, once again, only Q (price-to-book ratio) is significant at 1% significance level while all explanatory variables fail to explain the corporate investments at the two econometrical approaches. Hence, using system-GMM to correct the endogenous errors (Model 2). Finally, the coefficients and t-statistics are noted in the Table 5 below.

Table 5. Regression results on the impact of internal cash flow on investment (Model 2).

Invest	$Invest_{i,t} = \hat{\beta}_0 + \hat{\beta}_1 CF_{i,t} + \hat{\beta}_2 Cash_{i,t} + \hat{\beta}_3 Q + \hat{\beta}_4 NR + \hat{\varepsilon}_{i,t}$			
	Pooled OLS	FEM	REM	System GMM
CF	5.47 (a)	6.28 (a)	5.47 (a)	939 (a) ***
	[0.7495]	[0.743]	[0.749]	[0.006]
Cash	−0.03.14 (a)	0.747 (a)	−0.0314 (a)	99.5 (a)
	[0.999]	[0.969]	[0.999]	[0.668]
Q	0.1345012 ***	0.1353395 ***	0.1345012 ***	0.1354203 ***
	[0.000]	[0.000]	[0.000]	[0.000]
NR	5.33 (a)	8.60 (a)	5.33 (a)	0.0517 (a) **
	[0.874]	[0.856]	[0.874]	[0.023]
Cons	0.748	0.903	0.942	0.072
AR(1)				0.000
AR(2)				0.998
Sargan test				0.865

The symbols *, **, and *** denote the significance at the 10, 5, and 1% levels, respectively whereas t-statistics of the corresponding coefficients are reflected in square brackets. The Sargan test is a Sargan–Hansen test of over-identifying restrictions. AR(1) and AR(2) are tests for first and second-order serial correlation in the first-differenced residuals. Note that (a) means that the multiple of 10^{-13}.

As regards the system-GMM, internal cash flow has positively influenced corporate investments. Especially, this demonstrates a strong evidence because its coefficient is significant at 1% significance level. The greater the internal cash flow, the larger the corporate investment values. Hence, the result, once again, fails to reject the second hypothesis. In the context of other variables, the results share same patterns with the previous study of Kadapakkam et al. (1998). To be more specific, the Q (price-to-book ratio) influences corporate investment at 1% significance level. Furthermore, the NR (net revenue) significantly affects the corporate investments at 5% significance level. Unexpectedly, cash is insignificant in this regression estimations. This shows that corporate investment is not sensitive to internal cash flow in Vietnam. Meanwhile, the firms having greater net revenue are likely to invest more. The first-order and second-order correlation in the estimations showed that the results are robust. Furthermore, the Sargan–Hansen test also indicates that the instrumental variables are not correlated with the residuals. Once again, the results are unbiased and consistent. Therefore, the second research question is answered, which means that the internal cash flow also affect the corporate investment in Vietnam.

5.3. Third Hypothesis

By dividing the samples into two groups (i) small and (ii) large based on three criteria: (i) price-to-book ratio, (ii) net revenue, and (iii) total assets, the authors examine the scale effect of internal cash flow on corporate investment. The Table 5 demonstrates the results of pooled-OLS regression of model 2 by two sub-samples dividing by price-to-book ratio. The main reason for choosing pooled-OLS is to reexamine the sub-sample effects between the two groups. The previous results and findings are robust because of system-GMM techniques; therefore, the authors only employ the simple rule in statistics (known as parsimony) for testing the third hypothesis.

As can be seen from Table 6, the Q (price-to-book ratio) in the large group is significant at 1% significance level for the three criteria. In addition, there is a weak evidence that internal cash flow influences corporate investments in the large group at the sub-sample of Q (price-to-book ratio). Therefore, the authors fail to reject the third hypothesis. This proves that there are differences in the impacts of internal cash flow on corporate investment. Internal cash flows in large-scale firms have a weak impact on corporate investment, suggesting that financial constraint issues and asymmetric information do not affect the investment decisions of small-scale firms. Large-scale firms are more cautious in investing, not only in external capital but also in internal cash flow and the amount of money they hold to decide whether to increase the investment or not. The findings and results are similar to the study of Kaplan and Zingales (1997). Thus, there are differences between two sub-samples concerning the impacts of internal cash flow on corporate investment, which is the third research answer.

Table 6. Summary regression results by sub-samples based on three criteria by pooled-OLS.

Variable	Price-to-Book Ratio	
	Small	Large
CF	0.000322 [a]	371 [a]
	[0.02]	[1.87]
Cash	−0.00398 [a]	487 [a]
	[−0.22]	[1.27]
Q	−0.0865233	0.1348381 ***
	[−1.21]	[119.71]
NR	−0.0587 [a]	226 [a]
	[−0.75]	[0.35]
Cons	0.3279273	−2.675934
	[5.11]	[−0.08]

Variable	Net revenue	
	Small	Large
CF	0.04 [a]	5.44 [a]
	[0.11]	[0.22]
Cash	−4690 [a]	−9.07 [a]
	[−0.20]	[−0.03]
Q	−0.0169778	0.1345023 ***
	[−0.58]	[118.90]
NR	−10.4 [a]	7.59 [a]
	[−0.90]	[0.12]
Cons	0.3017064	−2.256631
	[6.64]	[−0.06]

Table 6. *Cont.*

Variable	Price-to-Book Ratio	
	Small	Large
Variable	Total asset	
	Small	Large
CF	−2460 [a] [−0.10]	292 [a] [1.63]
Cash	−5310 [a] [−0.21]	3.57 [a] [1.00]
Q	0.0195474 [0.62]	0.1347637 *** [118.10]
NR	−0.0546 [a] [−0.52]	26.9 [a] [0.41]
Cons	0.3123523 [6.37]	−1.486654 [−0.04]

The symbols *, **, and *** denote the significance at the 10, 5, and 1% levels, respectively whereas *t*-statistics of the corresponding coefficients are reflected in square brackets. Note that [a] means that the multiple of 10^{-13}.

6. Conclusions and Implications

6.1. Conclusions

By employing the rich set of quantitative techniques, the authors confirm that when the State Bank of Vietnam promulgates expansionary monetary policies, corporate investments increase. This explains why corporate investment is heavily dependent on external sources of capital. With the expansionary monetary policy, which means lower interest rates, businesses will tend to borrow and invest more and more. Obviously, borrowing for investment when commercial banks apply an expansionary monetary policy is ideal because interest expense is no longer too heavy. It also creates opportunity cost for shareholders to invest in many other fields instead of retaining profits to continue investing in fixed assets. On top of that, interest rates is a great tax shield for businesses. However, it is very interesting to witness that the monetary policy effect is quite weak. Therefore, apart from macroeconomic elements, corporate investment is also affected by the internal elements. To prove that, the authors have implemented further research on the impacts of internal cash flow on corporate investment. At the same time, cash holdings, market value, and net revenue are also considered in this study to explain corporate investments.

As the expectation of the theoretical research of Kaplan and Zingales (1997), internal capital flows have a significant impact on corporate investment. It can be interpreted that the more effective the business is, the more investment in fixed assets it can attract to expand the scale of business. Investigating an impact of internal cash flow on investment helps practitioners recognize that market value plays an important role in corporate investment decisions. In addition, the classification of the scale of business has shown that large-scale groups are more sensitive to internal cash flows than small-scale ones. Moreover, research results from both groups of companies show that cash holdings does not affect the investment decisions of enterprises. However, with different scale groups, research results found that cash holdings play an extremely important role in large-scale enterprise groups. Thereby, it shows that large enterprises are very careful in making investment decisions and allocating capital.

6.2. Implications

By the two main research models, the authors also conclude that both macroeconomic and internal factors always influence corporate investment. In particular, the macroeconomic factors are the most important and decisive factors. Monetary policy plays a vital role in the economy. The study demonstrates that expansionary monetary policy makes investment increases. However, it is not always true in the case that monetary policy is ideal as the more the inflation increases, the more the real value of the currency decreases. Also, the dependence on external financing of businesses is growing, and interest rates increase the risk of bankruptcy and lousy debts more and more. The study does not aim to promote expansionary monetary policy but to measure the degree and direction of impacts on investment. Based on that, SBV can consider in combination with the socio-economic situations to best-tailor the monetary policy.

Dependence on external financing of small business is understandable. However, small-business groups need to focus on the role of cash holdings in an investment in order to minimize the risks of interest and react timely to the economy as soon as the market fluctuates. The evolution of the economy is like a parabolic graph: growth and recession will take place from time to time, and this is indispensable. Therefore, the preparation to respond to the fluctuations is very important to help businesses survive and develop.

As regards the macroscopic aspects, the study must carry out in-depth research on each group of companies in order to have the most general overview of the problem. Especially, with an emerging economy like Vietnam, in which most of the businesses are small and medium, the research groups are the businesses that are listed on the stock exchange and all of which are well positioned in the Vietnamese economy. Therefore, the study cannot cover all enterprises with financial constraints, especially those in rural areas and underprivileged economic areas.

From the limitations of the research, the authors propose separate research on how monetary policy affects investment. The sample should be expanded to more enterprises and consider the impacts on each group of enterprises: large-scale, medium scale enterprises, small-scale enterprises, and enterprises with financial constraints (small enterprises, rural enterprises, etc.). Because this is a macro issue, further research should be more intensive and in-depth.

As regards the recommendations for monetary authority, the authors suggest that State Bank of Vietnam should remain the sustainable monetary policy. Any change in monetary policy should be carefully considered in the economic and political aspects. Furthermore, holding the expansionary monetary policies will encourage corporate investments; however, it also has to pay the prices for 'inflation'. This research suggests the further quantitative techniques to estimate the threshold of the M2 money supply to be optimal for Vietnamese economy.

The authors suggest researching the importance of cash holdings in businesses. Because the authors focus on the impacts of internal cash flow on investment, so cash is only a second variable and fail to be able to go into the problem. Investigating the role of cash holdings in investment is extremely necessary. However, in Vietnam, such studies do not receive as much proper attention as in European countries as well as in the US. In China, there has recently been many topics related to the topic of cash holdings in the business. The authors strongly believe that more studies as well as discussions will be held on this topic in Vietnam in the future.

Author Contributions: These authors contributed equally to this work.

Funding: This research was funded by University of Economics Ho Chi Minh City (Vietnam), Banking University of Ho Chi Minh City (Vietnam) and Foreign Trade University (Vietnam).

Acknowledgments: We are grateful for the anonymous referees for their remarks. Any remaining errors are our own responsibilities. The first author would also like to thank Bui Cong Duy (Banking University of Ho Chi Minh City) and Nguyen Thi Thu Hien (Institute of Banking Research and Technology, Banking University of Ho Chi Minh City) for their continuous guidance and encouragement. This paper was presented in the National Olympic Contest of Econometrics and Applications held by Academy of Finance (Vietnam) in 2018. The work is the outcome of the research group by Student Research Group (Banking University of Ho Chi Minh City) and Vietnamese Students' Association at Banking University of Ho Chi Minh City (Vietnam).

Conflicts of Interest: These authors confirm that there are no conflict of interest.

References

Ahiadorme, Johnson Worlanyo, Agyapomaa Gyeke-Dako, and Joshua Yindenaba Abor. 2018. Debt holdings and investment cash flow sensitivity of listed firms. *International Journal of Emerging Markets* 13: 943–58. [CrossRef]

Allen, Franklin, Jun Qian, and Meijun Qian. 2005. Law, finance and economic growth in China. *Journal of Financial Economics* 77: 57–116. [CrossRef]

Almeida, Heitor, Murillo Campello, and Michael S. Weisbach. 2004. The cash flow sensitivity of cash. *The Journal of Finance* 59: 1777–804. [CrossRef]

Arellano, Manuel, and Olympia Bover. 1995. Another look at the instrumental variable estimation of error-components models. *Journal of Econometrics* 68: 29–51. [CrossRef]

Athey, Michael J., and Prem S. Laumas. 1994. Internal funds and corporate investment in India. *Journal of Development Economics* 45: 287–303. [CrossRef]

Ayturk, Yusuf. 2017. The effects of government borrowing on corporate financing: Evidence from Europe. *Finance Research Letters* 20: 96–103. [CrossRef]

Batten, Jonathan A., and Xuan Vinh Vo. 2014. Liquidity and Return Relationships in an Emerging Market. *Emerging Markets Finance and Trade* 50: 5–21. [CrossRef]

Batten, Jonathan A., and Xuan Vinh Vo. 2015. Foreign ownership in emerging stock markets. *Journal of Multinational Financial Management* 32–33: 15–24. [CrossRef]

Bernanke, Ben S., and Mark Gertler. 1995. Inside the black box: the credit channel of monetary policy transmission. *Journal of Economic perspectives* 9: 27–48. [CrossRef]

Bloomberg. 2016. Vietnam's Economy Is an Emerging Market Standout. Available online: https://www.bloomberg.com/news/articles/2016-01-18/vietnam-growth-makes-it-emerging-market-standout-in-shaky-world (accessed on 7 February 2017).

Blundell, Richard, and Stephen Bond. 1998. Initial conditions and moment restrictions in dynamic panel data models. *Journal of Econometrics* 87: 115–43. [CrossRef]

Blundell, Richard, and Stephen Bond. 2000. GMM estimation with persistent panel data: An application to production functions. *Econometric Reviews* 19: 321–40. [CrossRef]

Bond, Stephen, and Costas Meghir. 1994. Dynamic investment models and the firm's financial policy. *The Review of Economic Studies* 61: 197–222. [CrossRef]

Brainard, William C., and James Tobin. 1968. Pitfalls in financial model building. *The American Economic Review* 58: 99–122.

Brandt, Loren, and Hongbin Li. 2003. Bank discrimination in transition economies: Ideology, information, or incentives? *Journal of Comparative Economics* 31: 387–413. [CrossRef]

Carlino, Gerald, and Robert DeFina. 1998. The differential regional effects of monetary policy. *Review of Economics and Statistics* 80: 572–87. [CrossRef]

Chang, Chun, Zheng Liu, Mark M. Spiegel, and Jingyi Zhang. 2018. Reserve requirements and optimal chinese stabilization policy. *Journal of Monetary Economics*. [CrossRef]

Chen, Xin, Yong Sun, and Xiaodong Xu. 2016. Free cash flow, over-investment and corporate governance in China. *Pacific-Basin Finance Journal* 37: 81–103. [CrossRef]

Chen, Kaiji, Jue Ren, and Tao Zha. 2018. The nexus of monetary policy and shadow banking in China. *American Economic Review* 108: 3891–936. [CrossRef]

De Jong, Abe, Rezaul Kabir, and Thuy Thu Nguyen. 2008. Capital structure around the world: The roles of firm-and country-specific determinants. *Journal of Banking & Finance* 32: 1954–69.

Devereux, Michael, and Fabio Schiantarelli. 1990. *Investment, Finacial Factors and Cash Flow: Evidence from UK Panel Data (No. w3116)*. Cambridge: National Bureau of Economic Research.

Dickinson, David, and Liu Jia. 2007. The real effects of monetary policy in China: An empirical analysis. *China Economic Review* 18: 87–111. [CrossRef]

Donaldson, Gordon. 1961. *Corporate Debt Capacity*. Cambridge: Harvard University Press.

Duchin, Ran, Oguzhan Ozbas, and Beck A. Sensoy. 2010. Costly external finance, corporate investment, and the subprime mortgage credit crisis. *Journal of Finance Economics* 97: 418–35. [CrossRef]

Fazzari, Steven, R. Glenn Hubbard, and Bruce C. Petersen. 1988. Financing constraints and corporate investment. *Brookings Papers on Economic Activity I* 1988: 141–206. [CrossRef]

Friedman, Benjamin M. 1978. *Crowding out or Crowding in? The Economic Consequences of Financing Government Deficits*. Cambridge: National Bureau of Economic Research.

Gertler, Mark, and Simon Gilchrist. 1994. Monetary policy, business cycles, and the behavior of small manufacturing firms. *The Quarterly Journal of Economics* 109: 309–40. [CrossRef]

Grunfeld, Yehuda, and Zvi Griliches. 1960. Is aggregation necessarily bad? *The Review of Economics and Statistics* 42: 1–13. [CrossRef]

Kadapakkam, Palani-Rajan, P. C. Kumar, and Leigh A. Riddick. 1998. The impact of cash flows and firm size on investment: 'The international evidence'. *Journal of Banking & Finance* 22: 293–320.

Kahn, George A. 2010. Monetary policy under a corridor operating framework. *Economic Review (Kansas City)* 95: 5–35.

Kaplan, Steven N., and Luigi Zingales. 1997. Do investment-cash flow sensitivities provide useful measures of financing constraints? *The Quarterly Journal of Economics* 112: 169–215. [CrossRef]

Kashyap, Anil K., Jeremy C. Stein, and David W. Wilcox. 1993. The monetary transmission mechanism: Evidence from the composition of external finance. *American Economic Review* 83: 78–98.

Kennedy, Peter. 1992. *A Guide to Econometrics*, 3rd ed. Cambridge: The MIT Press.

Keynes, John Maynard. 1936. *The General Theory of Employment. Interest and Money*. London: Palgrave Macmillan, Cambridge: Cambridge University Press, for Royal Economic Society.

Lamont, Owen. 1997. Cash flow and investment: 'Evidence from internal capital markets'. *Journal of Finance* 52: 83–109. [CrossRef]

Li, Bing, and Qing Liu. 2017. On the choice of monetary policy rules for China: A Bayesian DSGE approach. *China Economic Review* 44: 166–85. [CrossRef]

Maddala, Gangadharrao S., and Kajal Lahiri. 1992. *Introduction to Econometrics*. New York: Macmillan, vol. 2.

Majumder, Alauddin. 2007. Does Public Borrowing Crowd-out Private Investment? The Bangladesh Evidence. *Policy Analysis Unit Working Paper Series* 708.

Myers, Stewart C., and Nicholas S. Majluf. 1984. Corporate financing and investment decisions when firms have information that investors do not have. *Journal of Financial Economics* 13: 187–221. [CrossRef]

Miller, Merton H. 1977. Debt and taxes. *The Journal of Finance* 32: 261–75.

Mishkin, Frederic S. 2009. Will monetary policy become more of a science? In *Monetary Policy Over Fifty Years*. Abingdon: Routledge, pp. 93–119.

Morck, Randall, M. Deniz Yavuz, and Bernard Yeung. 2013. *State-Controlled Banks and the Effectiveness of Monetary Policy*. Cambridge: National Bureau of Economic Research.

Myers, Stewart C. 1984. The capital structure puzzle. *The Journal of Finance* 39: 574–92. [CrossRef]

Richardson, Scott. 2006. Over-investment of free cash flow. *Review of Accounting Studies* 11: 159–89. [CrossRef]

Terjesen, Siri, Niels Bosma, and Erik Stam. 2016. Advancing public policy for high-growth, female, and social entrepreneurs. *Public Administration Review* 76: 230–39. [CrossRef]

Tobias, Olweny, and Mambo Chiluwe. 2012. The effect of monetary policy on private sector investment in Kenya. *Journal of Applied Finance and Banking* 2: 239.

Tobin, James. 1969. A general equilibrium approach to monetary theory. *Journal of Money, Credit and Banking* 1: 15–29. [CrossRef]

Vogt, Stephen C. 1994. The cash flow/investment relationship: 'Evidence from US manufacturing firms'. *Financial Management* 23: 3–20. [CrossRef]

Windmeijer, Frank. 2005. A finite sample correction for the variance of linear efficient two-step GMM estimators. *Journal of Econometrics* 126: 25–51. [CrossRef]

Yang, Xingquan, Liang Han, Wanli Li, Xingqiang Yin, and Lin Tian. 2017. Monetary policy, cash holding and corporate investment: 'Evidence from China'. *China Economic Review* 46: 110–22. [CrossRef]

Zhao, Jing, Xiao Chen, and Ying Hao. 2018. Monetary policy, government control and capital investment: Evidence from China. *China Journal of Accounting Research* 11: 233–54. [CrossRef]

© 2019 by the authors. Licensee MDPI, Basel, Switzerland. This article is an open access article distributed under the terms and conditions of the Creative Commons Attribution (CC BY) license (http://creativecommons.org/licenses/by/4.0/).

Article

Asymmetric Effects of Policy Uncertainty on the Demand for Money in the United States †

Mohsen Bahmani-Oskooee * and **Majid Maki-Nayeri**

The Center for Research on International Economics and Department of Economics, The University of Wisconsin-Milwaukee, Milwaukee, WI 53201, USA; makinay2@uwm.edu
* Correspondence: bahmani@uwm.edu
† Valuable comments of four anonymous reviewers of this journal are greatly appreciated. Remaining errors, however, are ours.

Received: 12 October 2018; Accepted: 19 November 2018; Published: 20 December 2018

Abstract: A comprehensive measure of economic uncertainty, known as "Policy Uncertainty", which was constructed by the Economic Policy Uncertainty Group by searching popular newspapers for uncertain terms associated with economic factors and its impact on macro variables, is gaining momentum. Although some researchers have assessed its impact on the demand for money in a few countries, we considered the U.S.A. demand for money one more time and showed that when a linear money demand was estimated, policy uncertainty had no long-run effects. However, when a nonlinear model was estimated, the results showed that while increased policy uncertainty induces the public to hold less money in the long run, decreased uncertainty has no long-run effects, a clear sign of asymmetric response.

Keywords: policy uncertainty; money demand; the U.S.A., asymmetry; nonlinear ARDL

JEL Classification: E41

---

1. Introduction

Ever since the introduction of the new measure of uncertainty by Baker et al. (2016), response of macro variables to this new measure has gained momentum. Unlike other measures that are based on a single macro variable, such as volatility of money supply or output, under the new measure, which is known as "Policy Uncertainty", the Policy Uncertainty Group today relies upon the method by Baker et al. (2016) and constructs the policy uncertainty measure by searching popular newspapers in a given country for such terms as "uncertain' and "uncertainty" associated with such words as "policy", "tax", "spending", "regulation", "central bank", "budget", "deficit", etc. From the volume of news associated with these terms, an index of uncertainty is then constructed. The larger the volume of the news, the higher the index, and the higher uncertainty.[1]

As mentioned, the new measure has recently gained momentum and researchers are emphasizing its impact on macro variables. Examples include Wang et al. (2014) who investigated the link between policy uncertainty and corporate investment, Pastor and Veronesi (2013); Ko and Lee (2015); and Brogaard and Detzel (2015), who assessed its impact on risk premia and market returns, Baker et al. (2016) who assessed its impact on economic activity and firm-level outcome, Bahmani-Oskooee and Ghodsi (2017), who investigated its impact on house prices in each state of

---

[1] For more information and source of the data visit Economic Uncertainty Policy Group: http://www.policyuncertainty.com/europe_monthly.html.

the U.S.A., and Kang and Ratti (2013), as well as Bahmani-Oskooee et al. (2018), who looked into the link between the new uncertainty measure and oil prices.

Another macro variable that is said to be affected by an uncertainty measure is the amount of money that people hold as cash, i.e., the demand for money. Assessing the impact of an uncertainty measure on the demand for money must be first attributed to Friedman (1984), who emphasized volatility of monetary growth as a measure of uncertainty. Choi and Oh (2003) then added volatility of output as a measure of uncertainty that could affect the demand for money. However, Bahmani-Oskooee et al. (2015, 2016) argued that factors other than money supply and output volatility can contribute to an uncertain economic environment. Hence, they employed the new policy uncertainty measure and assessed its impact on the demand for money in the U.K. and in the U.S.A., respectively.[2]

All of the above studies have assumed that the impact of policy uncertainty on macro variables is symmetric. However, concentrating on the demand for money, Bahmani-Oskooee and Maki-Nayeri (2018a, 2018b) recently argued that the effects of policy uncertainty on the demand for money could be asymmetric. As they argued, while people hold more cash during times of increased uncertainty, people might hold even more cash during times of decreased uncertainty, as they might attempt shield themselves from an uncertain environment in the future. They demonstrated these asymmetric effects by estimating the demand for money in Korea and Australia, respectively.

As mentioned above, Bahmani-Oskooee et al. (2016) have already assessed the impact of the new measure of policy uncertainty on the demand for money in the U.S.A., and have shown that the new uncertainty measure has short-run and long-run positive effects, implying that due to policy uncertainty Americans hold more cash so that they can hedge against an uncertain future. The findings also imply that a decrease in policy uncertainty will induce the U.S.A. public to hold less cash, implying a symmetric response to policy uncertainty. How valid is this symmetric assumption in the U.S.A.? As our asymmetry analysis will show, the assumption is valid in the short run, though not in the long run. Therefore, the main goal of this paper is to investigate the asymmetric effects of policy uncertainty on the demand for money in the U.S.A. To gain some insight on the path of policy uncertainty measure in the U.S.A., see Figure 1. The rest of the paper is organized as follows: in Section 2, we outline the models and explain the methods. We then present the estimation results in Section 3 and provide a summary in Section 4. Data definition and sources are then explained in Appendix A.

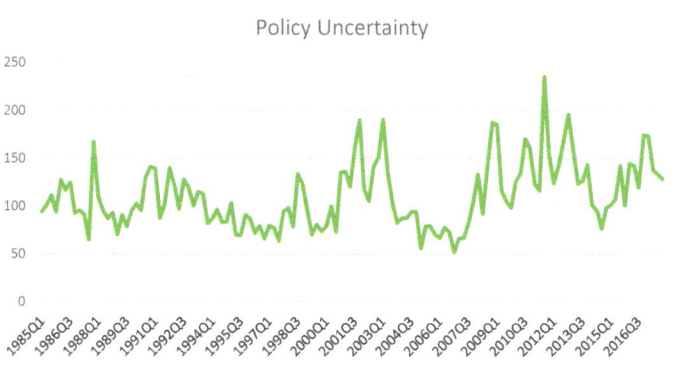

Figure 1. Measure of Policy Uncertainty for the U.S.A.

---

[2] Other measures of uncertainty have been used by others. For example, Sahin (2013) assessed the impact of inflation uncertainty on the demand for money in Turkey and found that increased uncertainty increased precautionary motives. Sahin (2018) looked at the impact of impact of the U.S.A. money supply volatility as a measure of uncertainty on the velocity of the money in Organization of the Petroleum Exporting Countries (OPEC) countries and finds significant long-run effects only in three countries.

2. The Money Demand Models and Methods

Since our main purpose is to extend the symmetric analysis of Bahmani-Oskooee et al. (2015) and engage in an asymmetric analysis, we borrow their specification as outlined by Equation (1):

$$LnM_t = a + bLnY_t + cLnr_t + dLn(P_t/P_{t-1}) + eLnEX_t + fLnPU_t + \varepsilon_t \qquad (1)$$

In specification (1), it is basically assumed that level of real income, *Y*, interest rate, *r*, rate of inflation proxied by $Ln(P_t/P_{t-1})$, the nominal effective exchange rate, *EX*, and policy uncertainty, *PU*, are the main determinants of the demand for money in the U.S.A. Real income was included to account for transaction demand for money and it was expected that income elasticity to be positive. Interest rate was included to account for the opportunity cost of holding money against other financial assets and inflation rate was included as opportunity cost against real assets. Estimates of both c and d were expected to be negative. The nominal effective exchange rate was included to account for currency substitution, and as discussed by Bahmani-Oskooee et al. (2015) and others in the literature, an estimate of e could be either negative or positive. As the U.S. dollar depreciates (i.e., *EX* declines), domestic currency value of foreign assets rises; if this is perceived as an increase in wealth, foreign asset holders at home will increase their spending by holding more cash, hence a negative estimate for *e*. On the other hand, as the dollar depreciates or foreign currencies appreciate, some may expect further appreciation of foreign currencies. They will then hold more foreign currencies and fewer dollars, hence, a positive estimate for e.[3] Similarly, since policy uncertainty could have negative or positive impact on the demand for money, an estimate of *f* could be positive or negative.[4]

Coefficient estimates of model (1) are the long-run elasticities. In order to infer the short-run effects of exogenous variables, we rely upon an estimation method that yields both short-run and long-run effects in one step, i.e., the Autoregressive Distributed Lag (ARDL) approach of Pesaran et al. (2001). Accordingly, we turned (1) to an error-correction model as follows:

$$\begin{aligned}\Delta LnM_t = \;& \alpha + \sum_{i=1}^{n1}\beta_i\Delta LnM_{t-i} + \sum_{i=0}^{n2}\delta_i\Delta LnY_{t-i} + \sum_{i=0}^{n3}\varphi_i\Delta Lnr_{t-i} + \sum_{i=0}^{n4}\gamma_i\Delta Ln(P_t/P_{t-1})_{t-i} + \\ & \sum_{i=0}^{n5}\eta_i\Delta LnEX_{t-i} + \sum_{i=0}^{n6}\lambda_i\Delta LnPU_{t-i} + \rho_0 LnM_{t-1} + \rho_1 LnY_{t-1} + \\ & \rho_2 Lnr_{t-1} + \rho_3 Ln(P_t/P_{t-1})_{t-1} + \rho_4 LnEX_{t-1} + \rho_5 LnPU_{t-1} + \varepsilon_t\end{aligned} \qquad (2)$$

As can be seen, once the error-correction model (2) is estimated, short-run effects of each variable are reflected in the estimate of coefficients attached to first-differenced variables. For example, short-run effects of policy uncertainty are inferred by the estimates of λ_i's. The long-run effects are inferred by the estimates of $\rho_1 - \rho_5$ normalized on ρ_0. However, in order to avoid spurious regression problem, we applied the F-test to establish joint significance of lagged level variables as a sign of cointegration. Pesaran et al. (2001) tabulated new critical values for the F-test that accounted for integrating properties of variables. Indeed, variables could be a combination of I(0) and I(1), but not I(2) and this is another advantage of this approach.[5]

As mentioned before, our goal was to extend the above symmetric analysis to asymmetric analysis. To this end, we followed Bahmani-Oskooee and Maki-Nayeri (2018a) and Shin et al. (2014) and decomposed the *LnPU* variable into two new time-series variables. For this purpose, we first form

---

[3] For more, see Mundell (1963); Arango and Nadiri (1981); and Bahmani-Oskooee and Pourheydarian (1990).
[4] Other studies that have estimated the demand for money in the U.S.A. without uncertainty measure are: Hafer and Jansen (1991); Hoffman and Rasche (1991); McNown and Wallace (1992); Ahking (2002); Wang (2011); Rao and Kumar (2011); Ball (2012); Jawadi and Sousa (2013); and Gupta and Majumdar (2014)Gupta and Majumdar
[5] Another advantage of this approach is that by including short-run dynamic adjustment process in estimating the long-run elasticities, the approach accounts for feedback effects among all variables (Pesaran et al. 2001, p. 299).

$\Delta LnPU$ which includes positive changes as well as negative changes in our uncertainty measure. We then used the partial sum concept to construct the two new series as follows:

$$POS_t = \sum_{j=1}^{t} \max(\Delta LnPU_j, 0), \ NEG_t = \sum_{j=1}^{t} \min(\Delta LnPU_j, 0) \qquad (3)$$

where POS_t, which is the partial sum of positive changes, reflects only increases in policy uncertainty and NEG_t, which is the partial sum of negative changes in uncertainty, reflects only declines in policy uncertainty. The next step is to move back to ARDL model (2) and replace $LnPU$ by POS and NEG variables. We then arrive at the following specification:

$$\begin{aligned}\Delta LnM_t = \ & \alpha + \sum_{i=1}^{n1} \beta_i \Delta LnM_{t-i} + \sum_{i=0}^{n2} \delta_i \Delta LnY_{t-i} + \sum_{i=0}^{n3} \varphi_i \Delta Lnr_{t-i} + \sum_{i=0}^{n4} \gamma_i \Delta Ln(P_t/P_{t-1})_{t-i} + \\ & \sum_{i=0}^{n5} \eta_i \Delta LnEX_{t-i} + \sum_{i=0}^{n6} \lambda_i^+ \Delta POS_{t-i} + \sum_{i=0}^{n7} \lambda_i^- \Delta NEG_{t-i} + \rho_0 LnM_{t-1} + \rho_1 LnY_{t-1} + \\ & \rho_2 Lnr_{t-1} + \rho_3 Ln(P_t/P_{t-1})_{t-1} + \rho_4 LnEX_{t-1} + \rho_5^+ POS_{t-1} + \rho_5^- NEG_{t-1} + \varepsilon_t \end{aligned} \qquad (4)$$

Since constructing the partial sum variables introduce nonlinearity into adjustment process, models like (4) are classified as nonlinear ARDL models (Shin et al. 2014), whereas (2) is labeled as the linear ARDL model. Shin et al. (2014) then demonstrated that the same estimation method and the same tests by Pesaran et al. (2001) could be applied to (4) as well. Indeed, they argue that the critical value of the F-test for cointegration should stay the same when we move from (2) to (4), even though (4) has one more variable.[6]

Once (4) was estimated, a few asymmetry assumptions could be tested. First, after using a specific lag selection criterion, if ΔPOS takes a different lag order than ΔNEG, that will be evidence of short-run adjustment asymmetry, implying that the public responds at a different speed to an increase in uncertainty versus a decrease in uncertainty. Second, at a given lag order such as $i = 1$, if estimate of $\lambda+$ differs from the estimate of λ^-, that will support short-run asymmetric effects of changes in policy uncertainty. However, stronger short-run cumulative or impact asymmetric effects will be established if we reject the null hypothesis of $\sum \lambda_i^+ = \sum \lambda_i^-$. The Wald test is commonly used to test this hypothesis. Finally, long-run asymmetric effects of policy uncertainty on the demand for money will be established if we reject the null hypothesis of $\frac{\rho_5^+}{-\rho_0} = \frac{\rho_5^-}{-\rho_0}$, again by applying the Wald test.[7]

3. The Results

In this section we estimate both the linear model (2) and the nonlinear model (4) using quarterly data from the U.S.A. over the period 1985I–2017IV. The main reason for restricting ourselves for this period was availability of data for policy uncertainty measure. In estimating each model we followed the literature and use Akaike's Information Criterion (AIC) to select the optimum number of lags. Furthermore, since there are different critical values for different estimates, they were collected in the notes to each table and were used to identify significant estimates. If an estimate was significant at the 10% level, one * is used. Those significant at the 5% level are identified by **.

One of the requirement of the ARDL bounds testing approach is to rule out potential I(2) variables. For this purpose, we applied the augmented Dickey-Fuller (ADF) test to the level, as well as first-differenced variables; the outcome is reported in Table 1 along with some descriptive statistics.

---

[6] See Shin et al. (2014, p. 219). This proposition is based on dependency between the two partial sum variables.
[7] For some other application of these methods in recent literature, see Gogas and Pragidis (2015); Al-Shayeb and Hatemi-J (2016); Lima et al. (2016); Nusair (2017); Aftab et al. (2017); Arize et al. (2017); and Gregoriou (2017). Furthermore, we have used statistical package Microfit 5.5 by Pesaran and Pesaran downloadable for free at: http://www.econ.cam.ac.uk/people-files/emeritus/mhp1/Microfit/Microfit.html.

From Table 1, we gather that while inflation rate and policy uncertainty variable were both I(0), other variables were I(1). There were no I(2) variables.

Table 1. Summary Statistics for All Variables.

		\multicolumn{6}{c}{Variables}					
		M	Y	r	$Ln(P_t/P_{t-1})$	EX	PU
Mean		3273.31	12402.14	3.33	0.53	115.55	110.44
Min		2244.30	7537.93	0.01	−0.20	92.51	52.09
Max		5578.80	17272.47	8.54	1.20	170.40	235.08
Std Dev		976.73	2899.15	2.57	0.24	14.01	34.20
Skewness		0.90	−0.11	0.09	0.14	1.00	0.86
Kurtosis		2.62	1.65	1.72	3.52	4.74	3.59
		\multicolumn{6}{c}{ADF Test Results (Augmented Dickey-Fuller test)}					
		\multicolumn{6}{c}{Variables}					
		Ln M	Ln Y	Ln r	$Ln(P_t/P_{t-1})$	Ln EX	Ln PU
With Constant	Level	−2.10(1)	−1.88(1)	−1.53(1)	−3.04(2) *	−2.88(2)	−5.22(0) **
	First Difference	−8.06(0) **	−4.88(1) **	−9.04(0) **	−12.33(1) **	−7.97(1) **	−12.22(1) **
With Constant	Level	−0.61(0)	−1.34(2)	−1.89(1)	−6.26(0) **	−2.99(1)	−5.54(0) **
and Trend	First Difference	−8.65(0) **	−7.78(0) **	−9.03(0) **	−12.28(1) **	−8.12(1) **	−12.17(1) **

Notes: Real money supply (M) is in Millions of U.S. Dollars. Std Dev is standard deviation. * and ** denote statistical significance at the 10% and 5% confidence levels, respectively. Number inside the parenthesis is the number of lags selected by AIC.

We are now in a position to estimate the linear ARDL model (2). The results are reported in Table 2. From the short-run results reported in Panel A, we gathered that all variables had short-run effects since each variable carried at least one significant coefficient. However, short-run effects of none of the variables last into the long run, since none of the normalized long-run estimates in Panel B were significant. This is supported by the lack of cointegration among the variables, since the F-test reported in Panel C was marginally significant at the 10% level and ECM_{t-1} was not.[8] The model seems to have been misspecified, since Ramsey's RESET test in Panel C was highly significant but there is no evidence of serial correlation, since the Lagrange Multiplier statistic reported as LM was insignificant. Finally, application of the CUSUM and CUSUMSQ tests for stability of all coefficient estimates reported in Figure 2 reveals that estimates were stable by the first test but not by the second test. These results are also indicated in Panel C by "S" for stable and "UNS" for unstable estimates. In sum, it appears that policy uncertainty has short-run effects on the demand for money in the U.S.A., though not long-run effects.

---

[8] The ECM_{t-1} test is an alternative test under which normalized long-run estimates and Equation (1) are used to generate the error term denoted by ECM as follows:

$$ECM_t = LnM_t - \frac{\hat{\rho}_1}{-\hat{\rho}_0} LnY_t - \frac{\hat{\rho}_2}{-\hat{\rho}_0} Lnr - \frac{\hat{\rho}_3}{-\hat{\rho}_0} Ln\left(\frac{P_t}{P_{t-1}}\right) - \frac{\hat{\rho}_4}{-\hat{\rho}_0} LnEX_t - \frac{\hat{\rho}_5}{-\hat{\rho}_0} LnPU_t.$$

We then move back to an error-correction model (2) and replace the linear combination of lagged level variables by ECM_{t-1} and estimate the new specification at the same optimum lags. A significantly negative coefficient obtained for ECM_{t-1} implies that variables are adjusting toward their long-run equilibrium values or cointegrating. The value of the estimated coefficient measures the speed of adjustment. Since the t-test is used to judge significance of the coefficient attached to ECM_{t-1}, the test is also known as the t-test for cointegration. Like the F test, Pesaran et al. (2001, p. 303) provided new critical values for this test too. Note also that the value.

Table 2. Full-information estimates of the Linear Autoregressive Distributed Lag (ARDL) Model (2).

Panel A: Short-Run Coefficient Estimates

Lag Order	0	1	2	3	4	5	6	7	8	9	10	11	12
ΔLnM	-												
ΔLnY	−0.32 [a] (−2.08) *												
ΔLn r	−0.01 (−2.02) *	−0.002 (−0.94)	0.002 (0.52)	0.004 (1.34)	−0.01 (−2.24) *	0.004 (1.57)	−0.004 (−1.32)	−0.003 (−0.60)	0.01 (1.97)				
ΔLn(P_t/P_{t-1})	−0.02 (−4.54) **	0.01 (1.33)	0.01 (2.67) **										
ΔLnLEX	0.11 (2.93) **	−0.04 (−1.24)	0.07 (2.11) *	0.003 (0.09)	−0.08 (−2.81) **	0.05 (2.80) **							
ΔLnPU	0.01 (3.98) **												

Panel B: Long-Run Coefficient Estimates

Constant	LnY	Ln r	Ln(P_t/P_{t-1})	LnEX	LnPU
131.45 (0.77)	−14.06 (−0.74)	0.39 (0.65)	0.51 (0.79)	0.69 (0.89)	−0.87 (−0.64)

Panel C: Diagnostics

F [b]	ECM$_{t-1}$	LM [d]	RESET [e]	$\bar{R}^2$	CUSUM (CUSUMQ)
3.46 *	0.01 [c] (0.64)	0.32	23.32 **	0.55	S (UNS)

Notes: a. Numbers inside the parentheses are t-ratios. * and ** indicate significance at the 10% and 5% levels, respectively. b. The upper bound critical value of the F-test for cointegration when there are five exogenous variables is 3.35 (3.79) at the 10% (5%) level of significance. These come from Pesaran et al. (2001), Table CI, Case III, p. 300). c. The critical value for significance of FCM$_{t-1}$ is −3.86 (−4.19) at the 10% (5%) level when k = 5. The comparable figures when k = 6 in the nonlinear model are −4.04 and −4.38, respectively. These come from Pesaran et al. (2001), Table CII, Case III, p. 303). d. LM is the Lagrange Multiplier statistic to test for autocorrelation. It is distributed as χ^2 with one degree of freedom. The critical value is 2.70 (3.84) at the 10% (5%) significance level. e. RESET is Ramsey's test for misspecification. It is distributed as χ^2 with one degree of freedom. The critical value is 2.70 (3.84) at the 10% (5%) significance level.

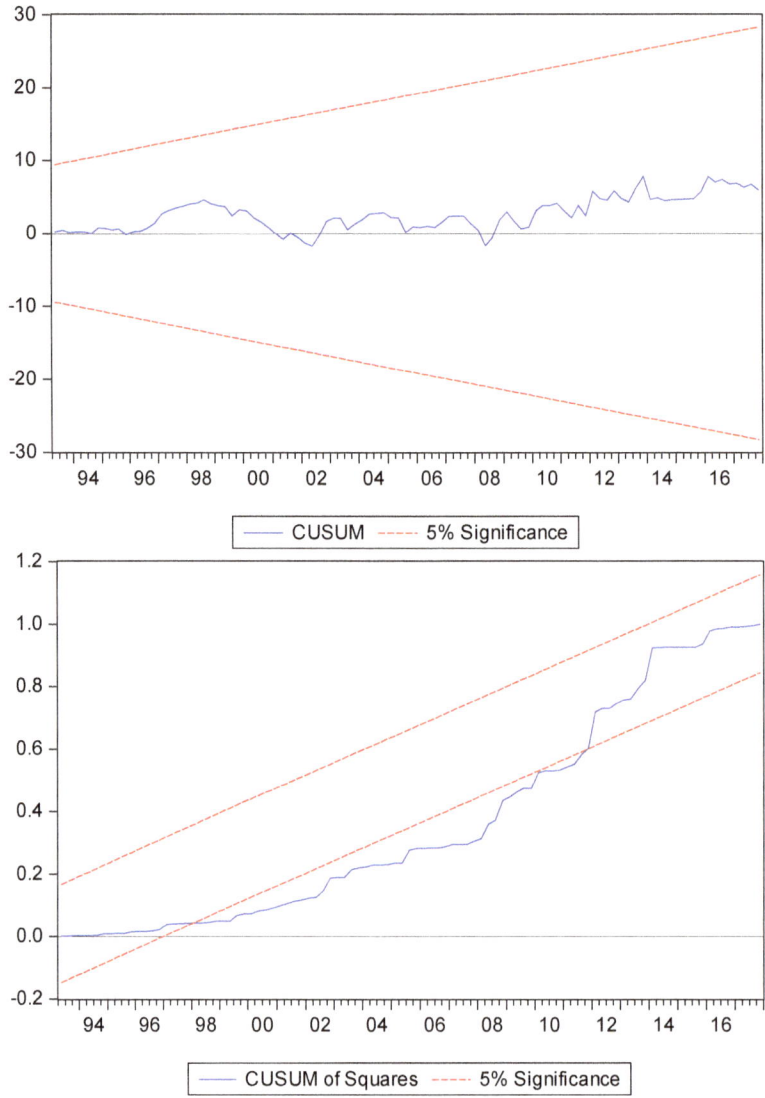

Figure 2. Graphical Presentation of the CUSUM and CUSUMSQ Stability Tests of the Linear Model (2).

The estimates of the nonlinear ARDL model in Table 3 show that introducing nonlinear adjustment of the policy uncertainty measure can change the outcome.

Table 3. Full Information Estimate of the Nonlinear ARDL Model (4) with 0% Threshold.

Panel A: Short-Run Coefficient Estimates

Lag Order	0	1	2	3	4	5	6	7	8	9	10	11	12
ΔLnM	-	-0.20 [a] (-2.93)**	-0.23 (-4.03)**	-0.09 (-1.34)	0.02 (0.38)	-0.19 (-2.26)*							
ΔLnY	-0.39 (2.53)**												
$\Delta Ln\, r$	-0.01 (-5.56)**	-0.002 (-1.13)	0.003 (1.31)	0.01 (2.31)**	-0.003 (-1.34)	0.004 (2.62)**	-0.005 (-2.34)**	-0.004 (-1.01)	0.01 (5.23)**				
$\Delta Ln(P_t/P_{t-1})$	-0.02 (-5.04)**	0.001 (0.40)	0.003 (0.84)	0.01 (1.26)	-0.003 (-0.65)	-0.01 (-1.51)	-0.01 (-1.29)	0.02 (3.24)**	-0.02 (-4.49)**				
$\Delta LnLEX$	0.08 (3.37)**	-0.02 (-0.63)	0.06 (1.70)	-0.01 (-0.31)	-0.08 (-2.88)**	0.02 (0.78)	-0.01 (-0.24)	-0.01 (-0.52)	0.07 (2.05)*	-0.10 (-4.24)**			
ΔPOS	0.002 (0.32)	-0.01 (-1.94)*	0.01 (1.22)	0.01 (2.35)**	0.004 (1.10)	0.01 (3.17)**	-0.01 (-2.27)*	0.01 (1.45)	0.01 (2.48)**	0.01 (2.35)**	0.01 (2.37)**		
ΔNEG	0.02 (2.60)**												

Panel B: long-run coefficient estimates

Constant	LnY	Ln r	$Ln(P_t/P_{t-1})$	LnEX	POS	NEG
-4.29 (-0.46)	0.49 (0.52)	-0.28 (-3.31)**	0.13 (5.10)**	1.52 (5.33)**	-0.78 (-3.81)**	0.22 (1.58)

Panel C: Diagnostics

F [b]	ECM_{t-1} [c]	LM [d]	$RESET$ [e]	$\bar{R}^2$	CUSUM (CUSUMQ)	Wald-L [f]	Wald-S
6.08**	-0.07 (-2.95)	0.29	2.57	0.67	S (UNS)	9.01**	58.30**

Notes: a. Numbers inside the parentheses are t-ratios. * and ** indicate significance at the 10% and 5% levels, respectively. b. The upper bound critical value of the F-test for cointegration when there are five exogenous variables is 3.35 (3.79) at the 10% (5%) level of significance. These come from Pesaran et al. (2001), Table CI, Case III, p. 300). c. The critical value for significance of ECM_{t-1} is -3.86 (-4.19) at the 10% (5%) level when k =5. The comparable figures when k = 6 in the nonlinear model are -4.04 and -4.38, respectively. These come from Pesaran et al. (2001, Table CII, Case III, p. 303). d. LM is the Lagrange Multiplier statistic to test for autocorrelation. It is distributed as χ^2 with one degree of freedom. The critical value is 2.70 (3.84) at the 10% (5%) significance level. e. RESET is Ramsey's test for misspecification. It is distributed as χ^2 with one degree of freedom. The critical value is 2.70 (3.84) at the 10% (5%) significance level. f. Both Wald tests are also distributed as χ^2 with one degree of freedom. The critical value is 2.70 (3.84) at the 10% (5%) significance level.

From the short-run results in Panel A we gathered that, again, each variable carries at least one significant coefficient, implying that all variables did have short-run effects. Almost all coefficient estimates obtained for ΔPOS and ΔNEG were positive, supporting the fact that an increase in policy uncertainty raises the demand for money and declines in uncertainty reduces it. However, the short-run effects were asymmetric, not just in terms of their sizes, but also in terms of the adjustment process. Evidence of adjustment asymmetry is borne out by the fact that ΔPOS takes much more lag order than ΔNEG. Strong evidence of short-run asymmetric effects is borne out by the fact that the sum of the coefficients attached to ΔPOS is significantly different than the sum attached to ΔNEG. This is reflected in the significant Wald test that is reported in Panel C as Wald-S, since the test is for short-run cumulative or impact asymmetry. However, only the short-run effects of the POS variable lasts into the long run, since the POS variable carried a significant long-run coefficient in Panel B but the NEG variables did not. This is a clear sign of long-run asymmetric effects, which is also supported by the Wald test reported as Wald-L in Panel C. Furthermore, since the POS variable carries a significantly negative coefficient, it appears that increased policy uncertainty in the U.S.A. induces the public to hold less cash in the long run and more safe financial or real assets so that they can hedge against an uncertain future.

The long-run estimates are meaningful since cointegration is supported by the F-test if not also by the ECM_{t-1} test. Other diagnostic statistics, such as the LM and RESET tests, indicate that there is no evidence of serial correlation and misspecification. Since the nonlinear model is correctly specified and it enjoys a relatively better fit as evidenced by the size of adjusted R^2, the nonlinear model is preferred to the linear model.

Finally, for sensitivity analysis, we excluded changes in the policy uncertainty that were less than 2%. This amounts to changing the threshold level from zero to 2% in generating the partial sum variables as follows:

$$POS_t = \sum_{j=1}^{t} \max(\Delta LnPU_j, 0.02), \quad NEG_t = \sum_{j=1}^{t} \min(\Delta LnPU_j, 0.02) \qquad (5)$$

The results using the new partial sum variables and nonlinear model (4) are reported in Table 4, and as can be seen, the outcome did not change. The only improvement was support for stability of all coefficient estimates by both CUSUM and CUSUMSQ tests.

Table 4. Full-information estimates of the Nonlinear Model (4) with 2% Thresholds.

Panel A: Short-Run Estimates

Lag Order	0	1	2	3	4	5	6	7	8	9	10	11	12
ΔLnM	-												
ΔLnY	−0.17 (−1.16) [a]	0.11 (0.66)	0.08 (0.47)	0.32 (1.69)	−0.86 (−4.99)**	0.46 (3.20)**	0.15 (1.06)	−0.15 (−0.97)	0.28 (2.12)*	−0.50 (−4.10)**	0.19 (1.97)		
ΔLn r	−0.01 (−5.34)**	0.005 (2.71)**	0.001 (0.33)	0.01 (2.29)*	−0.005 (−2.02)*	0.001 (0.56)	−0.001 (−0.62)	−0.003 (−0.88)*	0.01 (3.62)**				
ΔLn($P_t/P_{t−1}$)	−0.02 (−3.96)**	0.003 (0.88)	0.005 (1.15)	0.01 (2.46)**	−0.01 (−2.58)**	0.0004 (0.10)	−0.01 (−3.44)**	0.02 (4.03)**	−0.01 (−4.42)**				
ΔLnLEX	0.10 (4.06)**	−0.03 (−1.13)	0.01 (0.35)	0.01 (0.36)	−0.08 (−3.28)**	0.04 (1.43)	0.01 (0.45)	−0.06 (−2.17)*	0.07 (2.80)**	−0.14 (−5.15)**	0.07 (3.38)**		
ΔPOS	0.01 (3.09)**	−0.02 (−2.31)**	0.01 (2.59)**	0.01 (2.47)**	0.01 (1.71)	0.01 (1.23)	−0.004 (−0.79)	−0.01 (−1.21)	0.03 (6.24)**	0.01 (2.20)*			
ΔNEG	0.01 (1.67)*	0.01 (1.96)*	0.01 (0.74)	0.0001 (0.01)	−0.003 (−0.54)	0.01 (0.99)	0.004 (0.65)	0.02 (3.61)**	−0.02 (−5.62)**				

Panel B: long-run coefficient estimates

Constant	LnY	Ln r	Ln($P_t/P_{t−1}$)	LnEX	POS	NEG
1.81 (0.26)	0.12 (0.15)	−0.18 (−3.41)**	0.09 (3.33)**	0.95 (6.73)**	−0.50 (−4.03)**	−0.08 (−0.53)

Panel C: Diagnostics

F [b]	ECM$_{t−1}$ [c]	LM [d]	RESET [e]	$\bar{R}^2$	CUSUM (CUSUMQ)	Wald-L [f]	Wald-S
3.77*	−0.09 (−3.08)	0.03	2.36	0.68	S (S)	3.71*	31.62**

Notes: a. Numbers inside the parentheses are *t*-ratios. * and ** indicate significance at the 10% and 5% levels, respectively. b. The upper bound critical value of the F-test for cointegration when there are five exogenous variables is 3.35 (3.79) at the 10% (5%) level of significance. These come from Pesaran et al. (2001, Table CI, Case III, p. 300). c. The critical value for significance of ECM$_{t−1}$ is −3.86 (−4.19) at the 10% (5%) level when k =5. The comparable figures when k = 6 in the nonlinear model are −4.04 and −4.38, respectively. These come from Pesaran et al. (2001, Table CII, Case III, p. 303). d. LM is the Lagrange Multiplier statistic to test for autocorrelation. This is distributed as χ^2 with one degree of freedom. The critical value is 2.70 (3.84) at the 10% (5%) significance level. e. RESET is Ramsey's test for misspecification. This is distributed as χ^2 with one degree of freedom. The critical value is 2.70 (3.84) at the 10% (5%) significance level. f. Both Wald tests are also distributed as χ^2 with one degree of freedom. The critical value is 2.70 (3.84) at the 10% (5%) significance level.

4. Concluding Remarks

In the early 1980s, when the Fed missed its inflation target, Friedman (1984) attributed it to volatility of monetary growth rate. Since then, many studies have tried to assess the impact of alternative measures of uncertainty on the velocity of the money or on the demand for cash balances. The literature has advanced on two grounds. First, relatively more comprehensive measure of uncertainty is being used to assess public's demand for money in response to an uncertainty measure. The new uncertainty measure includes any factor that contributed to an uncertain economic and political environment. Second, in some countries such as Australia and Korea, previous research has discovered that public respond to changes in uncertainty measure in an asymmetric manner.

In this paper, we estimated the demand for money in the U.S.A. by including a new measure of uncertainty known as policy uncertainty that was constructed by Policy Uncertainty Group (see the Appendix A) by searching popular newspapers in the U.S.A. Bahmani-Oskooee et al. (2016), who used the new measure and assessed its impact on the demand for money in the U.S.A., assumed that the effects were symmetric. In this paper, we deviated from that assumption and argued for asymmetric effects. Since we used updated data, we first estimated the demand for money by holding symmetric assumption. This amounts to applying the linear ARDL approach from Pesaran et al. (2001). Then, we changed the symmetry assumption to asymmetry assumption and used the nonlinear ARDL approach by Shin et al.

Our findings are best summarized by saying that when the linear ARDL model was estimated, policy uncertainty had short-run effects but not long-run effects. However, estimates of the nonlinear ARDL model revealed that changes in policy uncertainty have both short-run and long-run effects on the demand for money in the U.S.A. Furthermore, both the short-run and long-run effects were asymmetric.[9] In the long run, we found that while increased policy uncertainty had adverse effect on the demand for cash, decreased policy uncertainty has no long-run effects. Increased uncertainty makes people more cautious about the future; however, they do not simply adjust their portfolio to decreased uncertainty, perhaps because they are used to some degree of uncertainty in their environment, or because they expect more uncertainty in the future.

Author Contributions: M.M.-N. collected the data, carried out the entire estimation, and tabulated the results, M.B.-O. wrote the paper.

Conflicts of Interest: The authors declare no conflict of interest.

Appendix A

Appendix A.1 Data Definition and Sources

Quarterly data over the period 1985I–2017IV were used to carry out the estimation. The main restriction for using data prior to 1985 was unavailability of data on policy uncertainty. Data were collected from the following sources:

(a) International Financial Statistics (IFS) of International Monetary Fund (IMF).
(b) Economic Policy Uncertainty Group: http://www.policyuncertainty.com/us_monthly.html
(c) Federal Reserve Bank of St. Louis (FRED)

Appendix A.2 Variables

$M2$ = Money supply measured by real M2. Data come from Source (c).
Y = Real GDP. Data come from Source (c).
r = Interest rate. Interest rate on 3-Month Treasury Bill from Source (c).

---

[9] These finding for the U.S.A. are similar to those of Bahmani-Oskooee and Maki-Nayeri (2018a, 2018b) for Korea and Australia respectively.

P = Price level used to measure the inflation rate is GDP deflator. Data come from Source (c).

EX = Index of nominal effective exchange rate of the U.S dollar. A decline reflects a depreciation of U.S dollar. Data come from Source (a).

PU = Policy uncertainty. Data come from Source (b).

References

Aftab, Muhammad, Karim Bux Shah Syed, and Naveed Akhter Katper. 2017. Exchange-rate volatility and Malaysian-Thai bilateral industry trade flows. *Journal of Economic Studies* 44: 99–114. [CrossRef]

Ahking, Francis. 2002. Model Mis-Specification and Johansen's Co-Integration Analysis: An Application to the U.S.A. Money Demand. *Journal of Macroeconomics* 24: 51–66. [CrossRef]

Al-Shayeb, Abdulrahman, and Abdulnasser Hatemi-J. 2016. Trade openness and economic development in the UAE: An asymmetric approach. *Journal of Economic Studies* 43: 587–97. [CrossRef]

Arango, Sebastian, and M. Ishaq Nadiri. 1981. Demand for Money in Open economies. *Journal of Monetary Economics* 7: 69–83. [CrossRef]

Arize, Augustine C., John Malindretos, and Emmanuel U. Igwe. 2017. Do Exchange Rate Changes Improve the Trade Balance: An Asymmetric Nonlinear Cointegration Approach. *International Review of Economics and Finance* 49: 313–26. [CrossRef]

Bahmani-Oskooee, Mohsen, and Seyed Hesam Ghodsi. 2017. Policy Uncertainty and House Prices in the United States of America. *Journal of Real Estate Portfolio Management* 23: 73–85.

Bahmani-Oskooee, Mohsen, and Majid Maki-Nayeri. 2018a. Policy Uncertainty and the Demand for Money in Korea: An Asymmetry Analysis. *International Economic Journal* 63: 567–91. [CrossRef]

Bahmani-Oskooee, Mohsen, and Majid Maki-Nayeri. 2018b. Policy Uncertainty and the Demand for Money in Australia: An Asymmetry Analysis. *Australian Economic Papers*, forthcoming. [CrossRef]

Bahmani-Oskooee, Mohsen, and Mohammad Pourheydarian. 1990. Exchange Rate Sensitivity of the Demand for Money and Effectiveness of Fiscal and Monetary Policies. *Applied Economics* 22: 1377–84. [CrossRef]

Bahmani-Oskooee, Mohsen, Sahar Bahmani, Alice Kones, and Ali M. Kutan. 2015. Policy Uncertainty and the Demand for Money in the United Kingdom. *Applied Economics* 47: 1151–57. [CrossRef]

Bahmani-Oskooee, Mohsen, Alice Kones, and Ali Kutan. 2016. Policy Uncertainty and the Demand for Money in the United States. *Applied Economics Quarterly* 62: 37–49. [CrossRef]

Bahmani-Oskooee, Mohsen, Hanafiah Harvey, and Farhang Niroomand. 2018. On the Impact of Policy Uncertainty on Oil Prices: An Asymmetry Analysis. *International Journal of Financial Studies* 6: 12. [CrossRef]

Baker, Scott R., Nicholas Bloom, and Steven J. Davis. 2016. Measuring Economic Policy Uncertainty. *Quarterly Journal of Economics* 131: 1593–636. [CrossRef]

Ball, Lawrence. 2012. Short Run Money Demand. *Journal of Monetary Economics* 59: 622–33. [CrossRef]

Brogaard, Jonathan, and Andrew Detzel. 2015. The Asset-Pricing Implications of Government Economic Policy Uncertainty. *Management Science* 61: 3–18. [CrossRef]

Choi, Woon Gyu, and Seonghwan Oh. 2003. A Demand Function with Output Uncertainty, Monetary Uncertainty, and Financial Innovations. *Journal of Money, Credit, and Banking* 35: 685–709. [CrossRef]

Friedman, Benjamin M. 1984. Lessons from the 1979–1982 Monetary Policy Experiment. *American Economic Review, Papers and Proceedings* 74: 397–400.

Gogas, Periklis, and Ioannis Pragidis. 2015. Are there asymmetries in fiscal policy shocks? *Journal of Economic Studies* 42: 303–21. [CrossRef]

Gregoriou, Andros. 2017. Modelling non-linear behaviour of block price deviations when trades are executed outside the bid-ask quotes. *Journal of Economic Studies* 44: 206–13. [CrossRef]

Gupta, Rangan, and Anandamayee Majumdar. 2014. Reconsidering the Welfare Cost of Inflation in the U.S.A.: A Nonparametric Estimation of the Nonlinear Long-Run Money-Demand Equation Using Projection Pursuit Regressions. *Empirical Economics* 46: 1221–40. [CrossRef]

Hafer, Rik W., and Dennis W. Jansen. 1991. The Demand for Money in the United States: Evidence from Cointegration Tests. *Journal of Money, Credit, and Banking* 23: 155–68. [CrossRef]

Hoffman, Dennis, and Robert H. Rasche. 1991. Long-Run Income and Interest Elasticities of Money Demand in the United States. *The Review of Economics and Statistics* 73: 665–74. [CrossRef]

Jawadi, Fredj, and Ricardo M. Sousa. 2013. Money in the Euro Area, the US and the UK: Assessing the Role of Nonlinearity. *Economic Modelling* 32: 507–15. [CrossRef]

Kang, Wensheng, and Ronald A. Ratti. 2013. Oil Shocks, Policy Uncertainty and Stock Market Return. *International Financial Markets, Institutions, and Money* 26: 305–18. [CrossRef]

Ko, Jun-Hyung, and Chang-Min Lee. 2015. International Economic Policy Uncertainty and Stock Prices: Wavelet Approach. *Economics Letters* 134: 118–22. [CrossRef]

Lima, Luiz, Claudio Foffano Vasconcelos, Jose Simão, and Helder Ferreira de Mendonça. 2016. The quantitative easing effect on the stock market of the USA, the UK and Japan: An ARDL approach for the crisis period. *Journal of Economic Studies* 43: 1006–21. [CrossRef]

McNown, Robert, and Myles S. Wallace. 1992. Cointegration Tests of a Long-Run Relationship between Money Demand and the Effective Exchange Rate. *Journal of International Money and Finance* 11: 107–14. [CrossRef]

Mundell, Robert A. 1963. Capital Mobility and Stabilization Policy Under Fixed and Flexible Exchange Rates. *Canadian Journal of Economics and Political Science* 29: 475–85. [CrossRef]

Nusair, Salah A. 2017. The J-curve Phenomenon in European Transition Economies: A Nonliear ARDL Approach. *International Review of Applied Economics* 31: 1–27. [CrossRef]

Pastor, L'uboš, and Pietro Veronesi. 2013. Policy Uncertainty and Risk Premia. *Journal of Financial Economics* 110: 520–45. [CrossRef]

Pesaran, M. Hashem, Yongcheol Shin, and Richard J. Smith. 2001. Bounds Testing Approaches to the Analysis of Level Relationships. *Journal of Applied Econometrics* 16: 289–326. [CrossRef]

Rao, B. Bhaskara, and Saten Kumar. 2011. Is the U.S.A. Demand for Money Unstable? *Applied Financial Economics* 21: 1263–72. [CrossRef]

Sahin, Afsin. 2013. Estimating Money Demand Function under Uncertainty by Smooth Transition Regression Model. Paper presented at the 6th Annual International Conference on Mediterranean Studies, Athens, Greece, March 26–29.

Sahin, Afsin. 2018. Staying Vigilant of Uncertainty to Velocity of Money: An Application for Oil-Producing Countries. *OPEC Energy Review* 42: 170–95. [CrossRef]

Shin, Yongcheol, Byungchul Yu, and Matthew Greenwood-Nimmo. 2014. Modelling Asymmetric Cointegration and Dynamic Multipliers in a Nonlinear ARDL Framework. In *Festschrift in Honor of Peter Schmidt: Econometric Methods and Applications*. Edited by Robin C. Sickles and William C. Horrace. New York: Springer, pp. 281–314.

Wang, Yiming. 2011. The Stability of Long-Run Money Demand in the United States: A New Approach. *Economics Letters* 111: 60–63. [CrossRef]

Wang, Yizhong, Carl R. Chen, and Ying Sophie Huang. 2014. Economic Policy Uncertainty and Corporate Investment: Evidence from China. *Pacific-Basin Finance Journal* 26: 227–43. [CrossRef]

© 2018 by the authors. Licensee MDPI, Basel, Switzerland. This article is an open access article distributed under the terms and conditions of the Creative Commons Attribution (CC BY) license (http://creativecommons.org/licenses/by/4.0/).

Commentary

China and Special Drawing Rights—Towards a Better International Monetary System

Matthew Harrison [1] and Geng Xiao [2,*]

[1] Hong Kong Institution for International Finance, K K Leung Building, University of Hong Kong, Hong Kong; matt-harrison@netvigator.com
[2] Peking University HSBC Business School, PHBS 734, Peking University, University Town, Nanshan District, Shenzhen 518055, China
* Correspondence: xiaogeng@phbs.pku.edu.cn

Received: 28 February 2019; Accepted: 3 April 2019; Published: 9 April 2019

Abstract: China and the international monetary system need each other. The international monetary system is strained, with crisis just around the corner, yet reform is not on anyone's agenda. Meanwhile China, deeply invested in the current system, faces narrowing options as trading partners question its moves abroad, debt levels rise at home, and its current account moves from surplus to deficit. RMB internationalization might appear to provide a way out, but the policy has its limits and tends to exacerbate rather than relieve tensions. We argue that a tension-reducing solution is at hand to the problems of both the international monetary system and China—IMF-style Special Drawing Rights (SDRs). If in a unilateral initiative China were to make the SDR central to its next phase of capital account opening, China's institutions, corporates and individuals—presently restricted in their access to international currency—would likely embrace it. Begun by China, with support from the international community and Hong Kong, promulgation of the SDR would usher in an era of lower tensions, providing space for development and avoidance of conflict within a reordered monetary system in which China would have a more prominent role.

Keywords: China; Special Drawing Rights (SDRs); international monetary system; RMB internationalization; Belt and Road Initiative; risk management

JEL Classification: F3; G1; P2

1. Introduction

In this commentary, drawing on ideas we first set out in Harrison and Xiao (2018), we argue that two major monetary problems, seemingly loosely connected, have a common solution. The two problems are, firstly, that of the international monetary system as a whole and, secondly, that of China's monetary relations with the rest of the world. We suggest a solution to these two problems in expanded use of the International Monetary Fund (IMF)'s Special Drawing Rights (SDRs). China would be in a position to unilaterally kick-start an SDR market, following which, broad international participation would likely snowball.

In the present paper, we firstly establish the nature of the two problems. Regarding the international monetary system, the signs of strain if not of imminent crisis are clear. Emerging markets were put under pressure by US interest rate rises, and Argentina and Pakistan have had to approach the International Monetary Fund (IMF). Global indebtedness has reached 225% of GDP—higher than in the aftermath of the Global Financial Crisis (GFC) (IMF 2019a). Central banks, which provided USD 10 trillion to the financial markets via monetary easing, have begun withdrawing their support (Fitch Solutions 2017). We argue that the current tensions in the international monetary system result from a systemic cause, namely reliance on a single national currency, the dollar, as the de facto global currency. Such a system is inherently prone to instability, yet unfortunately there is no prospect of systemic reform.

Regarding China's monetary relations with the world, there are again clear signs of building crisis, most obviously the US–China trade war and China's rising domestic indebtedness. There are also grounds for a more positive outlook, namely political will on both sides to resolve the trade war, China's huge accumulated foreign exchange reserves, and the policy of RMB internationalization, which creates new space outside the dollar arena. However, we argue that these factors at best defer the crisis. China will need to further open its capital account and, hence, step up its monetary relations with the world.

These two problems have a potential, common solution. Global imbalances would reduce if the world were to make wider use of SDRs as a fully-fledged currency. This is not a realistic prospect given that the willingness of states to cooperate on multilateral initiatives is diminishing, while the international monetary system is low among politicians' priorities. However, a currency version of SDRs would be useful to China as well in its capital account opening process. As a separate currency it would be easy to track and control, while its fungibility with the dollar and its inclusion of the RMB add further appeal. We argue for a unilateral initiative by China to promote use of the SDR by its own institutions, corporates, and individuals. With Hong Kong's help, this could kickstart a global SDR ecosystem to the benefit of all.

The remainder of our paper discusses the risks of the proposed SDR initiative to China and how these risks may be mitigated. The China authorities have more experience than most in the management of financial crises. Monetary quotas and geographical limits are among the tools available. Given China's prowess in FinTech there may even be a role for a cryptocurrency version of SDRs, which would in turn provide risk-mitigating control and transparency.

Neither the international community nor China have unlimited time to confront their respective monetary problems. The SDR is a solution whose time has come.

2. International Monetary System

2.1. Problems

The strains in the international monetary system are clear.

As we detail in Harrison and Xiao (2018), following the collapse in the early 1970s of the Bretton Woods arrangements under which global currencies were pegged to the US dollar, which in turn was pegged to the price of gold, the world gravitated to a de facto system centered on the US dollar. This de facto system is characterized by free-floating exchange rates, massive private capital flows, current account convertibility for most countries, and varying degrees of capital account convertibility for many, with the IMF available to lend balance of payments support to countries in difficulties. However, the post-Bretton Woods era has seen crisis after crisis, with defaults ranging through Latin America (1980s), East Asia (1997/98), Russia (1998) the developed West (2007/09), and emerging markets (2018–).

The present monetary setup has been described as 'a deficient non-system' (White 2015; see also Ocampo 2017). It is inherently crisis-prone because of the following drawbacks:

- Reliance on a national currency (the US dollar) as the de facto international currency. US dollar interest rates are determined with reference to US domestic conditions and may be too high for some other countries (currently) or too low (during the immediate post-GFC years). Moreover, the US authorities have 'weaponized' their currency by denying banking access to actors considered hostile to US national interests.
- Inequity. Poorer developing countries are obliged to accumulate precautionary dollar surpluses to insure against potential future balance of payments difficulties, so transferring resources to the world's richest country, the USA.

- Recessionary bias. Balance of payments debtors are forced to adjust when it is most painful for them to do so, while creditors face no such adjustment pressure.
- Lack of oversight. The IMF monitors developments and issues warnings but has little power to influence events until approached by a debtor nation.
- Limited policy coordination. The G20 is perhaps the closest to an economic policy coordinating mechanism, but it has not been very effective in this role.

The US benefits from the system and so has resisted change. However, while as issuer of the world's currency the US gains seigniorage, prestige, and even an instrument of foreign policy, these benefits come with costs. In order to provide the world with dollars, the US has to run extended current account deficits, while the (forced) willingness of other nations to buy its debt arguably encourages the US in fiscal irresponsibility, as exemplified in the Trump tax cuts of December 2017. In the long run, the present system may not be good for the US either.

We argue that the dollar-centric monetary system is in urgent need of reform. As Rickards (2015) puts it, 'If the dollar fails, the entire international monetary system will fail with it'.

2.2. Existing Reform Proposals

If the present global monetary system is deficient, why has it persisted for so long?

There has been no shortage of reform proposals. In 2009, then-governor of the People's Bank of China Zhou Xiaochuan (Zhou 2009) expressed dissatisfaction with the dollar-centric system and argued for more use of the SDR. The IMF (2011) took up the call and produced a paper on the potential of the SDR. Palais-Royal (2011) urged, '... the reconstruction of a fully-fledged international monetary order' with a central role for the SDR. Other commentators have called for a revival of Keynes' clearing union, a larger role for the IMF, development of the SDR as a true global currency, restrictions on private capital flows, and improved macro-economic coordination among others. Meanwhile, the IMF (2018a) continues to advocate a larger role for SDRs to moderate imbalances and counter weaknesses in the present system. However, none of these proposals has gained traction.

In line with Ocampo (2017) and Li (2016), we hope for an evolution of the international monetary system to a multicurrency one with a larger role for the SDR. However, even this evolutionary scenario is unlikely to materialize.

Firstly, geopolitical alignment is lacking. The US, although wielding veto power within the IMF, has lost moral authority because of the GFC, and in any case the world is now multipolar. With the GFC receding into memory, and with nationalism and populism on the rise, states have become less willing to cooperate in building a new monetary order.

Secondly, massive capital flows—often seen as the villain—can hardly be dismissed. Trading and investing freely across the world's markets and currencies has come to be seen as a right. The world's openness to private capital flows has, alongside its disbenefits, enabled multitudes of investors and institutions to diversify and improve returns in ways that in the Bretton Woods era would not have been possible. This is in many ways a good thing, and it is all but irreversible. The genie is out of the bottle.

Top-down reform of the international monetary system appears infeasible. Rather, we argue that any reform will have to be de facto and bottom-up, the initiative of a single state or group of states, and promulgated by the market process.

3. China's International Monetary Options

We now consider China's international monetary problem. Having established that there is a problem, we consider two possible solutions, namely RMB internationalization and the monetary implications of the Belt and Road Initiative (BRI), and argue that they cannot meet China's needs. In our view, a third solution is more promising for China—limited capital account opening via SDRs.

3.1. Need for Capital Account Opening

At first glance, it might appear that China does not have an international monetary problem, or at least not an unmanageable one. True, there is a building trade war with the US, but a settlement of some kind will surely be reached. Even if the trade war should go badly, China has cards to play. Internal consumption has room to take up the slack from exports; there are new trading partners cultivated by the BRI; the foreign exchange reserves provide a huge cushion; and while indebtedness is high at 266% of GDP, most of this debt is internal rather than external (Bloomberg 2018a). China's increasing technological prowess in areas ranging from FinTech to space exploration, supercomputing, and telecommunications opens up new areas of opportunity.

Our view, however, is that China is near the limits of its existing development model. Externally, that model is one of exploiting the openness of trading partners while keeping the domestic market relatively closed. Internally, notwithstanding the market reforms of the past forty years, China remains a state-permeated economy (Otero-Iglesias and Vermeiren 2015), even more so in recent years as the position of state-owned enterprises is boosted and control over opinion and information flow tightened.

Now, both dimensions of the development model are under threat. Externally, trading partners are pushing back against China's exports and overseas investments while demanding better access to China's domestic market. Even before these demands are addressed, rising consumption (including the overseas spending of Chinese tourists) has tilted China's current account balance towards deficit (The Economist 2019). Nor can the China authorities easily resist these trends without jeopardizing the high rate of economic growth on which their claim to legitimacy depends.

In order to finance its looming current account deficit, China must import capital. This would not be difficult, since China has a vast and diverse economy to which foreign investors are keen to gain exposure. However, given the restrictions and controls on capital movement, foreign investors tend to limit the amounts they invest, currently owning only 2% of China's bond market (CNBC 2018). In order to attract further capital on a large scale, China would need to substantially loosen capital account restraints. Yet this would allow China's own citizens to 'vote with their feet' financially, the resultant capital flight undermining the state-permeated system. Even the vast foreign exchange reserves might not be enough to stem the flood.

We argue that China has a pressing need to open its capital account but cannot readily do so without compromising the state-permeated system. Before turning to our preferred solution, we first explore two policies which appear to offer a way out—RMB internationalization and the monetary implications of the BRI.

3.2. RMB Internationalization

In the aftermath of the GFC, China embarked on a program of internationalizing its own currency, encouraging use of the RMB for trade, for reserve-holding, and for investment purposes, in order to reduce reliance on the dollar and in the longer run even supplant the dollar as a global currency. How has this initiative fared, and what are its prospects?

One school of thought, with Eichengreen (2014), expects the RMB to become an international currency alongside the US dollar relatively soon. Another school, with Frankel (2012), emphasizes the role of financial depth in determining a currency's international acceptability and sees RMB internationalization as a more distant prospect. Prasad (2018) considers that the RMB's potential will remain unrealized unless China embarks on a broad range of financial system and economic reforms.

China authorities have taken steps to support internationalization of their currency. To help ensure RMB supply, the People's Bank of China (PBoC) has concluded swap agreements with the central banks of some 36 countries (EIU 2018). These agreements appear to have supported bilateral trade between China and the countries concerned (Zhang et al. 2017). The IMF's inclusion of the RMB in its SDR basket provides justification for central banks to include the currency in their reserves. On 8 October 2015, China launched the Cross-border Inter-bank Payments System (CIPS) to rival the Society for Worldwide Interbank Financial Telecommunication, SWIFT (CCTV 2017). RMB has been allowed to accumulate offshore in Hong Kong and, to a lesser extent, other centers; in 2013, a link was set up between the Hong Kong Monetary Authority (HKMA)'s RMB Real-Time Gross Settlement System and the Shenzhen Financial Settlement System (HKMA 2016). Domestic financial markets have been opened somewhat with the launch of Stock Connect and Bond Connect, with quotas on these channels being relaxed over time. Meanwhile, the RMB was allowed to trade in a wider daily band, linked to an undisclosed basket of currencies rather than simply pegged to the US dollar (New York Times 2015). China also initiated the establishment of a new multilateral financial institution, the Asian Infrastructure Investment Bank (AIIB) launched in January 2016, in which it retained a 30% share (SCMP 2015).

From an almost negligible international profile the RMB contributed 1.7% of foreign exchange reserves in Q3 2018, ranking sixth globally (IMF 2019b), while in January 2019 it contributed 1.24% of SWIFT's international transactions, ranking eighth (SWIFT 2019). Russia has reduced the dollar share of its reserves and allocated 15% to RMB (Bloomberg 2019). However, there is still a long way to go to rival the dollar.

The above supporting initiatives have had limited impact so far. BRI lending has largely been in dollars (FT 2018), AIIB lending exclusively so (Global Times 2016). CIPS volumes are not disclosed[1], suggesting that they may not be too large. The RMB's international footprint is narrow, with 80% of RMB transactions passing through Hong Kong (SWIFT 2019). The Connect schemes (again through Hong Kong) are designed to prevent RMB straying outside the intended purposes. Offshore RMB (CNH) is not fungible with onshore RMB (CNY)—the two have a different price and a different interest rate, and approval is needed for conversion of one to the other (Currenxie 2016). Overall, as an international holder there are not too many things that one can do with one's RMB.

For RMB to become attractive enough for foreigners to want to hold it on a large scale, there would have to be much greater freedom to exchange it for other currencies and to spend or earn it within China or abroad. For there to be enough RMB in the international system, China would have to run large and extended trade deficits, as the US has done. For large-scale RMB investment and reserve holding by foreigners, China would need much deeper and more open financial markets. Long before these conditions were met, China would face capital flight, pressure on the exchange rate, and financial market turbulence—existential threats to the internal order.

Katada (2018) draws lessons from Japan's attempt to internationalize the Yen after the 1997/98 Asian Financial Crisis. Despite Japan's advantages in economic size and open, developed financial markets, the effort foundered on acceptance by the international community and domestic policy priorities. Although China today is bigger economically than Japan was then, in other respects it is less well-placed.

Moreover, the benefits of RMB internationalization for China are hard to find (Huang and Lynch 2013). The prestige or soft power accruing to the issuer of a global currency is a long-term and remote benefit; nor does China have fiscal deficits needing to be financed with international money. RMB internationalization would likely increase exchange rate volatility rather than reduce it; denominating trade in RMB rather than US dollars would create financial efficiencies but would not relieve China and its trading partners of the need to maintain international competitiveness by means such as wage cuts or unemployment.

In China's case, currency internationalization carries the further benefit of added impetus to domestic reforms (RBA 2018). Nonetheless, domestic imperatives carry greater weight. Facing internal financial instability, RMB depreciation and capital flight, the PBoC intervened in Hong Kong's offshore RMB market to buy up RMB and make offshore holding more difficult. This signaled readiness to

---

[1] Statistics not apparently available on CIPS website, http://www.cips.com.cn/cipsen/, viewed on 25 February 2019; for example, the press release, 'CIPS runs smoothly and hits new record', 14 April 2017, has no statistics.

'sacrifice' the offshore market in order to manage expectations of the value of the RMB (Long and Kroeber 2016).

Overall, we do not see RMB internationalization as coherent with China's state-permeated system. RMB internationalization is perhaps more a response to crises such as the Asian financial crisis and the global financial crisis, a short-term problem-solver rather than coherent long-term strategy. At best, RMB internationalization could be described as a matter of 'currency normalization' rather than 'currency dominance' (Bowles and Wang 2013).

3.3. Belt and Road Initiative

If RMB internationalization is problematic, there is the alternative, lesser goal of RMB regionalization.

As China began its efforts to promote wider use of the RMB, there was scholarly discussion about the possible formation of an RMB region in East Asia as a staging post on the RMB's journey to international acceptance (e.g., Chow 2013). China has substantial trade ties with the region, from which it is a net importer; the countries concerned could naturally accumulate RMB deposits. In this narrative, the RMB would become a major or even the dominant currency for China's relations with its nearby trading partners, leading to the formation of an East Asian RMB bloc. RBA (2018) finds evidence that the Asian monetary system is becoming bipolar, influenced by both the US dollar and the RMB. Nevertheless, it concludes that, 'the US dollar is still by far the most important anchor currency for most economies in the region.'

Could the BRI foster an RMB region? Among its aims, the BRI was intended to further RMB internationalization, and it is expected to expand RMB usage for trade and investment (See Chan 2017; also City of London Corporation 2018). It could be argued that BRI countries would be to a certain extent under China's sway and, thus, less destabilizing to the state-permeated system than the rambunctious foreigners of the developed West.

However, we question how much the BRI can help the cause of RMB internationalization.

Firstly, most BRI lending to date has been in dollars, not RMB. There are initiatives by BRI countries to explore RMB facilities such as the March 2018 issue of Panda bonds by the Philippines (PDI 2018), but the disincentives to RMB usage discussed in Section 3.2 still apply.

Secondly, the BRI strategy itself is controversial. As rising great power, China was in the process of reaching out in manifold ways internationally; the BRI announced in 2013 was in part a relabeling of these efforts in response to the US-led TPP (Brookings 2017)—the latter being intended to exclude China but, in the event, not ratified by the US). The drivers of the BRI—whether commercial or in the nature of 'Marshall Aid'-type grants, whether win-win for the participant countries or 'debt-trap diplomacy'—have not been thought through. The BRI has evoked mixed responses abroad, in that while investment and infrastructure are generally welcomed, host countries have shown concern about debt sustainability (Pakistan, Myanmar, and Sri Lanka), corruption (Malaysia), and the influx of Chinese workers (SCMP 2019). Within China responses have also been mixed, with critics wondering whether the resources might be better spent at home (Economic Times 2018).

According to Zhang (2018), while the West tends to see the BRI as China's strategy to ultimately rule the world, Chinese and most developing nations see it as China's international cooperation strategy to foster a more balanced and equitable world system. Liu et al. (2018) also see the BRI as promoting more inclusive globalization. Nonetheless, to support this narrative China needs to better explain its initiative as well as match its words with its deeds, so as to win more trust and support from the international community.

Thirdly, the more than one hundred countries participating in the BRI (HKTDC 2019) are a broad church, many of them in regions geographically remote from China (South America, Africa, and Oceania). The motivations of these countries are also diverse, with most subscribing to the goal of infrastructure and connectivity, but not necessarily fealty to China. It remains to be seen whether China can steer so diverse and extended a group.

3.4. Special Drawing Rights (SDRs)—The Best Available Monetary Option

In our view, China has reached a stage in its development at which there is no obvious or easy way forward. The existing model of keeping the domestic market relatively closed and relying on the openness of trading partners is nearing its limits, while the newly assertive posture abroad is arousing concern. Domestically, the renewed focus on state-owned enterprises, triggered partly by national security concerns, will likely slow economic growth, while Made in China 2025 is not a sustainable solution, given pressures from trading partners, and has been downplayed by the leadership (Bloomberg 2018b). The BRI provides an opportunity for new sources of global growth that could also increase China's global influence, but it brings substantial geopolitical and cultural challenges, which have yet to be mastered. RMB internationalization provides only marginal help and raises new challenges as well.

In terms of China's broader economic development, we have detailed elsewhere our proposal for controlled opening via Hainan free port and other special zones and areas (Harrison et al. 2019)—going far beyond the limited vision released by the authorities for the Hainan and for Greater Bay Area (Shira and Associates 2019). In the monetary dimension, the concern of the present paper, we propose a similarly calibrated initiative, this time of controlled capital account opening via SDRs.

4. A Unilateral SDR Initiative by China

As per the IMF (2018a), the SDR is an accounting unit used to express members' reserve balances. It is a basket of five currencies, currently US dollar (41.73%), euro (30.93%), Chinese RMB (10.92%, added in October 2016), Japanese yen (8.33%), and British pound sterling (8.09%). SDR204.2 billion (USD 291 billion) is extant—equivalent to less than 3% of global foreign exchange reserves.

As we propose in Harrison and Xiao (2018), wider use of the SDR, not only as, "the principal reserve asset in the international financial system", as the IMF intended per its Articles of Agreement (IMF 2016), but as a fully-fledged currency for use by governments, institutions, firms and individuals, would be beneficial in reducing dollar-related imbalances. This in turn should create space and a more favorable environment for structural reforms such as an SDR clearing account at the IMF, more effective monitoring, and better policy coordination. However, efforts to promote the SDR have foundered on the 'liquidity premium' (IMF 2011, p. 15)—the higher interest rate that issuers of an SDR asset would have to pay to compensate buyers for its lower liquidity.

How can the liquidity premium be overcome? The IMF has proposed 'official institutions' committing to act as market makers (IMF 2011, p. 26), but it is doubtful that these institutions' members would be prepared to bear the costs. Even with deep-pocketed market makers, SDRs will remain unattractive to users with ready access to the dollar.

4.1. China's Pivotal Role

China's support for the SDR was voiced strongly by then-PBoC Governor Zhao Xiaochuan in 2009. As noted by Wang (2017), this advocacy of the SDR was in line with China's longstanding position that the international monetary system needs rebalancing away from the dollar. China's support for the SDR continued up to the RMB's inclusion in 2016 and was followed by limited SDR bond issuance in Shanghai—albeit that these issues were settled in RMB (Reuters 2016), rather defeating the purpose.

We suggest that it is now time for a fully-fledged SDR initiative from China. Crucially, China users would face a lower, or even negative, SDR liquidity premium because they do not enjoy unrestricted access to international currency. If an SDR component were included in the next round of capital account liberalization, China institutions, firms, and individuals would likely take up SDR issuance and investment activity. Ideally, there would be some facilitative support from the IMF (including reform of its own SDR quota system—Bird and Rowlands 2006) and acceptance by SDR-constituent currency polities. Once China's SDR activity took off, it would prompt participation from international players and the development of an ecosystem. Hong Kong would have a key role to play in channeling the related financial flows and providing supporting services.

With increasing use of SDRs by the international community, the liquidity premium would reduce. Given their relative stability, SDRs would become attractive for the pricing of long-term contracts and commodities, and for reserve-holding and investment purposes generally. Greater use of SDRs would help moderate the imbalances and inequities in the current international monetary system. Because the change would be market-led and gradual, all parties would have time to adjust. Reduced monetary tensions would lead naturally to peace in a broader sense, with less reason for trade wars or currency wars.

A meaningful SDR market would be good for the world. It would also be good for China.

In our view, promotion of the SDR would have several advantages from China's point of view. Firstly, promulgation of the SDR achieves RMB internationalization at a stroke. The RMB's 10.92% share of the SDR compares rather favorably with its present 1.7% share of global reserves. Secondly, the SDR also incorporates the currencies of four other top trading powers—the US, the EU, Japan, and the UK. Expanded use of the SDR would cast China as a friend of these powers and as a multilateralist. Thirdly, initiation of an active SDR market would create a global public good, which would again enhance China's reputation as well as making for a more favorable external environment. Fourth, as initiator, China would be a maker rather than taker of rules in the emerging new global monetary order.

4.2. Implementation

If SDRs are a good idea for China, as well as for the world, how could they be implemented?

In Harrison and Xiao (2018), we detail unilateral steps that China could take to initiate a market in SDRs. These steps can be summarized as follows:

- Policy opening. Incorporation of SDRs into the next round of capital account opening measures for state and local government entities, firms, institutions, and individuals. Essentially, all qualifying parties would be allowed to hold, issue, and otherwise transact in SDRs as appropriate, and ancillary to that in the SDR component currencies, subject to overall limits.
- Facilitative measures. Establishment of infrastructure such as clearing facilities for SDRs and the component currencies; introduction of risk management tools such as derivatives.
- 'Ice-breaking' issues of SDRs by state entities, both domestically and internationally.
- Communication of the initiative both domestically and internationally.
- Enlisting the support of Hong Kong to extend the domestic SDR market internationally.

We expect that strong policy endorsement and communication coupled with 'ice-breaking' issuance by state entities would be enough to kick-start the initiative. Development would thereafter be market-led, subject to government-imposed limits, monitoring, and controls. The key deterrent to SDR usage—the SDR liquidity premium—would be lower or even negative for China-based users who do not presently enjoy unrestricted access to international currency. The market should take off once users understand the aims and conditions. International players, when permitted under the policy framework, would welcome the chance to participate.

Endorsement and facilitation by the IMF and other multilateral organizations, the SDR-component currency-issuing entities, and ultimately the G20 would of course greatly assist the SDR initiative and, at some point, would be essential to its further progress. However, we believe that a good start can be made on a bottom-up market-led basis, provided the China authorities supply the initial policy impetus.

Given the very limited use of the SDR at present, the supporting infrastructure provided by the IMF—an interest rate determined weekly, settlement (between member states through IMF auspices) taking several days, and rebalancing every five years (IMF 2018b)—is rather basic. To support the proposed SDR initiative, it would be necessary to consider enhancements to the IMF's infrastructure and to set up additional infrastructure in China.

Hong Kong could provide support on the infrastructure side as well as more broadly helping to link China's SDR market with the global market. The HKMA already has real-time gross settlement systems (RTGS) for three of the five SDR underlying currencies—US dollar, euro, and RMB.

5. Risk Management

We have described above the opportunity for China to take the global lead on SDRs, the benefits to China as well as the rest of the world, and the implementation steps. The remaining considerations are around risk. What measures can the China authorities take to mitigate the risks of the proposed SDR initiative?

5.1. China's Overall Resilience

Following the Risk Governance Framework of the International Risk Governance Council (IRGC 2017), there are five stages in the approach to risk:

1. Pre-assessment—Identification and framing.
2. Appraisal—Assessing the perceived causes and consequences of the risk.
3. Characterization and evaluation—Making a judgment about the risk and the need to manage it.
4. Management—Deciding on and implementing risk management options.
5. Cross-cutting aspects—Communicating and engaging with stakeholders, considering the context.

Regarding items 1–3, advance consideration of risk, we acknowledge that any market-based initiative in China's state-permeated economy raises the dual risk of excess—since users may embrace the new freedom too eagerly—and undermining of state authority. This is even more true of financial liberalization initiatives because of finance's immediacy, intangibility, and far-reaching effects. In China, where a large financial system operates to its own dynamic behind a capital account wall, ill-considered financial liberalization could be catastrophic.

The IRGC (2013) identifies slow-developing catastrophic risk (SLDR)—such as the build-up of credit that gave rise to the GFC, or today's crisis of global warming—as a crucial risk category. SLDR, as the name indicates, builds slowly, but reaches a tipping point at which crisis suddenly breaks. Systems—whether financial, economic, or climatic—comprise multiple interlinked feedback loops that, on reaching a critical point, flip from positive to negative effects, avalanching out of control. SLDRs, the IRGC argues, are consequently very difficult to prevent, indeed from time to time will happen regardless of risk management. It is therefore necessary to build resilience, so that in crisis the system quickly finds a new equilibrium, if necessary, with changed institutions and policies.

The risks posed by our SDR initiative are of this catastrophic nature. However, any financial opening initiative for China carries risks like this. As Xu (2018) puts it, ' ... further financial openness will expose China's flawed financial system to international capital flows and endanger the nation's financial and economic stability. Financial openness needs a solid foundation, such as an efficient and robust banking sector, which China lacks.' Moreover, the status quo carries heavy costs in terms of inefficiency, and it is not sustainable either. Our proposed SDR initiative is in some senses less risky than the status quo in that the targeted outcome is increased stability while the risks are very much in view.

Moreover, the China system has resilience. China authorities have shown themselves able to manage through multiple financial crises. Crisis-fighting initiatives of recent years have included the spending surge following the GFC (which helped forestall a global recession as well as one in China), the clampdown on shadow banking, the scaling back of excess credit, the re-imposition of capital controls in 2016/17, and the clampdown on stock market abuse in the same period. These initiatives involved policy reversals, changes in regulatory personnel, and even changes in institutions—such as establishment of a Financial Stability and Development Committee to lead the PBoC and a merger of the banking and insurance regulators into the China Banking Insurance Regulatory Commission (EAF

2018). This is not to say that another crisis would be welcome, but the system has demonstrated the capability to handle a crisis.

Turning now to IRGC item four, Management of risk, we propose a layered approach incorporating monetary limits (quotas), geographical limits, the use (in part) of a cryptocurrency version of the SDR, monitoring, responsiveness if a threat does occur, and building resilience generally. Monetary limits, geographical limits, and a cryptocurrency SDR are discussed in turn below.

5.2. Monetary Limits

An obvious way to limit the risk of new financial facilities is to set monetary limits on their use. China has extensive experience of setting financial quotas for the interaction of its citizens and institutions with the wider world—and indeed for foreign participation in China's markets. A quota regime for SDR usage could include an overall cap on the amount of SDR in circulation in China (to which other quotas would be subject), limits on each institution's SDR holdings, and limits on individual holdings. An initial overall quota of SDR200 billion (USD 280 billion), equivalent to 1.1% of the monetary base M2 of USD 25,600 billion-equivalent (CEIC 2018), would not seem too large. Ideally, SDR usage within the quota limits should require no further permissions, merely compliance with existing regulations on banking, securities offering, and so on.

The authorities could raise the quotas subsequently as experience was gained. In this regard, it is worth noting the recent experience of Stock Connect, the bilateral linkage mechanism for mutual access across the Mainland and Hong Kong stock markets. On 1 May 2018, the daily quotas for Northbound trading (by foreigners in the Mainland market) and for Southbound trading (by Mainland investors in the Hong Kong market) were raised to RMB 52 billion and RMB 42 billion from RMB 13 billion and RMB 10.5 billion, respectively, for each of the Shenzhen and Shanghai markets (HKEX 2018)—a fourfold rise.

5.3. Geographical Limits

Given China's vast geographical extent, the enclave model—whereby new ideas and institutions are trialed in a limited area before any application to the nation as a whole—has obvious appeal and has been extensively used in both historical and recent times. In Harrison et al. (2019), we advocate deepening the experimentation in Hainan and other free trade zones (FTZs) and the Mainland municipalities of the Greater Bay Area, with the support of Hong Kong and Macau. This 'Hainan-plus' platform, comprising some 8% of China's GDP and 5% of its population, could be used as the launchpad for the proposed SDR initiative. Including the 11 Mainland-based FTZs in the platform, this has the further advantage of providing the rest of the country with filtered access to the new facilities.

Setting geographical limits to the use of SDRs makes the initiative easier to control. Earlier attempts to use FTZs to spearhead financial reforms failed either because the scope of the initiative was too small (Shanghai Waigaoqiao), or too large (when FTZ accounts could be opened across the nation) such that the capital account wall was threatened. We suggest that the Hainan-plus platform would be 'just right'. Hainan-plus would be large enough for meaningful financial activity while still being controllable.

5.4. Cryptocurrency SDR

In common with some other central banks, the PBoC has been examining the potential to issue a crypto version of its currency for domestic use. There have been conflicting messages, the central bank on the one hand clamping down on cryptocurrency operations nationwide, while on the other, the central bank itself filing numerous patents for blockchain-related applications (Bitcoin.com 2018).

We suggest that the experiment be tried first in respect of SDRs, thus limiting the risks to the mainstream financial system. Cryptocurrency SDRs—say, 'E-SDRs'—would be backed by, with their value tied to, a basket of the SDR underlying currencies in the SDR composite ratio. The E-SDR would be a 'stable coin'. E-SDRs would be based on blockchain technology, thus providing new functions to support the digital economy. E-SDRs would be created by PBoC-authorized banks against deposit of the underlying currencies, and they would be available to retail and business users as well as banks.

Barrdear and Kumhof (2016) see substantial benefits potentially flowing from a central bank-issued digital currency (CBDC) version of the national fiat currency. Such issuance could allow everyone, rather than just banks, to use central bank money for payments, remittances, and holding, thus reducing financial frictions. CBDC would also provide transparency over monetary transactions, yielding real-time data for policy-making and risk management.

Kumhof and Noone (2018, p. 5) set four core principles to minimize the risk of bank runs:

1. CBDC pays an adjustable interest rate.
2. CBDC and bank reserves are distinct, and not convertible into each other.
3. No guaranteed, on-demand convertibility of bank deposits into CBDC.
4. The central bank issues CBDC only against eligible (principally government) securities.

We suggest that the last of these, issuance against eligible securities, may not be necessary in respect of SDRs, since SDR and RMB deposits would not be fungible with one another.

E-SDRs would be created/redeemed against baskets of the underlying fiat currencies by the banks on behalf of themselves or their customers, thus rendering the creation/redemption process accessible to anyone with a bank account and the requisite currency. As with exchange-traded funds (ETFs), the redemption/creation process for E-SDRs would allow arbitrage by nominated banks (and their customers) if the E-SDR price should drift out of line with the prices of the underlying currencies. The currency baskets would be held by the creating banks, but visible to the PBoC as supervising authority—and, via the blockchain mechanism, to the nominated banks (and via them, to their customers and information vendors). E-SDRs would be traded on the existing interbank currency market China Foreign Exchange Trade System and National Interbank Funding Center (CFETS). Transactions in E-SDRs would be validated by the nominated banks (under a 'proof of stake', i.e., authority, model), rather than by competing 'miners' under Bitcoin's 'proof of work' mechanism, thereby avoiding excessive consumption of electricity.

E-SDRs would possess the following other advantages—albeit that the scale of the benefits would be proportionate to the scale of E-SDR issuance, which would be minor initially:

- E-SDRs would enable everyone, not just banks, to transact securely and immediately in central bank money. This could relieve users of dependence on layers of financial intermediaries, with significant reductions in costs and risks.
- Transactions in E-SDRs would be transparent as to amount and timing via the blockchain mechanism, providing a granular view of transactions in the economy as they take place—allowing real-time risk management and financial policy analysis.
- Transactions would be relatively secure and unhackable.
- Transactions would be anonymous to external viewers of the blockchain, although known to the nominated bank concerned.
- Particular E-SDRs could be 'colored' (distinguished as a separate class or category) and used as vehicles for securities issuance (initial coin offerings, ICOs). Colored E-SDRs would not be fungible with non-colored E-SDRs, and their value would diverge as well since they would have securities-like attributes (part-ownership of a company).

Overall, the SDR proposal, if adopted by China, would provide useful space for experimentation with CBDC. If the experiment should go well in respect of E-SDRs, the PBoC could consider proceeding with an equivalent initiative for the RMB itself.

6. Conclusions

The present dollar-based international monetary system is perennially unstable, with emerging market crisis never far away and developed markets also at risk. Reform of this problematic system is needed, but in the current climate international consensus appears almost unreachable. Meanwhile, geopolitical tensions such as the US–China trade war increase the risk of crisis.

One element of a solution would be wider use of the SDR as an international currency to supplement the US dollar. Efforts in this direction have foundered on the SDR liquidity premium. However, for China users the liquidity premium would be less off-putting, and China is large enough for a unilateral initiative to make a difference. China is therefore able to launch an SDR initiative that, with multilateral support, could help stabilize the global monetary system. China itself, hard-pressed to reconcile its need for greater openness with domestic political imperatives, would benefit from the delimited and controllable market opening that this proposal represents. Overall, an SDR initiative would have win-win outcomes for both China and the international community.

Author Contributions: Conceptualization, M.H. and G.X.; methodology, M.H. and G.X.; validation, M.H.; formal analysis, M.H.; investigation, M.H. and G.X.; resources, M.H.; writing—original draft preparation, M.H.; writing—review and editing, M.H. and G.X.

Funding: This commentary received no external funding.

Conflicts of Interest: The authors declare no conflict of interest.

References

Barrdear, John, and Michael Kumhof. 2016. *The Macroeconomics of Central Bank Issued Digital Currencies*. Staff Working Paper No. 605. London: Bank of England, July 18.

Bird, Graham, and Dane Rowlands. 2006. IMF Quotas: Constructing an International Organization Using Inferior Building Blocks. *The Review of International Organizations* 1: 153–71. [CrossRef]

Bitcoin.com. 2018. A Chinese Government-Controlled Bitcoin Alternative Is Reportedly in the Works, 18 December 2018. Available online: https://news.bitcoin.com/a-chinese-government-controlled-bitcoin-alternative-is-reportedly-in-the-works/ (accessed on 25 March 2019).

Bloomberg. 2018a. China's Debt Bomb, 17 September 2018. Available online: https://www.bloomberg.com/quicktake/chinas-debt-bomb (accessed on 27 March 2019).

Bloomberg. 2018b. China's Made in 2025 Plan Is a Paper Tiger, 18 December 2018. Available online: https://www.bloomberg.com/opinion/articles/2018-12-16/china-s-made-in-2025-industrial-ambitions-are-a-paper-tiger (accessed on 25 March 2019).

Bloomberg. 2019. Russia Buys Quarter of World Yuan Reserves in Shift from Dollar, 10 January 2019. Available online: https://www.bloomberg.com/news/articles/2019-01-09/russia-boosted-yuan-euro-holdings-as-it-dumped-dollars-in-2018 (accessed on 25 March 2019).

Bowles, Paul, and Baotai Wang. 2013. Renminbi Internationalization: A Journey to Where? *Development and Change* 44: 1363–85. [CrossRef]

Brookings Institution. 2017. China's One Belt One Road initiative: A view from the United States, 19 June 2017. Available online: https://www.brookings.edu/research/chinas-one-belt-one-road-initiative-a-view-from-the-united-states/ (accessed on 25 March 2019).

CCTV. 2017. China Breakthroughs: New International Payments System Goes into Action, 19 October 2017. Available online: http://english.cctv.com/2017/10/19/ARTIXz5AbEqSewRu8jDIFRKO171019.shtml (accessed on 25 March 2019).

CEIC. 2018. China Money Supply M2, December 2017. Available online: https://www.ceicdata.com/en/indicator/china/money-supply-m2 (accessed on 25 March 2019).

Chan, Sarah. 2017. The Belt and Road Initiative: Implications for China and East Asian Economies. *The Copenhagen Journal of Asian Studies* 35: 52–78. [CrossRef]

Chow, Hwee Kwan. 2013. Is the Renminbi East Asia's Dominant Reference Currency? A Reconsideration. Paper presented at 9th APEA Asia Pacific Economic Association Conference, Osaka, Japan, July 27–28; pp. 1–22.

City of London Corporation. 2018. Building an Investment and Financing System for the Belt and Road Initiative. Available online: https://www.cityoflondon.gov.uk/business/asia-programme/greater-china/Documents/building-an-investment-and-financing-system-for-the-bri.pdf (accessed on 26 March 2019).

CNBC. 2018. Amid Trade Tensions and Stock Turmoil, China Cracks Open Its Bond Market Further to Foreigners, 12 October 2018. Available online: https://www.cnbc.com/2018/10/12/china-cracks-open-its-bond-market-further-to-foreigners.html (accessed on 27 March 2019).

Currenxie. 2016. How to Take Advantage of the CNY-CNH Spread? 10 April 2016. Available online: https://currenxie.com/blog/how-to-take-advantage-of-the-cny-cnh-spread-20160810.html (accessed on 25 March 2019).

East Asia Forum. 2018. Regulatory Reshuffle in China's Financial Governance, 4 July 2018. Available online: https://www.eastasiaforum.org/2018/07/04/regulatory-reshuffle-in-chinas-financial-governance/ (accessed on 25 March 2019).

Economic Times. 2018. China's BRI Comes under Severe Criticism on Its Fifth Anniversary, 4 January 2018. Available online: https://economictimes.indiatimes.com/news/international/world-news/chinas-bri-comes-under-severe-criticism-on-its-fifth-anniversary/articleshow/67384058.cms (accessed on 25 March 2019).

Eichengreen, Barry. 2014. *International Currencies Past, Present and Future: Two Views from Economic History*. Bank of Korea Working Paper No.2014-31. Seoul: BOK Economic Research Institute.

Economist Intelligence Unit. 2018. Renminbi Internationalisation and the BRI: Rebuilding Momentum? 10 April 2018. Available online: https://www.business.hsbc.com/china-growth/renminbi-internationalisation-and-the-bri-rebuilding-momentum (accessed on 25 March 2019).

Fitch Solutions. 2017. Unwinding QE: What Will It Look Like and What Impact Will It Have? *Executive Brief*. Available online: http://your.fitch.group/rs/732-CKH-767/images/fs-executive-brief-unwinding-qe.PDF?mkt_tok=eyJpIjoiWm1NM04yVTRaREF4TmpFMiIsInQiOiI0dzdsMFpSVHM2d0dYUG9CeXcxVDdC5WJwVWo5WEVMMnhURStRU3JITCtNcm1FQWl5enphRnkwcmV6YmdiaWtraG5WSW5Ib3lqa0xoc3Vqc3lTdW9SY3VFVEpPXC8yOUFFazlEa0ZrcExsWWphVhXZ211bHMrVmZnWGYwRkNQemwifQ%3D%3D,.%5bCrossRef (accessed on 25 March 2019).

Frankel, Jeffrey. 2012. Internationalization of the RMB and Historical Precedents. *Journal of Economic Integration* 27: 329–65. [CrossRef]

FT. 2018. The Belt and Road's dollar problem. *FT Alphaville*, December 18. Available online: https://ftalphaville.ft.com/2018/12/18/1545130791000/The-Belt-and-Road-s-dollar-problem/ (accessed on 25 March 2019).

Global Times. 2016. AIIB Decision to Use US Dollars for Loans Not a Response to Recent Slide in Yuan, 17 January 2016. Available online: http://www.globaltimes.cn/content/964106.shtml (accessed on 25 March 2019).

Harrison, Matthew, and Geng Xiao. 2018. Enhanced Special Drawing Rights—How China Could Contribute to a Reformed International Monetary Architecture. *China & World Economy* 26: 41–61.

Harrison, Matthew, Geng Xiao, Wendy Hong, and Shirley Lam. 2019. *Hainan Free Trade Zone—Realising the Potential*, Working Paper under Review for Publication.

HKEX. 2018. HKEX Comments on Stock Connect Daily Quotas Expansion, 11 April 2018. Available online: https://www.hkex.com.hk/News/News-Release/2018/180411news?sc_lang=en (accessed on 25 March 2019).

Hong Kong Monetary Authority. 2016. Hong Kong—The Global Offshore RMB Business Hub, Hong Kong Monetary Authority. p. 17. Available online: https://www.hkma.gov.hk/media/eng/doc/key-functions/monetary-stability/rmb-business-in-hong-kong/hkma-rmb-booklet.pdf (accessed on 26 March 2019).

Hong Kong Trade Development Council. 2019. The Belt and Road Initiative: Country Profiles. Available online: http://china-trade-research.hktdc.com/business-news/article/The-Belt-and-Road-Initiative/The-Belt-and-Road-Initiative-Country-Profiles/obor/en/1/1X000000/1X0A36I0.htm (accessed on 25 March 2019).

Huang, Yukon, and Clare Lynch. 2013. Does Internationalizing the RMB make sense for China? *Cato Journal* 33: 571.

International Monetary Fund. 2011. Enhancing International Monetary Stability—A Role for the SDR? *Discussion Paper*. January 7. Available online: https://www.imf.org/external/np/pp/eng/2011/010711.pdf (accessed on 26 March 2019).

International Monetary Fund. 2016. Articles of Agreement of the International Monetary Fund, April, Second Amendment (AoA XXII). Available online: https://www.imf.org/external/pubs/ft/aa/index.htm (accessed on 25 March 2019).

International Monetary Fund. 2018a. Special Drawing Right (SDR). *IMF Fact Sheet*, April 19. Available online: https://www.imf.org/en/About/Factsheets/Sheets/2016/08/01/14/51/Special-Drawing-Right-SDR (accessed on 25 March 2019).

International Monetary Fund. 2018b. Considerations on the Role of the SDR. *Policy Paper*, April 11. Available online: https://www.imf.org/en/Publications/Policy-Papers/Issues/2018/04/11/pp030618consideration-of-the-role-the-sdr (accessed on 26 March 2019).

International Monetary Fund. 2019a. New Data on Global Debt. *Blog*, January 2. Available online: https://blogs.imf.org/2019/01/02/new-data-on-global-debt/ (accessed on 25 March 2019).

International Monetary Fund. 2019b. Currency Composition of Official Foreign Exchange Reserves, 8 January 2019. Available online: http://data.imf.org/?sk=E6A5F467-C14B-4AA8-9F6D-5A09EC4E62A4 (accessed on 25 March 2019).

International Risk Governance Council. 2013. Preparing for Future Catastrophes—Governance Principles for Slow-Developing Risks that May Have Catastrophic Consequences, Concept Note, 11 March 2013. Available online: https://www.irgc.org/wp-content/uploads/2013/03/CN_Prep.-for-Future-Catastrophes_final_11March13.pdf (accessed on 26 March 2019).

International Risk Governance Council. 2017. IRGC Risk Governance Framework. Available online: https://irgc.org/risk-governance/irgc-risk-governance-framework/ (accessed on 25 March 2019).

Katada, Saori. 2018. Can China Internationalize the RMB? Lessons from Japan. *Foreign Affairs, SNAPSHOT*. January 1. Available online: https://www.foreignaffairs.com/articles/china/2018-01-01/can-china-internationalize-rmb (accessed on 26 March 2019).

Kumhof, Michael, and Clare Noone. 2018. *Central Bank Digital Currencies—Design Principles and Balance Sheet Implications*. Staff Working Paper No. 725. London: Bank of England.

Li, Ruogu. 2016. *Reform of The International Monetary System and Internationalization of The Renminbi*. Singapore: World Scientific.

Liu, Weidong, Michael Dunford, and Boyang Gao. 2018. A discursive construction of the Belt and Road Initiative: From neo-liberal to inclusive globalization. *Journal of Geographical Sciences* 28: 1199–214. [CrossRef]

Long, Chen, and Arthur Kroeber. 2016. Retreating from an International Renminbi. *Gavekal Dragonomics*, January 14.

New York Times. 2015. China to Track Renminbi Based on Basket of Currencies. *New York Times*, December 11. Available online: https://www.nytimes.com/2015/12/12/business/international/china-to-track-renminbi-based-on-basket-of-currencies.html (accessed on 25 March 2019).

Ocampo, José. 2017. *Resetting the International Monetary (Non)System*. A Study Prepared by the United Nations University World Institute for Development Economics Research. Oxford: Oxford University Press.

Otero-Iglesias, Miguel, and Mattias Vermeiren. 2015. China's state-Permeated market economy and its constraints to the internationalization of the renminbi. *International Politics* 52: 684–703. [CrossRef]

Palais-Royal. 2011. Reform of the International Monetary System—A Cooperative Approach for the Twenty-First Century, 8 February 2011. Available online: http://global-currencies.org/smi/gb/telechar/news/Rapport_Camdessus-integral.pdf (accessed on 26 March 2019).

Philippine Daily Inquirer. 2018. PH Sells P12B Panda Bonds Amid Strong Demand, 21 March 2018. Available online: https://business.inquirer.net/248021/ph-sells-p12b-panda-bonds-amid-strong-demand (accessed on 25 March 2019).

Prasad, Eswar S. 2018. The slow, uneven rise of the Renminbi. *Cato Journal* 38: 521–29.

Reserve Bank of Australia. 2018. RMB Internationalisation: Where to Next? *Reserve Bank of Australia Bulletin*, September 20.

Reuters. 2016. Standard Chartered Successfully Issues SDR Bonds in China, 26 October 2016. Available online: https://www.reuters.com/article/uk-china-bonds-sdr/standard-chartered-successfully-issues-sdr-bonds-in-china-idUKKCN12Q0WJ (accessed on 27 March 2019).

Rickards, James. 2015. The death of money: the coming collapse of the international monetary system. *Portfolio/Penguin*, March 15.

South China Morning Post. 2015. China to Hold 30 per Cent Stake in AIIB and 26 per Cent Voting Rights, 30 June 2015. Available online: https://www.scmp.com/news/china/policies-politics/article/1829095/founding-nations-attend-signing-ceremony-china-led (accessed on 25 March 2019).

South China Morning Post. 2019. 2018 was meant to be Xi Jinping's year. Then China's Belt and Road Unravelled, 11 January 2019. Available online: https://www.scmp.com/week-asia/opinion/article/2178778/2018-was-meant-be-xi-jinpings-year-then-chinas-belt-and-road (accessed on 25 March 2019).

Shira, Dezan, and Associates. 2019. What Is the Greater Bay Area Plan? *China Briefing*, February 21. Available online: https://www.china-briefing.com/news/the-greater-bay-area-plan-china/ (accessed on 25 March 2019).

SWIFT. 2019. RMB Tracker, January 2019. Available online: https://www.swift.com/our-solutions/compliance-and-shared-services/business-intelligence/renminbi/rmb-tracker/document-centre (accessed on 25 March 2019).

The Economist. 2019. China's Current-Account Surplus Has Vanished, 14 March 2019. Available online: https://www.economist.com/finance-and-economics/2019/03/16/chinas-current-account-surplus-has-vanished (accessed on 27 March 2019).

Wang, Hongying. 2017. China and the International Monetary System: Does Beijing Really Want to Challenge the Dollar? *Foreign Affairs, SNAPSHOT*, December 19.

White, William. 2015. Point of View: System Malfunction. In *Finance & Development*. Washington, DC: IMF, vol. 52, pp. 44–47.

Xu, Guangdong. 2018. China's Financial Repression: Symptoms, Consequences and Causes. *The Copenhagen Journal of Asian Studies* 36: 28–49. [CrossRef]

Zhang, Zhexin. 2018. The Belt and Road Initiative: China's New Geopolitical Strategy? *China Quarterly of International Strategic Studies* 4: 327–43. [CrossRef]

Zhang, Fan, Miaojie Yu, Jiantuo Yu, and Jin Yang. 2017. The Effect of RMB Internationalization on Belt and Road Initiative: Evidence from Bilateral Swap Agreements. *Emerging Markets Finance and Trade* 53: 2845–57. [CrossRef]

Zhou, Xiaochuan. 2009. Reform the International Monetary System. *Bank for International Settlements*, March 23. Available online: https://www.bis.org/review/r090402c.pdf (accessed on 26 March 2019).

© 2019 by the authors. Licensee MDPI, Basel, Switzerland. This article is an open access article distributed under the terms and conditions of the Creative Commons Attribution (CC BY) license (http://creativecommons.org/licenses/by/4.0/).

MDPI
St. Alban-Anlage 66
4052 Basel
Switzerland
Tel. +41 61 683 77 34
Fax +41 61 302 89 18
www.mdpi.com

Journal of Risk and Financial Management Editorial Office
E-mail: jrfm@mdpi.com
www.mdpi.com/journal/jrfm

www.ingramcontent.com/pod-product-compliance
Lightning Source LLC
LaVergne TN
LVHW071958080526
838202LV00064B/6785